Understanding Primary Education

D1104154

Understanding Primary Education will help trainees and newly qualified teachers reflect on the professional decisions that they make within their planning and classroom practice. Key issues and policies within contemporary education are analysed through reference to research and case studies of pedagogical practice to provide a broad perspective of the curriculum with a focus on what curriculum breadth and balance looks like in practice. The book encourages readers to think beyond the statutory curriculum and consider questions such as:

- What views of education are held in the twenty-first century?
- What possible alternatives might readers envisage?
- In what ways are children encouraged to be active participants in their own learning within different educational settings and communities?

Drawing on the voices of trainees, teachers, other education professionals and, most importantly, those of children, the authors illuminate how learning is facilitated and how knowledge and understandings are constructed collaboratively within the classroom and other settings. Each chapter begins with the identification of several key questions linked to such themes as curriculum planning, pedagogy, inclusion, assessment and children's learning, which readers are encouraged to relate to their own experiences.

With case study material drawing on a range of educational settings, activities and reflections that invite readers to consider the issues discussed, this book will prove an invaluable resource for all trainees and newly qualified teachers.

Penelope Harnett is Reader in Education at the University of West England, UK.

Understanding Primary Education

Developing professional attributes, knowledge and skills

Edited by
Penelope Harnett

NO LONGER
the property of
Whitaker Library

Routledge
Taylor & Francis Group

LONDON AND NEW YORK

First published 2008
by Routledge
2 Park Square, Milton Park, Abingdon, Oxon OX14 4RN

Simultaneously published in the USA and Canada
by Routledge
270 Madison Ave, New York, NY 10016

Routledge is an imprint of the Taylor & Francis Group, an informa business

© 2008 Penelope Harnett selection and editorial matter,
individual chapters the contributors

Typeset in Sabon and Gill Sans by
Keystroke, 28 High Street, Tettenhall, Wolverhampton
Printed and bound in Great Britain by
Bell & Bain Ltd., Glasgow

All rights reserved. No part of this book may be reprinted or
reproduced or utilised in any form or by any electronic, mechanical,
or other means, now known or hereafter invented, including
photocopying and recording, or in any information storage or
retrieval system, without permission in writing from the publishers.

British Library Cataloguing in Publication Data
A catalogue record for this book is available from the British Library

Library of Congress Cataloging in Publication Data
A catalog record for this book has been requested

ISBN10: 0–415–39924–6 (pbk)
ISBN10: 0–203–93286–2 (ebk)

ISBN13: 978–0–415–39924–1 (pbk)
ISBN13: 978–0–203–93286–5 (ebk)

Contents

Notes on contributors

Martin Ashley is Reader in Education at Edge Hill University. His major research interest is in boys, masculinity and culture and he is currently working on an AHRC-funded project, 'Young Masculinity and Vocal Performance'. He is also interested in pedagogy in the middle years and was recently a member of the DfES-funded Steiner Schools in England research team.

Alison Bailey is Senior Lecturer in the Department of Geography and Environmental Management at the University of the West of England. She teaches geography on primary ITE programmes and has published widely in this field.

Jo Barkham is a Senior Lecturer and Programme Leader at the University of the West of England, Bristol. She is researching the effects of the National Literacy Strategy – how it was developed and implemented by people at national and local authority level, and the views of teachers and children.

Steve Barnes has worked mainly in primary education, but has also taught across all phases of education during the past 36 years. His specialist areas are geography, citizenship and the philosophy of education.

Helen Butcher taught for 15 years in London and West Yorkshire schools specialising in the education of young children, in particular Reception age children. In 1997 she moved to the University of the West of England, Bristol where she helped develop an Early Years specialism on ITE programmes and is Programme Leader for Early Childhood Studies.

Juliet Edmonds is a Senior Lecturer in the School of Education at the University of the West of England. She teaches science and Early Years education on primary ITE programmes.

Richard Eke taught in inner London primary schools before moving to the University of the West of England. He is Associate Dean in the Faculty of Social Science and Humanities and has research interests in children's classroom talk, the use of contemporary media in education and issues of social justice in education.

Gordon Guest was a primary teacher with experience across the whole primary phase from nursery to Year 6. He taught in Lincolnshire and Devon as well as Germany and Botswana and has been both a head-teacher and Advisor. He is currently a Senior Lecturer and Programme Leader at the University of the West of England.

Penelope Harnett is Reader in Education in the School of Education, at the University of the West of England and a National Teaching Fellow. She is interested in teaching humanities, particularly history, and has published extensively in this field.

Sue Hughes is Senior Lecturer at the University of the West of England. She teaches on the undergraduate and postgraduate ITE courses and is English subject leader. Sue has a particular interest in language and communication and learning and has recently completed her Masters' dissertation on the use of on-line communities of practice within teacher education.

Lalit Kumar is a poet and teacher. He taught in Bristol schools before moving to the University of the West of England where he is now a visiting lecturer. His research interests include the nature of classroom talk and the national strategies, particularly from the perspectives of pupils for whom English is only one of the languages which they speak.

John Lee was Reader in Education in the School of Education at the University of the West of England. He is currently researching classroom discourse.

Mandy Lee is a Senior Lecturer at the University of the West of England, Bristol. She teaches on both undergraduate and postgraduate ITE courses and is ICT Subject Leader.

Christine Macfarlane trained as a secondary science teacher in the late 1960s/early 1970s. Her teaching experience has been in both secondary and primary schools and she has over six years experience of primary headship. Christine worked for two years at the University of the West of England and has recently returned to headship.

Jo Miller worked in primary schools for several years. She is Senior Lecturer at the University of the West of England and is Mathematics Subject Leader for primary ITE courses.

Helen Mulholland was a Senior Lecturer in Primary Mathematics Education at the University of the West of England. She has also worked in universities in London and has wide teaching experience in both primary and special education. She is particularly interested in issues of inclusion and mathematics and has worked with the Primary National Strategy to publish materials in this field for teacher educators.

Michael Nicholson joined the profession in 1969 as a teacher in a comprehensive school. After holding various academic and pastoral leadership roles in school he joined the University of the West of England (as Bristol Polytechnic) in 1987. Since then he has followed a variety of research and teaching interests including the development of technology in schools, the academic development of Health Service and Police Training professionals, primary education and comparative education.

Jane Tarr has a background of teaching in primary and special schools. She is Principal Lecturer at the University of the West of England. Her teaching and research interests focus on policy and practice in the area of inclusive education. She is also interested in the development of inter-professional collaboration between all those working with children and young people.

Maria Vinney was Senior Lecturer in primary art and design at the University of the West of England. She also works as an artist educator in schools. Current research interests include the impact of the arts in primary and Early Years education and strategies which encourage a more creative approach in the classroom.

Preface

Penelope Harnett

In this book we aim to support primary trainees and newly qualified teachers in reflecting on their own values and the impact which these values may have on the teaching and learning occurring in their own classrooms. We emphasise the importance of listening to learners in determining worthwhile learning experiences and in thinking holistically about learners' all round development.

During the last two decades there have been tremendous changes within the primary and Early Years curricula. The introduction of the National Curriculum moved most of the curriculum decision making away from teachers and children in schools. Instead, curriculum decisions were made in accordance with central prescription detailing specific content to be learned which could then be assessed and measured. Assessment was based on linear progression within ten levels of achievement; children's progress was seen as a steady, upward progression through these different levels. OfSTED provided a framework in which the effectiveness of curriculum implementation and assessment could be monitored.

This approach towards the curriculum, planning, implementation and assessment was consolidated throughout the 1990s and was central to the New Labour agenda in 1997 with its focus on targets and target setting. The National Literacy and Numeracy Strategies further extended central control, not only of the content of the curriculum, but also of the ways in which it was to be delivered. The Strategies removed teachers one step further away from curriculum planning and there was less opportunity for individual or creative responses to children's different learning needs and interests.

More recently, however, there is evidence that central control of the curriculum is beginning to relax. The Values and Purposes of Education described in Curriculum 2000 (DfEE and QCA 1999) signal opportunities for schools to begin to decide on ways in which they might best meet the needs and interests of children and their communities. Schools' responsibilities in tailoring the curriculum to meet the needs of children within their communities are further strengthened in the Primary National Strategy, which urges the need for creative interpretations of the curriculum (DfES 2003a). The

Guidance for the Foundation Stage (DfEE and QCA 2000) also supports teachers in their individual responses to children's learning across a range of different experiences.

However, it may take time to establish this renewed emphasis on teachers' participation in determining learning experiences within their classrooms and educational settings. We note that teachers' professional autonomy has been eroded in recent years.

A parallel trend has also appeared in teacher training. The concentration on the successful fulfilment of a narrow range of standards has often been at the expense of learning about more creative approaches to curriculum planning and children's learning. Newly qualified teachers and trainee teachers are trained to deliver the curriculum, yet if this curriculum has to have any relevance for the children whom they teach, they also need opportunities to question the values which underpin the curriculum. In this respect, we argue that both teachers and trainees require support to articulate their beliefs and values and to consider how they might be developed through the experiences which they plan for children. Policy initiatives such as the *Every Child Matters* agenda and the new workforce agreements require teachers to clarify their contributions to children's education and the different roles which they play within their communities.

Understanding Primary Education: Developing professional attributes, knowledge and skills is designed to help trainees and newly qualified teachers respond to the challenge of more active participation and support them in reflecting on the professional decisions which they make within their planning and work with children. We discuss the challenges of policymaking within different chapters and suggest alternative possibilities. A broad perspective of children's learning is outlined and we encourage readers to reflect on the practical implications of taking such a point of view. We explore such questions as: What experiences are important for children's learning and development? How may they be planned, organised and implemented within school and Early Years settings? What responsibilities do teachers and children have in developing these learning experiences? How might children's learning be enhanced through extending relationships with different communities?

Implicit within our discussion are questions such as: What views of education are held in the twenty-first century? What possible alternatives might readers envisage? In what ways are children encouraged to be active participants in their own learning within different educational settings and communities?

Using children as the starting point, we discuss how their learning may be developed beyond the statutory requirements to consider their education in its fullest sense. Teachers' roles as facilitators and collaborators within children's learning are identified. We draw on the voices of different participants within a range of educational encounters and include a number of case studies to reflect creative interpretations of the curriculum and children acting as agents in their own learning.

How this book is structured

In Chapter 1, *The social distribution of school knowledge in primary classrooms*, Richard Eke and Lalit Kumar discuss the social construction of knowledge by learners and ways in which teachers control the learning agenda through the way in which they talk to children. Teachers' interactions with their pupils are analysed and conclusions drawn on the extent to which classroom talk enables children to initiate and articulate their ideas. The centrality of talk for learning is emphasised and is a theme which is returned to throughout many of the subsequent chapters in the book.

The background policy context for the development of the National Literacy and Numeracy Strategies and more recently the Primary National Strategy is analysed in Chapter 2, *Support or straitjacket? A tale of three Strategies*. Jo Barkham and Jo Miller examine the outcomes of the Strategies and question whether they have really raised standards and at what price.

Helen Butcher and John Lee track policies which extend the notion of education for the Early Years in Chapter 3, *Social care, childcare and education: Exploring issues in the Early Years*. They argue that Early Years professionals need to be cognisant of the social as well as the educational policy frameworks in which their work is located. The impact of a broad range of policy on practice is a recurrent theme throughout the book and is discussed in several chapters.

Martin Ashley and Michael Nicholson invite the reader to consider *What makes a pedagogy fit for Key Stage 2?* in Chapter 4. They draw on two comparative studies to question whether Key Stage 2 children are developmentally any different from Key Stage 1 or Key Stage 3 children and ask whether this matters. Secondly, they question whether one teacher can ever know enough to teach the whole of the Key Stage 2 curriculum.

The impact of assessment on children's learning is discussed by Gordon Guest and John Lee in Chapter 5, *Current assessment practice: Driving or supporting practice?* They analyse the contribution which assessment for learning may make to children's development and recognise the potential tensions arising from this view of assessment with current governmental concerns for higher standards, target setting and league tables.

In Chapter 6, *Developing inclusive school communities*, Helen Mulholland and Jane Tarr consider the concept of an inclusive community. Different interpretations of inclusivity are explored through the voices of different community members (children, teachers, parents, community professionals) who represent views of communities in their broadest sense.

Sue Hughes, Mandy Lee and Juliet Edmonds investigate what happens when teachers weaken their grip on the prescriptive curriculum and children are given space for developing their own learning. Chapter 7, *Space for learning?* explores children's views and draws attention to the potential of ICT for developing creative learning opportunities.

Penelope Harnett and Maria Vinney ask *What has happened to curriculum breadth and balance in primary schools?* in Chapter 8. They trace the development of the primary curriculum since the Education Reform Act and explore the effect of government policy on curriculum breadth and balance. Teachers' views on the curriculum are analysed and the chapter concludes with discussion of children's views on their learning in different contexts.

Alison Bailey and Steve Barnes continue the theme of children's active engagement and control of their learning in Chapter 9, *Children's futures, our futures: Educating citizens for the twenty-first century*. They remind readers of education's role in preparing citizens of the future and explore ways in which this might be developed through different case study material.

Chapter 10 identifies the challenges currently facing teachers in terms of their professional identity. John Lee and Christine Macfarlane in *Facing the future: The primary teacher in the twenty-first century*, trace the development of the teaching profession and analyse the extent to which recent policy has questioned teachers' professionalism and their roles as educators.

Successful education is dependent on teachers who can critically analyse different aspects of learning and teaching and who have an informed vision of their role. The book aims to develop the ability of trainees and newly qualified teachers to analyse key issues through focusing on identified questions which are explored within different chapters. Reflections and Activities are designed to encourage the reader to develop their understanding of issues more fully and to identify potential implications for their own work with children.

Chapter 1

The social distribution of school knowledge in primary classrooms

Richard Eke and Lalit Kumar

Introduction

This chapter addresses some of the main themes of the book. We discuss the social construction of knowledge by learners in the context of the teachers' control of the learning agenda, through the way they talk about subject content when they assist pupil performances. The way teachers talk has direct consequences for the way in which pupils talk, and consequently for the sense they are able to make of their different lessons.

The chapter will help you to think about the following questions:

- How do teachers control learning in their classrooms through their interactions with pupils?
- How do pupils make sense of teachers' talk?
- What forms of classroom organisation support pupil talk and the articulation of pupils' ideas?

We draw on evidence from teacher–pupil interactions and ask questions about the opportunities pupils have to articulate their understanding. The extent to which arrangements for classroom talk allow pupils to initiate or share in the development of ideas is discussed. The chapter also flags the importance of whole-class interaction and the way in which this varies between pupils. The impact of gender, special educational needs and age is visited in an attempt to question the idea of a single audience for whole-class teaching. In conclusion, some broader issues related to such teaching are raised. What you will find here is discussion of the way knowledge and talk interact with each other, the way different pupils talk in classrooms, and the way talk supports learning in different curriculum subject areas. You will find plenty of extracts from the classrooms we have studied, which reflect the talk of skilled and experienced teachers.

Classroom talk and primary pedagogy

In recent years, Robin Alexander (2004) has raised questions about what it means to be a primary teacher and what pedagogy for the primary years might look like. In his exploration of primary teaching in an international context (Alexander 2000), he uses the term 'pedagogy' to mean 'the science of the art of teaching'. As Alexander's own work shows, and others so clearly demonstrate, the science is based in the theorised study of classrooms. Primary school teachers have always known, as Stenhouse (1984) reminds us, that the legitimacy of studying classrooms rests on the intention to improve the quality of learning for those in them. Clarity about what counts as improving the quality of learning requires clarity about links between learning and teaching. A key way of understanding this process is to look at what goes on inside primary classrooms – we shall refer to some studies that do this shortly – and perhaps most tellingly, look at how people talk to each other in classrooms. Indeed, much of Alexander's work draws on the careful analysis of transcripts, and we have used this approach in writing this chapter. Where extracts from classroom talk or reports of classroom activities are used to inform an analysis of practice, it is important to know whether what is being reported are exceptional events that demonstrate what can happen under special circumstances or are typical events that are run-of-the-mill happenings as far as the authors are concerned. It is also good to know whether the evidence is intended to give the account greater depth, to bring it life or to offer inspirational examples.

The choice to look at classroom talk at the very beginning of this book reflects a commitment to understanding how meanings are produced and circulated in classrooms. We could hardly prioritise the voice of the child without drawing on classroom talk. We want to emphasise that looking at how children learn involves looking at how they make sense of their world, and we know this by looking at the way they represent it – that is, the way they use all the symbolic meaning-making devices available to them to show what they have learned and want to say about it. This focus on children's meanings and the many forms in which they might be expressed carries an implicit recognition of the importance of the voices of learners; this recognition is essential if we are to both understand what pupils learn from us and to value their contributions in the classroom.

In making these connections we recognise that the study of primary peda-gogy is a value-laden activity. All involved in writing this book have sought appropriate spaces to articulate the values embedded in their work. Without exploring these in detail now, we can note that questions of inclusion, both in terms of additional need and social class, gender-appropriate education and the recognition of cultural diversity, underpin our recommendations for primary practice based on research activity. This spectrum of commitments raises questions of the learning of these particular groups of children in enhancing the learning of all children, as well as considerations of how helpful it is to group children in this manner. It might be that we end up balancing the tensions of teaching the whole class whilst personalising learning.

Reflection

What opportunities have you observed for children to use talk to support their learning in the classroom? If possible, ask children if they think talking helps them learn. In what ways do they think it helps?

Supporting classroom learning: pupils' and teachers' roles

Debates about teaching have often been premised on psychological accounts of learning and now generally locate learning in a social context (see, for example, Wood 1998). In diverse social contexts teaching may prioritise the nature of children's learning and thus the processes of assimilation, accommodation and adaptation. These Piagetian terms remind us of the ways in which children's thinking responds to experience and that this response is essentially individual. The Piagetian teacher follows the developing pattern of children's thinking, and learning is generated through the perturbation of a learner's existing schema (wobbling their thinking).

An alternative or parallel approach is to prioritise what is worth knowing and to assist children in coming to know what is deemed worth knowing in our culture. In this Vygotskian account of learning, a selection is made based on what is considered worthwhile knowledge, and this cultural selection is chunked (made into handy learner-friendly sized portions) and then structured into a sequence appropriate for the acquisition of the desired skill or knowledge (see, for example, Newman and Holzman 1993). The National Strategies for Literacy and Numeracy in England (DfEE 1998, 1999a) are good examples of this and, as the guidance associated with these documents illustrates, learning is then about recognising and extending the learner's zone of proximal development. Consequently, teaching is about showing and telling, assisting pupil performance through appropriate scaffolding. So the Vygotskian teacher identifies children's positions on a map of learning and arranges talk and activities to take them the next small step along a pre-planned route.

In both of these psychological accounts of learning attention to the voices of the learners is seen as essential for the study of teaching and for teaching itself. For many years classroom studies have shown the importance of the voice of the teacher in determining both the form and content of pupil talk. It is now a common place that the metaphors of scaffolding and handover (Bruner and Haste 1987) are used to describe the ways in which teachers arrange for talk and activity in primary classrooms (see, for example, Tharp and Gallimore 1988). It often seems that teachers are very good at scaffolding learning, getting the learning chunks the right size, organised in a sequence and embedded in appropriate activity and talk, but are less effective at handing over the activity to children, at giving them the space to make sense of things through their own talk and activity. The metaphors do imply that teachers will help children make their own sense of learning and thus reinforce the importance of listening to the children's voices in classrooms.

Studies of primary classrooms are sometimes concerned with effectiveness and have implications for teaching. One important study (Mortimore et al. 1988) indicates that in the most effective classrooms there are only one or two subjects on offer at any one time. This makes it very difficult for children to follow their unique and specific interests and gives the teacher the job of appealing to learners' interests in a more general way. The individual voice of the child can only be articulated against a backdrop of arrangements made by the teacher for all children. For example, when Jonathan was 9 his class was studying the houses across the road from the school. He wanted to write a story in which the house was haunted by a man who had lived in the house and died of wounds from a war. He found out that the Crimean War fitted the dates he had in mind. He did some independent reading about the war to gain contextual information for his ghost story and then settled into writing a narrative of several thousand words. The articulation of this very individual voice began from a common starting point, but required some very individualised arrangements by the teacher.

A second important study, known as the Oracle study (Galton et al. 1980), focused closely on what went on in primary classrooms. Like the Mortimore study, many issues for primary teaching were reported, but from the point of view of talking and learning perhaps the most important lesson was that classroom interaction is best focused on learning when an adult is involved, and the majority of adult involvement springs from teachers talking to whole classes. It is easy to see how these two studies can lead to a view that effective primary teaching involves a teacher talking to a whole class with a single subject focus. The voices of children may thus be most frequently linked to learning in whole-class settings where the teacher's authority is at its greatest. This focus on learning will most likely be maintained through teacher control of subject knowledge and its boundaries. In such circumstances it is unlikely that the Crimean War will be linked with a study of local housing and an extended piece of creative writing. You can see how arrangements like this make it difficult for learners to experience any explicit control over their learning or for teachers to take up learners' enthusiasms.

The National Literacy Strategy as an example of knowledge-driven pedagogy

A central feature of what it is to study and enhance primary pedagogy is the question of what counts as worthwhile classroom knowledge, and this has become the subject of a continuing range of policy initiatives. Policy agendas have led to the production of the National Curriculum requirements defining worthwhile classroom knowledge and the prioritisation of English and mathematics and the related pedagogic strategies (The National Literacy Strategy, DfEE 1998; The National Numeracy Strategy, DfEE 1999a). The implementation of these Strategies has provided a focus for the interrogation of classroom practice from a range of perspectives (e.g. Earl et al. 2003; OfSTED 2002a; Lee and Eke 2004). The final report of the external evaluation of the National Literacy and Numeracy Strategies (NLS and NNS) in England asserted they were, with a few reservations, successful policy innovations (Earl et al. 2003). You will find further discussion on the implementation of the NLS in Chapter 2.

OfSTED (2002a), however, in an HMI overview of the Literacy Strategy, reported reservations about the underachievement of pupils in just over half the schools in areas of social deprivation in which good progress was not made. The challenge and potential difficulties of reconciling the Strategy with the requirements for children with special educational needs have also been identified and in particular how whole-class interactive teaching can involve content and discussion that includes all the pupils in the class (Wearmouth and Soler 2001). In this connection the OfSTED report commented favourably on subtle changes in pace employed by a teacher. OfSTED reports are rarely explicit on what they mean by pace and this may not be surprising given the variety of definitions we shall explore shortly. Despite the NLS, the literary achievements of boys and of those pupils with special educational needs or in areas of social and economic deprivation continue to cause concern. It is a real challenge for teachers to ensure the presence of the voices of all learners in the kind of whole-class teaching, promoted by the Strategies, where what counts as knowledge is very tightly defined and time is precious. The NLS in action is one place where we can see how teachers respond to these challenges.

A tight, teacherly, control of talking for learning can be associated with a tight control of the pace of lessons. Bernstein's use of the term 'pace' would suggest both explanations and challenges for the classroom implementation of the NLS. Pacing is defined by Bernstein as the rate at which learning is expected to occur – the speed at which the sequencing rules are transmitted and acquired and thus 'regulate the rhythm of the transmission' (1990: 76).

The NLS lists learning outcomes by school term and by school year and thus has strong pacing. The pacing rules determine when new topics are to be introduced and can be linked to the forms of questions asked and the anticipated duration of pupil response. The form and length of utterance are bound up with each other and so determine who can say what and when. Following Bernstein's (1990) argument, this has two consequences for the present discussion. Since time is at a premium, what counts as appropriate talk, in both length and form, will reduce pupil speech and increase teacher talk. It may be that pace is a central issue for our understanding of teaching and learning in literacy. Writing of the Reading Recovery Programme, Cazdan (2000) observes strong pacing with little time for chat. Disadvantaged children are doubly disadvantaged by these pacing rules and unless the pacing rules are modified they will need some form of remediation and/or receive a diminished curriculum. While we are aware of NLS materials that are responsive to these agendas, the challenge of inclusive teaching in the introductory session remains.

Alexander's (2000) analysis of pace argues that there are four kinds of pace: organisational, task, interactive and semantic or cognitive pace. Organisational pace refers to introductions, transitions and conclusions. His task pace is an indicator of the speed at which learning tasks are undertaken. Interactive pace refers to the pace of exchanges, corresponding with utterance length. Alexander defines semantic or cognitive pace as the speed at which conceptual ground is covered and new or old learning outcomes are introduced. This form of pace is adjacent to the way in which Bernstein (1990) uses the term and corresponds closely with links between learning outcomes and utterance length, although they all seem to correspond with the number of learning outcomes visited. Learning pace corresponds with the degree of on-task talk and evidence of learning in the session. The speed at which learning is expected to occur seems to be directly related to the access to learning that different children have in the classroom and this is managed through the children's and teachers' talk. Children whose language is valued and replicated in the classroom will learn at a different rate to those whose talk is not, and this seems to be reflected in the OfSTED (2002a) study.

Issues of the pace of teaching in NLS have concerned researchers with regard to the opportunities available for the development of critical language and reasoning capabilities (Riley 2001). The analysis of English et al. (2002) concludes that if pupils' contributions were not extended, it was unlikely that the talk would begin to resemble discussion, and a central concern identified was that of pace (see also Mroz et al. 2000). A similar concern with pace is apparent in discussion of children's understandings of the literacy hour (Hancock and Mansfield 2002). The pace at which classroom talk and activity has been arranged has consequences for pupils' opportunities to make their own sense. This has impact on children's engagement with knowledge. How we talk to children has consequences for what they can say, how they can say things and thus for the learning they engage with.

Classroom examples of nomination and the distribution of knowledge

Literacy lessons

It is tempting to try and present pace as a characteristic of classroom talk, perhaps as the 'speed' of a lesson. Whilst a teacher or an OfSTED inspector may experience the speed of the lesson in a unified way, our work has suggested that different groups of children will experience pace differentially. Teachers manage these different rates of learning through the ways in which they call on different children to speak (Young 1992). Children are frequently asked checking questions (where the teacher establishes what pupils know, if they are on the ball), sometimes they are asked guessing questions (about technical terms or the way language is used) and less frequently they are asked for judgements (what they think or feel). Sometimes teachers ask a question to which the whole class is invited to reply in unison; sometimes they ask questions and then invite an individual to respond; sometimes they name an individual respondent in the course of the question. Only very occasionally and under specific circumstances (for example hot seating) will a pupil's nomination of a speaker be accepted.

This process of speaker nomination and the kind of talk involved has the effect of differentially distributing knowledge in the classroom. Work with which we have been associated (Eke and Lee 2004) leads us to believe that pace proceeds at different rates for different groups of learners in the classroom. In the case of the NLS it seems that if there are large numbers of children who have additional needs in the classroom their experience will be distinct from that of other groups. Their voices are likely to be under-represented in the to and fro of classroom talk. They will be invited to speak less often than other children and will say less. The scaffolding for their learning will be restricted and they will visit fewer learning outcomes than their peers. Teachers are likely to ask these pupils checking questions and the speed of exchange will be fairly rapid while the pace of their learning will be slower.

Gender differentiation is frequently apparent in the teaching of literacy, and again nominations mean that the pace of the lesson is different for boys and girls. In our studies boys are asked more assessment questions than girls, visiting a slightly wider range of learning outcomes leading to a faster pace for them than for girls. The girls are more likely to be nominated for discursive questions, where they are asked about what they think or feel about the subject. This means that although they are likely to be asked fewer questions, they are likely to make longer responses. There are fewer learning outcomes that lend themselves to this approach than to assessment questioning and so fewer learning outcomes are visited, thus the pace is slower for girls. The girls have the space to give a fuller voice to their interests and concerns than do the boys.

For example, during the literacy hour with a class of Year 5 and Year 6 pupils, the teacher nominates girls to answer questions in a comparatively straightforward manner:

Teacher: *Stop there. Excellent! What are they looking at? What sort of piece of writing are we looking at already? Ebony?*

Here we see an instruction, positive feedback and an assisting question that is likely to require a technical response and guessing what the teacher is thinking. The pupil responds appropriately.

Pupil: At a newspaper (inaudible . . .)
Teacher: Good girl! So you think immediately we're talking about a newspaper article.

During the same session we find:

Teacher: Thank you. Who is going to put that in their own words? Hayley, yes.
Pupil: It's saying while the prisoners are in jail, but they're getting computers . . . um . . . um . . .. and 2 million pounds spent on them but they're not in jail.
Teacher: Good girl – sorry go on.
Pupil: . . . and they have to work in worse conditions.

Here there is space for Hayley to think on her feet (the 'ums' suggest she is formulating a subsequent utterance) and the teacher apologises when he occupies this space. The girls are congratulated as people in these examples. This contrasts with boys, who find their questions embodied in more complex utterances involving feedback, assisting questions, some modelling, and a speaker nomination. They are likely to be congratulated on a specific performance in English sessions with the teacher saying, 'That was good because you . . .' rather than simply 'Good boy'. In our studies we have found this kind of differentiation between boys and girls was present in Key Stage 1 sessions and becomes more sharply defined with older children.

Activity

Re-read the example of Year 5 and 6 pupils working with a newspaper article. Make a list of questions which you could ask pupils about a newspaper article. Sort your questions into assessment and discursive questions. Think about the answers you would expect from the different questions. Are some questions more useful for extending children's understanding? Why?

Working in mathematics

Differentiation has been a particular concern in the teaching of primary mathematics, and nowhere is this concern more apparent than in small rural primary schools where two or more age groups are taught in the same lesson. The skilled teachers we studied adapted the NNS to provide for the differences between age groups, boys and girls and to a limited degree between different learners. Askew (2001) makes the point that notwithstanding the prescriptions of the NNS to engage almost entirely in whole-class teaching, teachers still seek to differentiate. Our analysis of teachers at work in a rural primary school confirms this. The psychomotor modelling (showing pupils), the cognitive structuring offered (explanation and demonstration) and the assessment questions that followed indicated that our teachers were showing pupils what to do, providing explanations and then checking that they understood through task completion. Such talk made up a large part of the lessons we observed. Our skilled teachers distributed questioning during whole-class sessions to ensure that the youngest age group were engaged by questioning them first and by finding opportunities to return to them during the session. In the case of the older age group they are specifically addressed in the middle of the session. The end of the session is marked by an opportunity for discursive talk that focuses on either the youngest or oldest age group. In the sessions we analysed, the opportunities for the pupils to voice their understanding are very limited indeed. Our teachers distributed classroom knowledge to target pupil groups and individuals; in so doing the regulatory and instructional aspects of the session are bound up with each other and with the means of assistance. Working with a Year 2/3 class we found a substantial number of utterances could be coded for monitoring and checking pupil understanding with pupils responding in kind:

Teacher: *Yes, it would change that number completely. So you leave a space please to show me it's a new number. Right – which would be the next number? We are going in order. Now which one will be next? Katie.*

Pupil: *Twenty-eight.*

Teacher: *Twenty-eight – that's right. And what would I write down for the next one? James.*

Pupil: *Thirteen.*

Teacher: *Thirteen – and the smallest number would be? Lou.*

Pupil: *Seven.*

Teachers maintained tight control over classroom talk and kept it closely focused on their designated learning outcomes. They kept to a steady progression through one learning outcome at a time and visited a very restricted number of learning outcomes.

One exception to this control came with a Year 5/6 class:

Pupil: *Er . . . I done zero point one.*
Teacher: *Say again, Michele.*
Pupil: *Zero point one.*
Teacher: *Good girl.*
Pupil: *Sir, we decided to add them all up.*
Teacher: *Good – you can tell me the answer in a minute. A little challenge for the boys over there. Just to add them all. Er right – next one, Helen.*

Here the teacher follows up a pupil suggestion about lesson activity and at the end of the whole-class session encouraged exploratory and investigatory talk. Both teachers in our study did this at the end of the whole-class sessions, suggesting that the status of pupil talk where pupils engage with making mathematical meanings for themselves is of secondary importance to the requirements set out in official documents.

The children's voices in English sessions are sometimes discursive (where pupils discuss their responses to a text), although they are mostly confined to responding to requests for display, that is, answering questions from adults even though they know that the adults already know the answer. In mathematics their voices are even more restricted, with only a small space at the end of the lesson when they can articulate their own sense and understanding. This suggests that the opportunity for children's voices to be heard will vary with subject content.

Reflection

What difference does it make when a teacher adapts the flow of the lesson to accommodate learners' ideas? Reflect on examples how this might occur and in what subjects. In over 10,000 lines of transcript we found five examples of 'uptake' by teachers (you will find other examples in this chapter). Why do you think it is so unusual?

Religious education

For nearly 60 years religious education (RE) has been a mandatory subject in primary schools, although not every pupil is required to study it or every teacher to teach it. The current curriculum descriptions offer two key learning outcomes that are prioritised through two curriculum models (QCA 1996).

We can characterise these as 'learning about main faith traditions' and 'responding to puzzling questions'. Classroom talk in RE seems less constrained by subject learning outcomes than in the other two subjects discussed. There are differences between the two approaches we have flagged above and, as might be anticipated, talk in sessions focused on the main faith traditions is more constrained than that where puzzling questions are discussed.

In sessions focused on main faith traditions, a limited number of learning outcomes were visited and the pupil and teacher talk matched well with national expectations. In a Year 3 class where the story of Abraham was discussed:

Teacher: *What sort of questions do you think might be going through his head after God's promise . . . to sacrifice his son . . . Ricki.*
Pupil: *Erm . . . What a waste of time . . . why shall I do it?*
Teacher: *Yes, he might be thinking 'Why should I do it'. Helen?*
Pupil: *Why has He given me this son when He wants to take him away . . . wants me to sacrifice him?*

In a Year 5 class where the topic of Buddhism was being introduced, pupils were encouraged to discuss a range of images before they heard a story.

Teacher: *Lovely . . . well that . . . and we've a lot to add this afternoon. Would anyone like to have . . . might . . . I don't think you might know . . . you might have worked out what or who Buddhists worship.*
Pupil: *I think they worship the Buddha.*
Teacher: *OK. Anybody think of anything different?*
Pupil: *Erm . . . I think all the different Buddhists do different things. They . . . works . . .*
Teacher: *Ella.*
Pupil: *Buddhists still worship Buddha but I don't think as a person. His is just a statue that they worship.*
Teacher: *Cathy.*
Pupil: *I think . . . Gods . . . worship. In a picture there was all little gods.*
Teacher: *Annie.*
Pupil: *The . . . er . . . special book.*
Teacher: *They actually worship the book itself. Stuart.*
Pupil: *Well, they might worship statues.*
Teacher: *Jamie.*
Pupil: *They usually give grown-ups.*
Teacher: *Jordan, sit here. In fact you know the answer to this don't you? Now come on Jordan, please. I did tell Buddhism is slightly different from other religions. Jordan.*

Pupil: *Erm . . . Buddha isn't really a god. Has just a . . . has somebody that you should . . . you should. . . erm . . . like a right life for everyone.*

There was some evidence of talk designed to promote pupil cognition and some indication that this influenced pupil talk. The teachers worked hard to ensure pupils remained aware of the purpose of the lesson and reminded pupils of this as they managed change from one activity to another. The teachers told stories related to the content of the session and the pupils listened attentively, as was apparent in pupil responses.

Sessions which offered pupils the opportunity to discuss and respond to puzzling questions were the most open and discursive of all sessions we observed. The emphasis was on the attainment target which related to responding to puzzling questions and the teachers were able managers of whole-class discussion. Much of the talk was relevant to the topic but not all of it readily fitted with learning outcomes set out in national documents. Even so, the pupils produced some utterances which seemed to us to be above national expectations. In these exchanges, rather like the discussion of Buddhism above, where there is one instruction from the teacher and several invitations to speak, the pupils are willing to try answers and to speculate. A little later in the session the teacher asks the children what religious symbols and worship are for. The Year 2 children are happy to speculate:

Teacher: *(Writing comments from pupils on board) OK. So. We all die . . . die. Lollipop . . . .I'll just write them in shorthand. What was yours. . . erm . . . I have forgotten . . . erm . . . what was yours, Juliet?*
Pupil: *To live.*
Teacher: *Live – what did you just say? To make God real.*
Pupil: *No, I said so that people think that God is real.*

Here a 7-year-old is correcting the teacher as he writes on the board and demonstrating a grasp of the discussion which is above the expectations set out in QCA guidance. It is not specific questions that have produced this outcome but an approach to classroom talk in RE sessions, for example later in the same lesson:

Pupil: *Maybe people want to know what they are going to be when they die.*
Pupil: *(chuckles)*
Pupil: *She's hit the jackpot – that it is it.*

These pupils provided each other with feedback and made judgements based on their learning through talk. Analysis showed similar exchanges with a Year 5/6 class, who were also speculating about an afterlife.

Teacher:	*Up there somewhere. Yes. Most people think of heaven as above don't they? Yes. OK. We are not quite sure where and what it would . . . it would be like in heaven, Mike, if you went there. What do Christians think it would be like?*
Pupil:	*Like down here but it's different than here.*
Teacher:	*So it would be like down here but . . .*
Pupil:	*But posher kind of.*
Teacher:	*Bit posher (laughs). OK, that's one way of putting it. Nick.*
Pupil:	*White.*
Teacher:	*Yes, everything is white. I wonder why it's white.*
Pupil:	*Because it's like clouds and things.*
Teacher:	*Oh, I see. Right, heaven is white. Jane.*
Pupil:	*It could be like have your own one. It would be whatever you want it.*
Teacher:	*Like your own personal one.*
Pupil:	*My own heaven.*
Teacher:	*Yes, strange isn't it in a way, we all think of it a bit differently don't we? Lyn.*

Where the talk showed the teacher modelling cognitive activity or provided evidence of pupil thinking, through such things as pauses mixed with repetitions and fillers, then the talk was more likely to link with a published learning outcome. Our teachers regularly reminded pupils of the focus and purpose of the discussions but were not afraid to allow the children opportunities for sustained talk.

Reflection

You have seen examples here of classroom talk in English, mathematics and religious education. You might want to reflect on the ways in which they are similar and different. Why is the talk so tightly focused in mathematics lessons and why do children seem more prepared to risk more tentative responses in other lessons, especially in religious education?

Summary

Our evidence shows that there are many ways in which teachers assist pupil learning. This scaffolding is common to all the teachers we have studied in all the subjects we have discussed and with whatever age they are teaching. What is different is the way in which the learning outcomes, age and sex of the pupils and the attribution of additional learning needs are related to the kind of assistance the teachers offer. This means that teachers make a selection of means of assistance that reflect the subject and children they are teaching. This selection sets and usually determines the form of pupil response. The lesson content and pacing depends on the pupil positioning and this determines what the children have an opportunity to say. Pupil voices vary not only with the way they are identified, but also with the discourse of the subject.

There is a cogent argument that the form of knowledge children are learning about has an impact on the talk and activities they engage with, and this in turn impacts on what they learn. Our detailed analysis of a small number of lessons suggests that classroom talk is most restricted, with little space for pupil voice, where the knowledge content is tightly defined by the teacher. It becomes more relaxed, with greater opportunity for pupil voice, as the teacher cedes control of knowledge to the pupils. In addition, it could also be argued that alongside the forms of knowledge children engage with, consideration should also be given to the forms of representation (the means for representing meaning) children engage with (Eisner 1996).

In *Excellence and Enjoyment* (DfES 2003a) there is some recognition of the need to engage children's voices, to involve children as active meaning-makers using a diversity of means of representation, although Alexander (2004) questions whether this is more than gloss and capable of taking forward our grasp of the art of the science of teaching.

In conclusion, we want to suggest that engaging with these challenges will present a key dilemma to teachers who are concerned to engage all the learners they are responsible for in worthwhile activity. Given the nature of school learning and its distribution through classroom talk, success for all requires a response to the agenda set out by Tharp et al. (2000). He reminds us that it is 'unwise and unkind' to ignore what children come to school with and prevent the development of pupils' full potential. Our talk should not systematically ignore the voices of children. At the same time we should not allow the ways of speaking and modes of representation pupils bring from home to determine classroom activity because this would limit academic and social learning. If we take 'text' in the big sense of the word (a representation of ideas of some form, print, televisual, formulaic and so on), the learning that succeeds for all is about democratic engagement with texts.

To achieve such democratic engagement pupils should expect to have their culture acknowledged and extended by the school as they engage with making meaning utilising a diversity of forms of representation. They will learn in a context where they are asked few questions to which there is one knowable right answer and many questions which require them to think. The pace of learning will not be rushed and will be varied to meet the needs of individuals and groups within the classroom. The consciousness of the children will be in the mind of the teacher as the starting point for their education. This kind of reflective practice can take as its building blocks the way teachers talk to children and expect children to talk to them.

Reflection

In what ways has this chapter encouraged you to think about how teachers arrange classroom talk and activities for children's learning?

Drawing on your own experiences and from your reading, begin to identify some implications for your own teaching and explain reasons for some of your decisions.

Ask yourself:

- What opportunities will I provide for classroom talk?
- In what ways will I support children in representing their meanings through talk?
- How will I listen to children and develop my teaching from the children's contributions?

Chapter 2

Support or straitjacket?
A tale of three
Strategies

Jo Barkham and Jo Miller

Introduction

In September 1998, virtually every primary school teacher in England was trained to use the National Literacy Strategy (NLS). This became, in educational terms, one of the largest educational reforms world wide and, unlike the existing National Curriculum, prescribed not only *what* was to be taught, but also *how*. It was followed a year later by the National Numeracy Strategy (NNS). These initiatives are sometimes jointly referred to as 'the Strategies' or National Literacy/Numeracy Strategies (NLNS). In 2003 they became the heart of a re-launched Primary National Strategy (PNS), with its vision of 'excellence and enjoyment' (DfES 2003a) being recognised through increased flexibility for schools to innovate and to raise (literacy and numeracy) standards through a rich, broad and balanced curriculum. These Strategies have had a profound influence on primary education throughout England.

This chapter will help you to think about the following questions:

- Why were the Strategies introduced and what did they hope to achieve?
- Did the Strategies actually work?
- How has the curriculum changed, especially in relation to literacy and mathematics?

Throughout the chapter we use acknowledged sources together with our own research. We use data based on interviews with those who have worked at the heart of the Strategies – key policymakers who were writers and implementers at national level – and further data gathered from teachers and trainees. And perhaps, most importantly, the voices of some children who have 'benefited' from the Strategies are also heard.

What is the background to the National Literacy and National Numeracy Strategies?

Politics and 'education, education, education'

The seeds of the National Strategies found fertile ground following a change in government in 1997. After 18 years of Conservative rule, Tony Blair led New Labour to power, promising that his three priorities would be 'education, education, education'. What was it that inspired New Labour to focus its first priorities on education?

New Labour, like most European social democratic parties, believes that whilst their ideal of full employment is impossible within a world economy driven by market forces, the state *can* work to improve the ability of companies to compete in the global marketplace. For New Labour, improved education and training are essential to this end. Hence Blair's assertion that education is the best economic policy there is: 'The main source of value and competitive advantage in the modern economy is human and intellectual capital. Hence the over-riding priority New Labour is giving to education and training' (Blair 1998: 10).

For Blair, the dogma of the right leads the education system to defend and increase middle-class privilege whilst the dogma of the left, with its ideological insistence on uniformity of provision, results in the levelling down of standards, which has similarly perpetuated low working-class achievement: 'Too many children are written off. Too many talents are wasted' (Blair, cited in Hatcher 1996: 32). A decade later, Blair's rhetoric continues: 'Our task is to level up systematically . . . to make success the norm . . .' (Blair 2005a: 2). There is little doubt, therefore, that New Labour's commitment to social justice lies at the heart of their education policy.

Data from international comparisons caused concerns to the politicians of the 1990s. A particular feature of British educational performance was that a long 'tail' of underachievement existed. This was significantly greater than in other countries (Brooks et al. 1996: 10) Furthermore there is the argument summarised by Beard (2000: 8) that very low levels of literacy are associated with unemployment and crime.

Therefore, in 1997, the new government brought fresh energy to challenge underachievement; it meant to make its mark – and quickly. The Department for Education and Employment found not only a new minister (David Blunkett), but a new unit within its walls – a 'Standards and Effectiveness Unit' headed by Professor Michael Barber. Barber had chaired a Literacy Task Force, formed by Blunkett in 1996, whilst Labour was still in opposition. This group monitored the work of the 'Literacy Project', which was running in fourteen Local Education Authorities using selected schools whose standards of achievement in literacy were deemed to be low. Barber was very influential – his book *The Learning Game was* published in 1997, the front cover of which has a bold endorsement by Tony Blair, who calls the work 'provocative and timely, illuminating and optimistic'. Barber argues that to make a real difference in standards at secondary level, it would be necessary to begin with primary.

School effectiveness and school improvement: riding the juggernaut

Barber's area of expertise was managing change within systems. In his new role as head of the Standards and Effectiveness Unit, Barber (2001: 20) set out a model of 'high challenge, high support'. His stated position refers to winning hearts and minds by **imposed** structures and a **requirement** of adoption, following which, according to Barber, teachers would come to understand the principles behind their new practice. The requirements on the profession were couched in terms whereby schools were told that the Strategies were 'voluntary', but OfSTED inspection frameworks would test alternatives, requiring schools to demonstrate that they were as good or better. There is little wonder that implementation was not universally welcomed by the profession, particularly amongst officers in Local Education Authorities, for whom the Strategies were never 'voluntary'. For them, funding through the Standards Fund (which represented a significant increase in budgets for Local Education Authorities) depended directly on their compliance.

The Strategies are founded within the highly influential 'school improvement movement' whose work is based on research into 'school effectiveness' described by Slee and Weiner (1998: 3) as a 'juggernaut as it rides roughshod over educational policy-making and research'. This school improvement movement rejects the idea that outcomes are pre-determined by social class and that schools do not make much difference. In 1988, Mortimore et al. identified some characteristics of effective primary schools as having a purposeful leadership team, a structured school day and limited foci in lessons (their work was pre-National Curriculum) with elements of whole-class teaching rather than purely individualised learning, all of which resonates with the Strategies some ten years later. Reynolds (1999) explains that the research of the early 1990s extended Mortimer et al.'s work, resulting in a 'significantly enhanced' understanding of the key features of an effective school. These include strong leadership and good working relationships between head and deputy, a 'mission' which actively involves all staff and a balance between managerialism and collegiality. High quality teaching is reduced by Reynolds to a list which includes clarity of presentation, a restricted range of goals, structuring of curriculum content, questioning skills, matching the task to ability, appropriate grouping strategies, high expectations and 'pace' (by which he appears to mean some element of speed – without 'slack' in the timing). Each and every one of Reynold's definitions can be uncovered in the detail of the National Literacy and Numeracy Strategies with their highly structured list of objectives and prescriptive pedagogy.

Yet the research is contested and highly controversial. In reviewing the seminal work of 1988, Mortimore later expressed reservations that the research had failed to demonstrate advantage to *all* students and that 'the capacity of the advantaged to get more out of any situation . . . poses a serious problem to school improvement' (Mortimore 1992: 159). Pointing out that schools in England at that time were having to contend with the implementation of a National Curriculum with an attendant regime of assessment, local management of schools with funding allocated by a formula, competition between schools for pupils and a media hostile to the teaching profession, Mortimore appealed: 'having provided a reasonable legislative framework, governments – in my opinion – would do well to encourage . . . co-operative endeavour rather than the bullying and deriding tactics that are more commonly employed' (ibid.).

Many would doubt that his appeals were ever heard. The National Literacy Strategy was imposed by 'insiders' from the profession with parental and media support guaranteed by a universally acceptable appeal to raise standards for all; to reduce the 'unacceptably high' proportion of school leavers with little or very low levels of qualification (Barber 2001: 18); and to tackle fears that an unacceptable number of failing teachers were damaging the life-chances of children (Blair 1996, cited in Jones 1996: 20).

With a focus on **teaching** (rather than learning) and a drive to ensure high standards for all, the questions which arise in the mind of educators include: 'What (and who) is education for?' For the members of the school improvement movement, answers appear to lie principally in narrow economic terms of employability.

Reflection

What do YOU think education is for?

Who do you think education is for?

Compare and contrast your ideas with the views expressed above.

The Literacy and Numeracy Projects

The forerunner of the National Literacy Strategy was a National Literacy Project (NLP), which ran under the Conservative Government during 1996 and early 1997. Schools from fourteen local educational authorities (LEAs) were identified at a local as well as national level where there were concerns about attainment standards.

The Secretary of State for Education and Employment at that time declared that 'the first task of the education service is to ensure that every child is taught to read, write and add up' (DfEE 1997: 9), which also prompted the establishment of the Numeracy Task Force whose recommendations led to a National Numeracy Project (NNP). The NNP focused on proficiency with basic number skills in response to supposed concerns by workplace employers that significant numbers of school leavers had skill levels which inhibited their ability to fulfil everyday tasks. It should be noted, however, that there is very little workplace research to support this claim. That which does exist suggests the problem lies with a lack of relevance between what is perceived as traditional 'secondary school mathematics' and the everyday skills required for life. This appears to be a recurring concern as McIntosh, back in 1981, provided quotations showing that officials have deplored what they have seen as falling levels of numerical skills since at least the middle of the nineteenth century!

As with the Literacy Project, there was a bid for national funding and the Numeracy Project was taught within the schools and local authorities that supported them. Consultants in these projects developed materials and frameworks of objectives were devised under the leadership of national project co-ordinators. These projects were evaluated positively; NfER (1998) published the results of the Literacy Project in December of 1998, three months after the National Literacy Strategy (DfEE 1998) had been rolled out nationally.

The Numeracy Project framework, after very few modifications, became the *Framework for Teaching Mathematics* that appears under the National Numeracy Strategy (DfEE 1999a). As literacy had replaced English, the word Numeracy became synonymous with mathematics in spite of the term being specifically adopted for a project which was originally only concerned with improving proficiency of numerical skills. Crucially, neither project had ever been devised, designed or intended as pilots for the Strategies that they ultimately became.

Did the Strategies actually work? Implementation and evaluation

Implementation at school level: the lunchbox arrives

Outside the original projects, teachers began to become aware of the significant changes in their working practices to be required from September 1998 when the first of the Strategies, the NLS, was to be implemented. Across the country, heads, literacy co-ordinators and a governor from every school attended training events – that is when they knew this was, in the words of one teacher 'very big – a serious business'. Never had anything like this happened before.

Following this launch, headteachers and literacy co-ordinators returned to their schools with a heavy pack of training materials (the 'lunchbox'). These materials had been assembled by a team of people with great expertise in literacy but who had worked towards very tight deadlines. Nothing like this had been attempted previously – none of them had had the experience of making video material to exemplify what was expected and, according to one of those who held responsibility for this work, the whole process included 'compromise' and 'amateurism'. The headteachers and literacy co-ordinators became trainers – deliverers of professional development material which was unreliable in its quality. The success of this process was, to say the least, variable. Some teachers and leaders wholeheartedly embraced the materials, whilst others used them to impose unwanted changes on school staff. In a minority of schools, the materials were simply ignored. In most cases, however, schools began the process of transformation, if only as a result of leverage from OfSTED's expectations. In addition, considerable support was given to schools by consultants, recruited to work in each LEA. They represented the 'support' part of a 'lever' ensuring that change would take place effectively across the whole country.

The following year the process was repeated, with headteachers, mathematics co-ordinators and other identified key teachers attending either three- or five-day training sessions, depending on whether the school had been identified as having weaknesses. Again, the process turned from a waterfall to a fountain effect as the teachers who had attended mathematics training were expected to cascade all they had learned to their colleagues in school. Limitations on time, including the practicality of disseminating five days of training in relatively brief staff meetings, made this impossible.

Following the implementation of the Literacy Strategy, teachers generally took the Numeracy Strategy on board quite willingly. They were, by now, used to the idea of delivering many fragmented objectives from frameworks and those who felt they had less expertise in mathematics enjoyed the comfort and security of a prescriptive scheme of work. The question remains whether the Numeracy Strategy really supports children's mathematical development adequately – as so many teachers report that they still find little time to develop the area of mathematical enquiry as a result of the fast and relentless pace of the requirements.

Activity

What forms of teaching organisation for numeracy and literacy have you observed in schools? Are there daily lessons in these subjects? Do the lessons follow a particular structure?

Success (or otherwise) as measured by test results

To dispel the myth that Labour would simply increase spending to address priorities in education, the Chancellor, Gordon Brown, held the Department for Education to a contract with the Treasury where money would only be released if they kept to their plans with tightly written targets and objectives. The National Strategies were to be measured by success in Standardised Assessment Tests (SATs) with national targets at Key Stage 2 to be achieved by 2002. Of all primary children, 80 per cent would be expected to attain level 4 in English and 75 per cent in mathematics. Thus, the drive for standards replaced a concern for an appropriate primary curriculum (Davies and Edwards 1999).

There is a debate about whether or not SATs are a valid measure of pupils' learning, but nonetheless it is the one employed by the critical friends of the Strategies, the Ontario Institute for Studies in Education (OISE) team in analysing the effects of the Strategies in their final report. At first, Key Stage 2 SATs results between 1997 and 2000 showed substantial gains in the number of children reaching their expected level. OISE was rightly cautious about confusing causal factors with correlative ones and they argued that improvements in SATs results were most significant *before* the introduction of the Strategies, and that in the period following implementation the gains quickly began to level off. Other factors may therefore be at work here. The improved SATs results may result from teachers preparing their pupils more carefully for the tests. Also, the implementation period of the NLS and NNS was accompanied by a so-called amnesty, whereby schools were not expected to maintain a focus on foundation subjects and OfSTED's attention was centred on the Literacy Hour and daily mathematics lesson. By 2003, OfSTED agreed that standards were initially lifted but that further improvements were proving increasingly difficult to achieve (OfSTED 2003a: 54).

Of some interest, perhaps is a study by Machin and McNally. The authors compared GCSE results for English between pupils who had been involved in the National Literacy Project in Year 6 and those who had not. Their study 'strongly corroborates the view that the literacy hour under the NLP significantly raised pupil performance in the primary schools that were exposed to it' (Machin and McNally 2004: 5). But again, it might be appropriate to exercise caution in identifying the NLS (in general) as a support for pupils' learning in this instance, bearing in mind that the pilot schools chose to be involved and had a clear commitment to raising achievement. The apparent success as identified in the GCSE scores could be the product of this commitment and involvement, rather than any specific innovative pedagogy. In addition, the research and scrutiny of the pilot cohorts could itself induce the continued development and the later achievements. The new initiative might have enjoyed a measure of success because it is new, thus refreshing and energising practice: the 'Hawthorne effect'.

Reflection

Do SATs influence the way subjects are taught? List some ways in which you think SATs might influence the curriculum, particularly in relation to literacy/English and numeracy/mathematics sessions.

Success (or otherwise) according to the critical friends

The Strategies were closely monitored by OfSTED, who were a powerful influence on some of the details of the framework and implementation, as was the team of critical friends from the Ontario Institute of Studies in Education, led by Michael Fullan, a world authority on large-scale educational change (see Fullan and Stiegelbauer 1991; Fullan 2000, 2003). The series of reports from OISE is entitled *Watching and Learning* (Earl et al. 2000, 2001, 2003). The aims of the Strategies, according to OISE, were 'to improve classroom practice and pupil learning in literacy and mathematics' and provide 'clear direction and support for change' (Earl et al. 2003: 4). If improvement in pupils' learning was to be identified by an increase in the number of pupils meeting their 'expected level' (i.e. level 4) in Year 6, then presumably improvement in classroom practice was to be measured by the same outcome.

In their final report OISE concluded that the Strategies were generally well implemented and supported by schools and that elements of the Strategies appeared in virtually all classrooms. They recognise that ' there have been indications of improved teaching practice and pupil learning as well as a substantial narrowing of the gap between the most and least successful schools' (Earl et al. 2003: 8).

There was also evidence of a substantial improvement in the quality of teaching cited from other evidence – including HMI/OfSTED reports; amongst the successes noted was that teachers held a very positive view about their own professional development. OISE themselves, however, reported that it was more difficult to draw conclusions about the effect of the Strategies on pupil learning, and they go on to warn that, 'although the Strategies have made a good beginning in a relatively short period of time, the intended changes in teaching and learning have not yet been fully realised' (Earl et al. 2003: 8–9).

The view of many teachers and headteachers in the OISE reports seemed to be that pupils showed increased understanding and skill in many aspects of English and mathematics, but the picture was unclear. Furthermore, some reference was made to teachers' perceptions of pupils' dispositions towards the Strategies, particularly in terms of motivation and engagement. Some teachers indicated that the Strategies were effective in raising motivation (e.g.

'pupils really want to do the numeracy work': Earl et al. 2003: 86) whilst a headteacher stated, 'the downfall of the Literacy Strategy is that there is nothing on how to motivate children' (ibid.: 88). Consultants were reported as feeling that both Strategies had been helpful in engaging unmotivated pupils, the implication being that this was not necessarily a view shared by most practitioners. Nevertheless, what may be of significance in this context is the attitude of teachers themselves to the Strategies. It is reasonable to assume that negative attitudes may hinder learning whilst enthusiasm and enjoyment on the part of the teacher is likely to impart similar attitudes in their pupils.

Evaluation – research evidence

Research evidence at the start of the National Literacy Strategy shows that many teachers were positively disposed towards the Literacy Hour (Fisher et al. 2000), and Fisher (2002) presents further evidence from a research study into the implementation in small rural schools. Meanwhile, following criticism that NLS documentation lacked reference to research evidence, an academic review of evidence on which the pedagogic principles underpinning the NLS was commissioned (Beard 1999).

But the NLS had other early critics. Riley (2001) questioned the extent to which the NLS was able to accommodate the implications of research findings. She also suggested that the searchlights model of reading outlined in the Strategy documentation was inadequately explained – the underpinning theories were not illuminated – and the model was handled cursorily. Meanwhile, Mroz et al. (2000) challenged the success of whole-class inter-active teaching which, they assert, was ill-defined and resulted in a recourse to traditional whole-class, directive teaching with less emphasis on active learning. English et al. (2002) took this argument further, focusing parti-cularly on what they argue is 'contradictory pedagogical advice' on 'inter-active teaching'. Their research concludes that the classroom discourse of teachers in the Literacy Hour is quantitatively and qualitatively different from pre-NLS discourse. What had perhaps been intended was not what these researchers were finding in practice.

The NNS was also criticised for its lack of research base. The government had claimed in the original proposals that the NNS would be based on evidence concerning what works without making adequate reference to the actual evidence. Brown et al. (1998) examined these claims and found that some of the proposals and recommendations, such as in the use of calculators, actually ran counter to the evidence.

Further examination of the early Numeracy Strategy documentation leads to concerns which have resonance with those put by critics of the Literacy Strategy. In its focus on direct teaching, high quality interactive teaching is described by the Numeracy Strategy framework as a two-way process (DfEE

1999a) in which pupils are expected to play an active part through answering questions, contributing to discussion and by explaining and demonstrating their methods. However, of the eight elements identified as being components of quality teaching, the truly interactive element is sparse; teacher direction, instruction, demonstration and explanation dominate the recommended teaching styles. The comparison with the recommendations of the Cockcroft Report of 1982 is striking (Cockroft 1982). This report suggests discussion (including *between* pupils), investigative work, practical activity and problem solving are key elements of effective teaching of mathematics. In one scenario, the teacher dominates the interactions to direct children's thinking; in the other, pupils' voices are heard. There is danger in that the passive role of the learner in the first scenario leads to boredom, frustration and detachment.

Reflection

Do you think that the Strategies have been successful? In what ways?

Ask teachers and other professionals for their opinions and compare with your own views.

What has happened to the curriculum?

Fragmentation: from English to Literacy

The National Curriculum has a skills-based set of programmes of study for English. These are broken down into Speaking and Listening, Reading and Writing. Such fragmentation of language is questionable but appears positively holistic when compared with the National Literacy Strategy Framework of objectives (1998): here there are 807 objectives, divided into word level, sentence level and text level over the year groups from Reception to Year 6. Fragmentation within the hour where word level work was separated from the text level work featured in early literacy hour teaching. Cohesion between different literacy lessons over a week or a fortnight was another challenge that teachers initially found difficult to resolve. In short, the teaching of English had been replaced by Literacy. With a misguided assumption that teachers would ensure the rightful prominence of oracy in their work, it was not until 2003 that the Primary National Strategy, in one of its first publications, issued guidance on *Speaking, Listening, Learning: Working with Children in Key Stages 1 and 2* (DfES 2003d). In this, another 67 objectives are detailed, from Year 1 to Year 6. Linking objectives into a unit of work which makes sense to learners is one of the many challenges that faced teachers in their planning. The renewed Primary Framework of 2006 structures these objectives into a more holistic package.

The phonics debate

The argument over whether, and how, phonics should be taught has raged in the earlier years of children's schooling for decades. The NLS required teachers in Reception and Year 1 classes to use analytic and synthetic phonics regularly (15 minutes per day), from a detailed progression that was significantly faster than had historically been the case. In the NLS framework, the word level work (phonics) was deliberately placed first so that teachers would attend to that aspect of literacy. Yet in some LEAs, until the arrival of the Strategy, phonics had been discouraged as a method by which children should be taught to read, and in 1998 an ideological clash resulted. The debate is, in some circles, a furious one, and politicians sitting on a select committee in the House of Commons became involved. They commissioned a report (Rose 2006) into methods of teaching early reading which depend on a systematic, synthesised approach to phonics. This is a more prescriptive approach to phonics teaching than the NLS suggests, and advocates of this approach argue that early readers should be taught by this method alone, rather than encouraging early readers to use inference from cues such as the pictures. Rose suggests that a 'vigorous' programme of phonic work should be securely embedded within a broad, language-rich curriculum; that decisions about when to introduce phonic work should be a matter of principled professional judgement based on careful observation and robust assessment; and that for most children this will be worthwhile to begin before the age of 5. He concludes, however, that high quality phonics teaching is not enough. He also emphasises the importance of nurturing positive attitudes to literacy; developing spoken language; recognising that all areas of learning/subjects give opportunities for children to develop their language capabilities; and raising the quality of 'classroom talk' (Alexander 2006).

Rose acknowledges that significant amounts of time have been wasted by those who amplify strongly held, conflicting views, whilst most teachers have quietly continued with their mixed-methods approaches. Futile debate, Rose argues, distracts attention from the important questions around understanding how young children learn to read and write; some excellent principles underpinning the acquisition of early reading skills are sometimes dismissed by understandably confused (and annoyed) teachers. At least Rose gives readers the courtesy of a full explanation of his findings, together with academic references to the key research on which he has based his conclusions. Interestingly, his report suggests that the searchlights model of the NLS should be replaced. National prescription in 1998 was imposed with a flawed model and will now be superseded by another set of prescriptions until, of course, that, too, is perhaps found to be inadequate.

Activity

Ask practitioners how they teach phonics, particularly in Reception and
Year 1. Ask them for their views on the methods which they employ.

Time to read: what the children say

The time to read with and to children has seemed to decrease since the advent
of the National Curriculum. With the Literacy Hour, another indictment has
been added – it encourages the illumination of small chunks of literature
rather than the whole story. In addition, commentators have questioned
whether the Strategy has damaged the love of reading – the author Philip
Pullman was vitriolic in his condemnation to the annual conference of
National Association for the Teaching of English (NATE) in 2002. Yet there
are children who will give a different voice – whose teachers have introduced
them to a range of literature they would not otherwise have known and
whose passion and knowledge of appropriate children's literature is
infectious. In interviews with a group of twenty-six Year 6 children, not one
of them agreed that Pullman was right and Harry's comment below reveals
that the Literacy Hour had enabled him to access a wide range of texts that
he might not otherwise have thought of. He had just enjoyed a book which,
in his account, the author had written for another audience: '*We've had a
clump of books that were put on the table; we had to read from one that we
thought we would never choose . . . then I ended up doing a book which is
probably aimed at girls . . . but I enjoyed it.*'

These children went on further to say that they enjoyed the support
provided by reading in groups. Rebecca explained, '*In our class we've got
the Hobbit and . . . Carrie's War and everything and . . . they're really big
books and I really enjoy reading like in a group.*'

They were also supported well by their families. Emily's account was
typical:

> '*I like reading at home because I've got a lot of books at home – like at
> the moment at home I'm reading the new Harry Potter book . . . and my
> dad as well likes reading them so I get the books from him.*'

Their teacher was able to capitalise on their interest and love of books,
extending their selection of reading successfully, as Harry's account shows.
This will come as no surprise to those who recognise that access to books,
avid reading and home support for readers are paramount. As one who
vehemently argues this point, Krashen (2005) campaigns tirelessly for access
to good public libraries and a good stock of books in schools which are too

often limited in areas of economic deprivation. The children speaking here demonstrate to us how crucial this access is.

Reflection

Think about the ways in which you learned to read. What were your favourite books? Who encouraged and helped you learn to read and talked to you about books?

Activity

Ask a range of children what they think of their literacy sessions

What are their views on reading?

What sort of literature do they enjoy?

Narrowing of the curriculum: a drive towards a new Strategy

The dedicated hour of literacy was prescribed following an era in the 1990s when the Programmes of Study for English in the National Curriculum were delivered within the context of a variety of curriculum areas – children would write in history, read to extract information to inform their knowledge of science or debate the merits of a new by-pass in geography. A real purpose and audience for English was established alongside a rich seam of evidence that effective teachers of English shared their passion and knowledge of children's literature with their class (Medwell et al. 1998). However, the focus on the teaching of reading and writing in particular was becoming lost in the initial years of the National Curriculum's implementation, and in 1996 OfSTED were reporting that standards had fallen. As we have seen, this led to the requirement to introduce a daily, dedicated literacy (and mathematics) lesson. However, the separation of literacy from the rest of the curriculum in terms of this dedicated daily hour led to the fracturing of foundation subjects from literacy work. From our own research, a Year 1 class teacher recalled how, on 5 November 1999, she had not considered bringing the story of Guy Fawkes into the Literacy Hour until her colleague suggested it. Indeed, a highly influential OfSTED report identified precisely this issue when case studies of thirty-one highly successful primary schools demonstrated the need for a broad, balanced and enriching curriculum to raise standards further (OfSTED 2002b). This was the point at which the Strategies were recognised as stagnating – a change of direction was needed. Policy levers were adjusted and turned towards the leadership of schools – another key factor identified within the 2002 report. Therefore, responsive as ever to the agenda for reform, the Primary National Strategy (PNS) was launched in 2003. The first publication setting out the vision of the PNS was entitled *Excellence and Enjoyment* (DfES 2003a) in which schools were given significant freedom to innovate – assuming that they had the courage to do so.

What has happened to mathematics?

Whilst English was superseded by literacy, mathematics, through the advent of the NNS, became synonymous with numeracy. Furthermore, the objective-led framework, as with literacy, deconstructed the subject matter and compartmentalised it in discrete elements. Numeracy was also treated as a distinct curriculum subject, decontextualised from other curriculum areas. The very nature of the daily mathematics lesson divorced learning from the rest of the curriculum and made it challenging for the uses and applications of mathematics to be integrated into contexts that give sense and meaning. A purpose and context for calculation can be found in any curriculum area, and often another curriculum area is more relevant, and more powerful, than within numeracy. There is evidence (OfSTED 2002a) to suggest that the clear connections with other subjects were neglected and that this was at the expense of both subjects and of children's development.

The introduction of the Primary National Strategy in 2003 with its creativity agenda could have, and should have, been the catalyst for this to change. It clearly states that, 'it is for schools to decide how they are going to organise their timetable. QCA guidance suggesting how much time should be allocated to each subject is not statutory' (DfES 2003a:17). Furthermore, 'There is no requirement for subjects to be taught discretely – they can be grouped or taught through projects' (ibid.). Here, schools are being explicitly told that they can devise a broad and balanced curriculum pertaining to their children's needs, which can be creative and cross-curricular.

By 2005, OfSTED were acknowledging that headteachers had welcomed the flexibilities and freedoms, but that few changes had yet been made in the management of the curriculum. Schools were still focusing on the daily literacy and mathematics lessons and these had 'not been affected by the publication of *Excellence and Enjoyment* (OfSTED 2005b: 2). Also, according to this report, few schools had taken steps to incorporate the effective development of speaking and listening as part of a whole school approach despite having accessed the relevant training materials. Whilst most schools were aware of the PNS publications of a set of Learning and Teaching materials, consisting of another 'lunchbox' but this time made up of useful materials produced to a high standard, too few had accessed them or used them effectively to review their practice. Assessment for learning (a key module in this training pack) was still the least successful element of teaching (OfSTED 2005b). By this point in time, therefore, the PNS seems to have been less effective than might have been anticipated and desired.

These OfSTED findings are corroborated in a small-scale study carried out by groups of first year undergraduate teacher trainees at the University of the West of England. This survey was carried out in Foundation Stage and Key Stage 1 settings where it may be expected that the Early Years principles, ensuring that learning takes place through play, would support an integrated approach to the learning and teaching of mathematics and English. Worryingly, out of a total of 39 settings, 21 of which were Foundation Stage and 18 Key Stage 1, it was found that mathematics was taught within a discrete session in 33 of them, with the other 6 favouring an integrated approach. The NNS was being used as the main scheme of work in 19 settings, the National Curriculum in 3 and the Curriculum Guidance for Foundation Stage in 17.

Interestingly it was found that, even in these Early Years settings, over half of those surveyed taught mathematics to children who had been grouped by ability *even where the setting did not group by ability for any other subject area*. Further research would need to be carried out to ascertain possible reasons for this, but it gives an indication that cross-curricular, creative and diverse approaches to the learning and teaching of mathematics may still be a fair distance away despite the urgings of the Primary National Strategy.

Renewed Primary Framework for Literacy and Mathematics

In September 2006 the Primary Framework for Literacy and Mathematics was launched as an online resource. It updates and replaces the NNS and NLS. It contains some key changes in guidance for mathematics, one of the most fundamental being the 'pull-back' from the three-part mathematics lesson since ' Overuse of this structure has, for some teachers, been seen to constrain learning' (DfES 2006b).

The renewed Framework promotes planning across a sequence of lessons that offer children continuity with a blend of approaches that sustain challenge and maintain an interest in learning. It also seems to be promoting the broadening of the curriculum by advocating that links are made between curriculum subjects and areas of learning which deepen ' children's understanding by providing opportunities to reinforce and enhance learning' (DfES 2006b). There seems to be a clear recognition that there is no requirement to keep mathematics as a discrete subject, as originally prescribed by the NNS, and that this continued practice is very likely to be to the detriment of children's learning.

Reflection

Think about the different ways in which you have observed literacy and or/numeracy being taught. Is literacy and/or numeracy always taught discretely and separately from the rest of the curriculum? Have you observed any occasions when literacy and/or numeracy have been combined with other subjects? Are there any benefits/disadvantages in linking different subjects together in your view?

Structures within the classroom

Grouping by ability

Ability grouping for mathematics in the Early Years is not uncommon. Within the Literacy Hour, the expectation explicitly suggested is that children work in ability groups. Those who are working with their teacher during the second half of the hour on guided reading, guided writing or independent work can then be challenged at a level appropriate for their group. These groupings may, in effect, become permanent with children working in their so-called ability groups for all subjects. This is the scenario in the class of Year 6 children interviewed below. Warnings about the effectiveness of such within-class ability groupings have been given by MacIntyre and Ireson (2002), who found that learners were rarely moved between groups in mathematics and the self-esteem of lower attainers was often affected. Their level of attainment was more often limited than enhanced. Wall (2004) also reveals some of the complexities and dangers of setting for the Literacy Hour.

The children interviewed here have strong and critical opinions about ability grouping. Whilst they made many positive comments about the opportunities they had for group discussions, there were important issues in the way their table groupings were treated. They felt a sense of unfairness about teacher attention. In their words, the class teacher is seen to '*treat the top two tables different from the bottom*'. Explaining further, two children pointed out: '*well if everybody's got their hand up, he normally first chooses the top two tables . . . I think it's because he knows that they will probably get the right answer first time . . .*' and: '*he doesn't make us feel equal because he's always like asking the top two tables, not the bottom and it makes us feel like we're different, they're the smart ones, we're the dumb ones . . .*'

There is no doubt in these children's minds what the ranking is in this classroom, confirmed by the seeking of the right answers to questions from particular groups. These children seem here to be describing the classic 'initiation, response, feedback' form of didactic teaching used to their detriment. Children on the bottom table in this class have labelled themselves as 'dumb' and challenge the effectiveness of teacher questioning.

Reflection

What forms of groupings have you observed for children in literacy and mathematics lessons? Are there differences between arrangements for literacy and mathematics and other subjects?

What might be some of the advantages/disadvantages for learning and teaching within the different sorts of groupings which you have observed?

Activity

Ask the children for their opinions about the grouping arrangements in their class. Is there a difference between what the 'higher-achieving' children say and children in other groups? Analyse the responses you get from a range of children, including those with additional educational needs.

A good lesson: plenty of fun and talking in class

When asked what makes a good literacy or numeracy lesson, the answers given by almost all the young participants included some comment about good lessons being 'fun' or 'enjoyable'. James explains why: *'when you make it more fun, all the memories stick in your mind. But when like you do boring lessons, they just like goes through you 'cos when you make it fun you remember it.'*

From using a calculator to find strange words or searching for clues in a murder mystery, these children talked about the enjoyment they had had in their more engaging lessons. Other factors given were when their teacher *'explained things clearly'*. Discussing what made a really effective lesson began with a debate between James and Jodie about whether writing as little as possible or having the opportunity to write extensively was ideal. Their opinions differed. However, the opportunity for discussion was agreed as a crucial factor. The children made it clear that they often had discussion in their groups and as a whole class. Matthew was emphatic about the benefits: *'I prefer it in a lesson when we are just talking instead of having to write a lot of stuff down, 'cos I think it sticks in your head a lot more hearing things with words instead of reading things with paper.'*

Others agreed, responding: *'it's easier to express yourself when you're talking instead of writing it down – you can say more when you're talking.'*

These children also debated about how much opportunity there was for dialogue in the Literacy Hour. James decided that the best debates happen in their RE lesson: *'there's so many questions you need answering about whether Jesus did this or whether he did that or how can he have done this because of this and we have really long discussions.'*

This account by children echoes points made by English et al. (2002) about the quality of classroom discourse, and is discussed more fully in Chapter 1. What is more, these young people are telling us that when they are talking it *'sticks in your head a lot more'*. Vygotsky (1986) showed how social interaction aided cognitive development and determined the structure and pattern of internal cognition. Pupil talk becomes a 'collaborative discourse through which meanings are shared and constructed' (Edwards and Westgate 1994: 7). Matthew understands himself as a learner. He is a talker and a listener – for him the written word is less powerful than the spoken. He can clarify his ideas by talking them through and commit his ideas to long-term memory. These are all features of effective learning (Deakin Crick 2006) which are considered more fully in Chapter 8. Matthew was being challenged by his friends, too. In this classroom, children often get to nominate the speaker – they don't have to put up their hands – they get to agree (or agree to differ) as Jodie pointed out, *'It's nice because you don't have to put your hand up. You just put your point across and everybody listens and then you put your point across and then somebody else listens and puts their point across and it's nice because you all eventually get to a point where you've all got to agree about something.'*

The work of Alexander (2006) on pedagogic discourse is significant here. These children are talking themselves into an understanding, which their group work can encourage.

Although children in this case study, as is commonplace in English classrooms, are seated in groups and even given collective tasks, there is significant evidence that the kind of collaboration that Jodie seems to be suggesting is rare. As Bennett and Dunne (1992) have noted, children work *in* groups rather than *as* groups. Yet Ogden (2000) demonstrates that even the youngest children in Reception and Year 1 demonstrate a capacity for reciprocal interaction and by Year 2 the children were significantly more responsive and demonstrated a greater capacity for extended interactions. The children in this case study have clearly benefited from becoming confident at expressing themselves in such discussions.

Activity

Make some observations of how children respond to their learning activities in different sessions, particularly in literacy and mathematics lessons.

Ask the children what makes a 'good' lesson.

The problems in Reception and transition: what a waste of time

The idea of Reception and Year 1 children sitting through half an hour of whole-class teaching at the start of every Literacy Hour was never intended by the Strategy implementers. Lively, interactive suggestions for playing phonics games, devoid of worksheets, are at the heart of Strategy support material for early teaching of phonics. Indeed, Reception-aged children were not expected to have a dedicated Literacy Hour, but to be prepared for one in Year 1. But intentions and reality are two different things, as listening to young informants, suffering from excess of carpet time can reveal. The Literacy Framework contains thirty-three objectives for the Reception year and detailed support material in the form of Progression in Phonics, Playing with Sounds and Developing Early Writing exist. The NNS, similarly, has objectives for the Reception year. The links to the legal documentation – the Curriculum Guidance for Foundation Stage – are unclear, a fact which the Rose review (2006) acknowledges. Reception class teachers have been confused as to the status of the Literacy Hour and daily mathematics lesson in Reception and often become pressured by senior managers who are without a secure understanding of Early Years pedagogy. Sometimes an inappropriate curriculum for 4- and 5-year-olds has resulted.

Activity

Try and find out about the transition arrangements for children in the schools where you have worked. Are there differences according to the age range of children involved? For example – what changes might you note between Reception and Year 1 in literacy and mathematics? Are there so many differences between Year 2 and Year 3? What transition arrangements can you find out about between Year 6 and Year 7?

Further challenges

A de-skilled profession

Whilst the executive summary from the critical friends of the Strategy (Earl et al. 2003) congratulates many successes, there are important statements of caution. The first is around what the report's authors refer to as teacher capacity. They explain that, in order for the Strategies to succeed, 'many teachers will need to be highly skilled and more knowledgeable about teaching literacy and mathematics than is currently the case', and that there is a misconception within schools that 'the job is done'. Yet the pressure for compliance, with centrally driven directives, has the danger of leading to 'a culture of dependence, reducing professional autonomy'. This is surely a dangerous possibility. Furthermore, the report goes on to state that 'the magnitude of the task has meant that many teachers have had relatively little opportunity for the sustained professional development and consolidation that is needed' (Earl et al. 2003: 6). The case for high quality, continuing, professional development for teachers has never been more strongly made.

The emphasis on teaching – where is learning?

It is no coincidence that much of this chapter so far has debated the effects of the Strategies on teachers and teaching. This is the emphasis of the framework where the many objectives are introduced by the mantra that 'Pupils should be taught . . .' The framework dictates what should be taught – and when. The terms and the year groups are laid out in rigorous progression. As Wyse (2003) has challenged, the Literacy Framework is devoid of a theory of child development; the *learner* is absent. A question that needs to be asked is whether the frameworks, with their linear view of progression, are appropriate and whether this view of progression supports (or hinders) the cognitive development of the learner.

In 1989 the National Curriculum non-statutory guidance for mathematics stated that:

> progression is to do with the ways in which teachers and pupils together explore, make sense of and construct pathways through the network of ideas, which is mathematics. Each person's 'map' of the network and of the pathways connecting different mathematical ideas is different, thus people understand mathematics in different ways. The 'map' is also changing as the result of experiences and insights
> (National Curriculum Council 1989: C1–C2)

This view of learning (in this case in mathematics) is conspicuously at odds with the construction and teaching styles embedded in the NNS framework.

The view expressed by the National Curriculum Council is that effective development starts with the child and is based on individual needs, experiences and existing knowledge, rather than with a set of objectives attached to a nominal year group. Development is achieved through responsive teacher–pupil interaction and exploration. The framework for the Strategies, on the other hand, is essentially hierarchical, linear and largely inflexible. The same programme is presented to all children with extension materials or additional practice for the more and less able. Although the frameworks advocate group activities, this may be identified as an organisational strategy in order to teach the same topic to a 'matched' ability group rather than a means of identifying and working with individual development or as a principle acknowledging 'working together' as a practice underwriting the curriculum. It is difficult to assess what effect this aspect of the Strategies might have on children's learning development, but Ahmed (1987: 51) stated, unequivocally, that 'It is not possible to produce a definitive scheme of work which will apply to all pupils or situations, even within a specific ability range.'

Some ways forward

Whilst some implementers have described the Literacy Hour itself as a highly questionable tool, taken too literally by teachers and becoming a restrictive straitjacket, there are children who have been taught by inspirational teachers who have thrived within its supportive structures. The children whose voices we have heard can analyse an effective lesson – it includes a good debate, where they can engage with the issues in the text. Dialogic teaching is a common feature in their classroom, although not exclusively so, as the children from the 'bottom table' have so eloquently told us. But their teacher is an English graduate who had had five years' experience in the classroom before the NLS. This teacher has very firm views about the Literacy Hour, and most of them positive, as this statement demonstrates:

It's cut a lot of rubbish out of people's lessons and made them focus on what's important . . . . You know we're telling kids about why this book is good and why this isn't. Why this is an effective author, why this piece of writing makes your spine or your hair tingle, that's what it was about because that's the craft. On one of the training videos – the grammar for writing, one of the teachers says 'I'm going to share with you the tools of the trade'. That was what it was about. It was about showing kids how they too could do it and that's what I found exciting. You know, it wasn't about drafting work, it wasn't about lessons about full stops. Yes, it came into it, of course it had to, but it was about, to me it was about content work. It was about making it

*exciting and kids saying 'shut up now, I want to write now'. You know
if you can get that kind of feeling in your lesson, you've won.*

*And I don't feel that my first five years' worth of teaching, those
lessons compared to the Strategy. I think I can draw a line between pre-
literacy and after-literacy. Because I think the whole Strategy just made
you think about what was important, what's worth teaching.*

This teacher recognises the importance of the question 'What is education
really for?'

The future

As the NLNS merges deeper into the heart of the Primary National Strategy,
the outlook for learners and their teachers may, potentially, become brighter.
Those who have found the Strategies more of a straitjacket than a support
will be reassured that the PNS articulates its desire to build on Early Years
principles, where starting with the child and using an active, play-based, first-
hand curriculum, is paramount. Transition points, such as that from
Foundation Stage into Key Stage 1, is an example of one of the foci of PNS's
attention. Speaking and Listening materials, published in 2003, contain useful
video examples of group talk, drama and role play. In addition, the continuing professional development package *Learning and Teaching in the
Primary Years: Professional Development Resources* (DfES 2004b) was
offered to all schools in September 2004. These materials focus on learners
and learning rather than on teachers and pedagogy. They support teachers
in taking leadership roles in continuing professional development and remind
us, through sharing of good practice and using research-based evidence to
raise standards, that teaching is a research-based activity. We must be
mindful, however, that effective professional development does not simply
come in another lunchbox. However excellent the materials, they need
teachers in school to engage with them and mediate them. We have noted
that OfSTED (2005b: 5) reported that few schools have used these materials
effectively in professional development.

The importance of teacher engagement is also echoed in a position paper
published by the Advisory Committee on Mathematics Education (ACME
2006: 1–2), who warn that the useful materials published by the NNS in
1999 have led to the passive and uncritical continued use of resources without
sufficient attention to the needs of the individual learners. This committee
also endorses concerns that they have noted from OfSTED that the three-
part lesson, which was at the heart of NNS pedagogy from 1999, is not
always ideal. The 'uncritical adherence to the three-part lesson structure has
a less than positive impact on learning' (ACME 2006: 3). In terms of pedagogy, the paper recommends that, 'mathematics lessons need to encourage

good quality mathematical discussion through increased group and pair work and mathematically rich tasks' (ibid.).

Ultimately, therefore, the success or otherwise of Strategies, whether centrally or locally controlled, will depend upon the people who live with them. It will be their sustained commitment to continued professional development that will determine the quality of learning (and teaching) in the future. This is the responsibility of all 'reflective practitioners' (Pollard 2005). Ongoing attention needs to be paid to research and what we know about how children learn. Crucially, outcomes of research need to be disseminated efficiently to busy practitioners. More support is needed for teacher development through research done by practitioners on their practice and their local context. Teachers would do well to research with their own children – listening to the voices of their learners might alert the reflective practitioner to the perspectives of the children they work with. The 'dumb' ones in this study were very smart indeed, and very insightful when reflecting on good teaching. Through initiatives such as local learning networks funded by the Primary Strategy in 2006, this might begin to become a possibility.

If the Strategies can be a support, a scaffold or a flexible model, then they will continue to be adopted and adapted. Riley's early optimism that teachers move forward 'with considerably more insight and confidence than previously . . . the future looks promising' (Riley 2001: 54) may still be true. In 2006, the frameworks for literacy and numeracy were reviewed constructively. Mathematics is acknowledged as the correct title of the relevant area of learning and the emphasis on teaching is rightfully replaced with more of an emphasis on learning. The new frameworks are web-based and contain a wealth of links between year group objectives and useful references across the whole curriculum. Rather than a straitjacket of conformity, they must become a springboard, freeing the imagination of teachers and learners. The excellence, led by the creative, reflective practitioner, should then become truly enjoyable.

Summary

In this chapter we have discussed the background to the Strategies and explained some of their consequences in schools. We have explored the extent to which the Strategies have imposed a rigid structure for teaching on schools and questioned the extent of the benefits of such a structure. We conclude by asking you to reflect on your own experiences in school and to consider how the Strategies will influence your professional thinking.

Acknowledgements

The authors would like to acknowledge the contribution of Ruth Sharpe in the early development of this chapter and the detailed comments of Richard Waller, and of UWE students, on later drafts.

Reflection

In what ways has this chapter helped you to consider your own practice of teaching in literacy and mathematics?

What are the key points concerning children's learning which you have identified in the chapter? How will these influence your teaching and ways in which you organise learning in the classroom?

Chapter 3

Social care, childcare and education

Exploring issues in the Early Years

Helen Butcher and John Lee

Introduction

In this chapter we discuss recent social policy and indicate its influence on Early Years education. We view this discussion as important for Early Years teachers and also for primary teachers who need to be aware of policies and principles affecting children in the early years. UK social policy concerning children, including early childhood has, since 1992, been set within the context of the United Nation Convention on the Rights of the Child (UNCRC 1989). Beneath this global umbrella of children's rights sits European legislation, the European Social Charter (1996) and Human Rights Act (1998), and within this national legislation most notably the Children Act (2004), which launched *Every Child Matters: The Next Steps for Children* (DfES 2004a).

This chapter will help you to think about the following questions relating to the work of Early Years teachers:

- What is the interplay between educational policy frameworks, social policies and practice?
- What understanding of child development and play support Early Years teachers in their work?
- In what ways may the voices of children and their families be heard?

Despite evidence (Sylva 1999) that life-long dispositions to learning can be powerfully influenced by children's earliest experiences of educational settings, there remains a lack of national confidence (DfES 2003e; OECD 2001) about what knowledge Early Years teachers currently have and more importantly, what they need. In this chapter we argue that all those working with children need to be cognisant of different policy frameworks and their practice. Underlying such capabilities, a confident knowledge of child development, including understanding of learning theories and brain development, is needed. Consequently the enduring significance of an understanding of play and the importance of articulating children's right to play in order to promote confident learners are emphasised.

Core principles

The importance of well trained, highly qualified staff in Early Years settings has been asserted by Abbot and Pugh (1999), David (1999), and Sylva et al. (2003). The longitudinal study Effective Pre-school Provision (EPPE) demonstrates a high correlation between levels of staff qualification and children's progress.

In this chapter we emphasise that the most significant skill needed by all those working with children is critical thinking. In order to develop critical contextual thinking, teachers require an understanding of the processes and purposes of policymaking as well as the specifics of contemporary social and educational policies. Such an understanding will enable future teachers to evaluate and argue for appropriate provision for children in their care.

A critical understanding of both policy and child development is important to be able to create the kinds of analytic frameworks that guide provision through observing children playing and learning in a variety of contexts. A substantial understanding of play as a critical site of learning in conjunction with an awareness of the history and significance of policymaking will equip Early Years teachers with sufficient knowledge to critique new proposals as they emerge in the course of their career and ensure that children continue to receive their entitlements to decision making and shared sustained thinking in a stimulating learning environment.

Overall the core principles can be summarised as: a rigorous understanding of playful learning; listening to and consulting with children; and critiquing policy.

Understanding of playful learning

We argue that teachers need to be knowledgeable about and confident in articulating not only children's right to play (UNCRC 1989), but their need to play, if their learning is to develop confidently and vigorously (Bruce 2004; Broadhead 2004; Siraj-Blatchford et al. 2002). Play, described by Winnicott (1971) as 'the very business of childhood', has a long tradition of being valued in English Nursery education and demonstrates the influence of the work of educationalists such as Maria Montessori (1995) and Susan Isaacs (1933). Isaacs' naturalistic observations, of children playing freely has contributed much to our understanding of children's responses to their immediate environment.

Play is not a random activity, nor is it always fun. Picture the absorbed facial expressions of children struggling to create a den or the concentrated determination when trying to balance the final brick on the 'highest ever' castle. It is essentially exploratory – a 'brain event' as individuals attempt to make sense of their worlds, and it is in this respect that Vygotksy's (1978) claim that play assists the brain to function at a higher level is so important. Unfortunately in the UK, though significantly not in other European countries, play is often belittled as a frivolous activity – *'they're only playing'* or *'now that you have done your work you can go off and play'*. Such comments neglect the significance of play as the application of young minds challenging and testing, whether at an emotional or practical level, their immediate environments.

Viktor is 4 months old. He is lying on his play mat and becomes interested in tapping a plastic toy suspended above him. He reaches towards it and knocks it. It moves. He watches it swing backwards and forwards and then stop. He reaches out with his hand to knock it again, and again and again.

He is instinctively testing out if it always moves if he taps it. This is an example of a baby testing out his environment, checking what he has observed and storing information in his brain for future use.

At some point information stored in the brain will be challenged.

Aisha is 11 months old. She is pulling herself up confidently by reaching for the chair and finds that she can use the table too. Her working hypothesis based on evidence so far – everything I touch will support my weight begins to develop. However, the next table has wheels – Aisha reaches out for support but finds herself flat on her face with alarm and surprise as the table moves away.

It is at this point that Aisha's initial hypothesis is challenged, creating, in Piagetian terms, disequilibrium, an essential accelerant for cognition. She is likely to approach the next item of furniture with some caution.

The examples above illustrate young children testing out their physical environments, but play is also about investigating social relationships – what triggers other people's reactions to you? Babies search out different shapes and facial expressions and as they grow older play games and construct hypotheses to test out their expectations of people's responses to their behaviour. For example a 5-year-old child may try to persuade the babysitter that bedtime is really 8 o'clock when in reality it is half past 6. In the classroom children may test out a new teacher's responses to familiar classroom routines. One of the key drivers in these interactions is the search for consistency. Lack of awareness by teachers of schematic learning (Athey 2006) will seriously limit their ability to understand and engage meaningfully with the intentions of young learners' explorations.

We challenge the notion therefore that children are '*only playing*'. It is unlikely that we would walk past a laboratory dedicated to researching some scientific phenomenon and comment that the scientists were '*only playing*'. However, if you talk to scientists about their processes of speculation, data gathering, analysis followed by speculation and hypothesis, the same pattern of working as children engaged in play may be observed (Athey 2006). A more appropriate response to young children engaged in different forms of play may be, '*ssh scientists at work*'.

> As I watched my sister, a developmental biologist I could tell that her lab processes were not much different to my studio ones. In science at the bench much as the potter at his wheel or sculptor at her block of wood there is a process of preparation some questions posed, early on and a distinct feeling of grafting away until a result wins through. There follows a period of stepping back, more questions, what does this result say to me? What can this failure teach me and then back again, to retry or reshape the work in hand.
>
> Professor Helen Storey (DfEE 1999b)

For the Early Years setting such insight has great significance. An understanding of playful learning and creativity as fundamentally purposeful, allows the practitioner to conceptualise ways of arranging an environment which supports children's exploration and conceptual development. The Early Years Foundation Stage (DfES 2007a) acknowledges this by the inclusion of Enabling Environments as one of its four principles. The principle is illustrated with the statement 'the environment plays a key role in supporting and extending children's development and learning' and amplified by references to children's needs, working together, emotional, outdoor and indoor environments and the wider context.

Viewing play as trivial and the opposite of work or educational progress leads to Early Years settings with children engaging in arid, adult-devised pen and paper exercises. A deeper understanding of play and its relationship to brain development leads to the construction of purposeful environments where, for example, there might not be a chair for every child because activity-based opportunities such as role play, scientific investigation areas and construction centres feature, both inside and outside. In such environments opportunities for mark making, individual and collaborative, are held at a higher premium than copywriting.

Contemporary educational research affirms the importance of play (Athey 2006; Moyles 2005; Bruce 2001). The Effective Provision of Pre-School Education Project (Sylva et al. 2003) tracked the development of children, aged 3–5, in 141 settings and provides conclusive evidence about the significance of, amongst other things, play as a condition for children's learning.

Furthermore, the influence of this project may be traced in recent government policy and publications including *Key Elements of Effective Practice* (DfES 2005) and The Early Years Foundation Stage (EYFS) consultation by DfES and DWP (2006). We can end this section on understanding playful learning on an optimistic note. The EYFS states in the Statutory Framework (DfES 2007b: 11) 'All the areas must be delivered through planned purposeful play, with a balance of adult led and child initiated activities'.

Given the research evidence, it is perhaps surprising that children's opportunities for play-based activities within both Key Stages 1 and 2 are often very limited. We would argue that primary practitioners need to be aware of the importance of play and to organise opportunities for older children to engage in playful learning.

Reflection

How is play valued in the schools/settings where you have worked? Share your observations on the provision for play which you have observed. Discuss your observations taking into account views expressed in the preceding pages of this chapter.

Critiquing policy

The early years' workforce has a vital role to play in improving the lives of our children, young people and families. The first five years of life are critical in a child's development, and high quality early years provision can help children achieve their potential.

Jane Haywood, Chief Executive of CWDC (DfEE 1999b)

It is important to remember that in the UK statutory school age still begins in the term after a child has their fifth birthday. Consequently the National Curriculum (1989) did not incorporate the work of Nursery classes. It was 1996 when *Desirable Goals for Children's Learning before Entering Compulsory Education* was published (SCAA 1996), as non-statutory guidance for learning in Nurseries, followed in 2000 by *The Curriculum Guidance for the Foundation Stage* (CGFS) (DfEE and QCA 2000). This introduced unified play-based provision in Nursery and Reception classes. In the 2002 Education Act *The Curriculum Guidance for the Foundation Stage* became statutory for all settings inspected by OfSTED.

These developments occurred during the 1990s and critically aware Early Years teachers noted the changing use of language. In little more than ten years the language of provision moved from the gentle and permissive, for example *Desirable Outcomes* (SCAA 1996) and *Curriculum Guidance* (DfEE and QCA 2000), to statutory goals which have subsequently been extended to include babies from 0, where they are in registered childcare, in the *Early Years Foundation Stage Framework* (EYFS) (DfES 2007). The high degree of specificity evident in the EYFS stands in contrast with European practices, particularly those of Nordic countries.

The integration of education and care, sometimes called 'educare', is to be welcomed, because it provides a policy context for deconstructing the unhelpful division between social and other kinds of cognition. When 2-year-old Sushma brings a crying 3-month-old in the same room her special teddy, she is demonstrating sophisticated manipulation of the environment. She is also manifesting our most important human traits of compassion and empathy, 'human beings social intelligence is their pre-eminent skill' (Dunn 1988). Concomitant with this awareness of children's capabilities we are reminded of their needs by Maslow (1999) and Gerhardt (2004). Until the basic, including emotional, needs of learners are met, no worthwhile or sustained learning is possible. This is affirmed throughout the EYFS documentation.

The most important change between the EYFS consultation (May 2006: see DfES 2007b) and the published framework is the introduction of the four principles: A unique child; Positive relationships; Enabling environments; and Learning and Development. In addition children's learning has, under Personal, Social and Emotional development, been expanded to cover dispositions and attitudes, making relationships and a sense of community. We see these strands as detailed acknowledgment of the multifaceted texture and vital importance of social cognition. This is emphasised in the document where it states on p. 11 of the Statutory Framework for EYFS, 'None of these areas of Learning and Development can be delivered in isolation from others. They are equally important and depend on each other to support a rounded approach to child development '(DfES 2007a).

At Key Stages 1 and 2 we see these areas being developed through the guidelines of the Framework for Personal, Social and Health Education and Citizenship, although these are non-statutory.

The work of teachers in different Early Years settings as they attempt to integrate the new framework with the five outcomes from *Every Child Matters* will be at its most valuable and beneficial to children's learning and development where teachers are equipped with a clear rationale for children's learning and development and are confident in their skills of analysis and critique.

Activity

Although OfSTED inspects the five outcomes from *Every Child Matters* separately, rich learning opportunities may be lost by planning for them separately. A local children's centre has developed a project which includes children, parents, a local special school and an organic restaurant. The centre has acquired an allotment and the project's aim is for young children to be actively involved in the cultivation and preparation of food for themselves. It is easy to see how such a project unites being healthy, enjoying and achieving and making a positive contribution – some might argue that staying safe and economic well being are also implied.

Explore the areas of overlap between the five different outcomes, perhaps using Venn diagrams or mapping arrows to help you. Analyse different learning features in your setting or school and consider the implications for your planning and structuring of the learning environment which follow from your analysis. What strategies do you have for eliciting children's perspectives on your provision? One example where OfSTED have successfully linked two outcomes, 'staying safe' and 'being healthy', is the document *Early Years: Safe and Sound* (OfSTED 2006b). It may provide a useful starting point.

Expanding the role of Early Years teachers

Recent developments in social policy focused on young children require that teachers' evaluative skills should cover the wider policy context in which their work is set. In order for teachers to consider the implications of policy developments for their work with children, their families and the communities in which they live, an awareness of the context in which these initiatives has arisen is important.

Teachers need to ask why children, and in particular young children, are currently in the forefront of social policy. The answer is complex and multifaceted. Not since the beginning of the twentieth century have the care and education of children been so closely related. We would describe current UK policy as an attempt to create a seamless web of care and education, readily recognised in the current OfSTED framework for the inspection of child care and early education (2005). These policy changes have also been driven by the recommendations in reports of child abuse cases such those in the Laming Report (Laming 2003). Alongside this the Labour government has set targets to improve the economic well being of children and families by focusing on provision for children. Tax credits and the expansion of childcare places, with funding of a free nursery place for all 4-year-olds, whose parents wanted it, offer the possibility of wage earning, particularly to mothers (DfES and DWP 2006; Tizard 1988; Sylva 1999).

Since the 1997 general election there has been a shifting emphasis, which we would describe as seeing children as investments in the future. The Children Act (2004) enshrines in law proposals for care and education. The aim of the act is described by the Department for Children, Schools and Families in the following way:

> The overall aim is to encourage integrated planning, commissioning and delivery of services as well as improve multi-disciplinary working, remove duplication, increase accountability and improve the coordination of individual and joint inspections in local authorities. The legislation is enabling rather than prescriptive and provides local authorities with a considerable amount of flexibility in the way they implement its provisions
>
> (DfES 2004c)

Since 1997 the Treasury has made unprecedented investment in Early Years provision. Sure Start was originally an intervention designed for young children and their families in the most deprived electoral wards and many of its ideas are now embodied within the Children Act (2004). One of most significant ramifications of this Act for educators is the development of the extended school with its 'wrap-around care' from before-school breakfast clubs to after-school provision. In addition, teachers will be involved in the closer working practices required between all teachers involved with children's welfare. Further examples of such collaboration between teachers are discussed in Chapter 6. What originally was aimed at the most disadvantaged has now been expanded, at least in part, to create universal provision.

Increased training, funding and facilities for the early years are very welcome but there are far-reaching implications regarding the relationship between state intervention and family boundaries which need careful consideration. The kind of question which thoughtful professionals will wish to consider is the extent of the state's right to intervene in the life and family arrangements of children. Does the state have the right to create and impose a curriculum for children below statutory school age? In the last ten years, guidance for children's learning in Nursery and Reception classes has changed from desirable, to guidance, to statutory. DfES have now published The Early Years Foundation Stage, which addresses the learning requirements for children from birth to 5 and will be operational from September 2008 (DfES 2007a).

What needs to be asked is not merely does the state have the moral right, but in what sense does it have a legal right of imposition? Beyond this we need to ask on what basis the state can claim the wisdom to design such curricula. Daniel and Ivatts (1998) comment that little policy around children has been developed for their benefit, rather it is for adults or adult needs. We find little evidence that the apparatus set up to design and implement these curricula and care provisions draw on profound knowledge of the nature of childhood and the needs of children. This stands in stark contrast to contemporary proposals for the extension of state controlled arrangements characterised by lip service to the importance of play and an emphasis on meeting assessment targets.

Listening to and consulting with children

What is generally absent from the policy process in England is any sense of the voices of children. The state is doing things to children and their families not responding to their requests. Since publication of the United Nations Convention on the Rights of the Child (UNCRC 1989) and the UK Children Act in the same year there has been an increasing awareness of the need to listen to children and explicitly acknowledge and value their experiences. This has been evidenced in Early Years research (Clark and Moss 2000), academic discourse and policy initiatives, for example the provision of Children's Commissioners for Wales and in Scotland a Children's Minister. The Green Paper *Every Child Matters* (2003), which preceded the Children Act (2004) and grew out of Lord Laming's inquiry into the death of Victoria Climbié (Laming 2003), was notable for its inclusion of the results of consultation with children and young people whose priorities fortuitously coincided with those of the government, namely 'being healthy, staying safe, enjoying and achieving, making a positive contribution, economic well being'. The problem though, is that these have become moral and pedagogical imperatives directed at children usually via teachers and educational institutions.

The Children Act (op cit) may be seen as a move towards recognition of the relevance of the child's voice but the voices are muted, for all the claims of the DfES publicity material. Their statement begins, 'Children tell us. . .', but unfortunately they offer no information about which children, nor when or where they did the telling.

The Laming Report was clear on the need for children to have powerful representation.

> **Recommendation 1** With the support of the Prime Minister, a ministerial Children and Families Board should be established at the heart of government. The Board should be chaired by a minister of Cabinet rank and should have ministerial representation from government departments concerned with the welfare of children and families.
>
> (Laming 2003: 371)

The timescale for the implementation of this recommendation in the original Report was three months so not only was it not followed, but the government was very tardy even with its low key response. In contrast to the requirement on the Children's Minister in Scotland and the Commissioner in Wales, the English version does not prioritise consultation with children nor is the Commissioner their representative.

Reflection

Although the UNCRC has been part of the UK policy context since 1992, not all adults are fully aware of it. Given the national *Every Child Matters* agenda and an increased focus on listening to and respecting children's perspectives, how can we ensure this oversight does not continue?

What do you think teachers' roles might be in promoting awareness in children of their entitlements?

From the individual to the family

Despite the centralised curriculum of recent years, there is an enduring legacy of the Plowden Report (Central Advisory Council for Education 1967). What Plowden put firmly on the agenda was the relationship between family and educational performance. Plowden's survey showed how the best indicator of educational success was social class and thus family background. A major recommendation of the Report was to improve the relationship between Nurseries and families. In 2001 the Commons Select Committee on Education produced its first report examining early education. Of its fifty-five recommendations the first four all address the importance of establishing links with parents. Children are no longer viewed as isolated individuals – rather they are part of a family unit, which in turn lies within a social context (Bronfenbrenner 1979).

The Plowden Report led in a few places to the creation of new inter-professional relationships. A specific instance of action arising from the Report was the creation of a Nursery home visiting team in an outer London borough. Trained Nursery teachers were employed to visit the families of pre-school children in the most disadvantaged parts of the borough. This example of recognising the significance of the family context for children's development pre-figured both Sure Start and the familiar practice of Early Years teachers undertaking home visits to smooth transitions, gain insight into children's domestic achievements and, where relevant, establish links with allied professionals.

The period from the 1970s to around 2003 can be characterised by teaching children in schools set apart from communities and families except at a very basic level. In other words, education has been disengaged from other agencies intent on improving opportunities and social justice for disadvantaged groups. These images of discontinuity and detachment are set to change further in the next five years. The Children Act (2004) brings together and develops a set of interventions and policy decisions which conceptualise provision for young children not as separate individuals but rather as members of a peer group, family and community. The proposals for children's centres, neighbourhood nurseries and extended schools will change these citadels of education into hubs for community services including parenting support, employment advice and wrap-around care. Support staff and other professionals are acknowledged as key colleagues in a network of shared responsibility. This network of shared responsibilities discussed in Chapter 6 will be fundamental to the success of multi-agency/inter-professional working. It has become all too evident that education on its own cannot remedy social injustice and all those with responsibility towards young children are required to pool resources and integrate their working practices in order to bring about the most benefit for children. In other words, the 'expanded schools' of the Children Act 2004 expands our definition of learning and educational opportunities.

The current policy context and the future

It has become clear that current policy related to young children is not simply a matter of education, but is one of the major weapons in the government's arsenal aimed to reduce poverty and inequality. In a political climate that has rejected the redistribution of wealth, this focus on children and their families offers the possibility of targeting resources on the most needy. It is more important to the Treasury that these policies also aim to put the parents of families back into the workforce. An important aspect of these policies, then, is the removal of people from social welfare and an attempt to destroy the 'welfare trap' whereby successive generations of the same families are entirely dependent on what the right wing press and many politicians call 'state handouts'.

It is worth reminding ourselves here that the earlier interventions that came in the wake of the Plowden Report focused entirely on education and the parallel Community Development Pilot Programmes funded by the Home Office were as short lived as the Educational Priority Area Projects. Perhaps the best 'historic' model is that of President Johnson's war against poverty and in particular its influential Head Start Program which was launched in 1965. Many of these programs incorporated the High Scope approach, based on Piagetian principles and the significance of a cyclical 'plan, do, review' learning process (Hohmann and Weikart 1995), in which teachers organise daily routines and a structured environment to encourage children to initiate their own learning activities. Scientific evaluations have shown that for every $1 invested in Early Years in the High Scope Project the state got $7+ back, most of that coming from taxation, from income and the fact that families are no longer reliant on welfare.

The evidence that high quality Early Years provision has long-term benefits to individuals, families and communities has been used by politicians and policymakers to argue for among other things, Sure Start and latterly Children's Centres.

The scale of the funding being made available is large and moreover it is funding which is being guaranteed for a period of time. The budget statement of 2004 announced the settlement for Sure Start and Children's Centres would include an additional £669 million by 2007–2008 in comparison to the baseline figure for 2004–2005. The effect of these measures will be to establish Children's Centres in all of the 20 per cent most disadvantaged wards in England by 2007–2008, as a consequence it is estimated that 56 per cent of the poorest children living in these areas will have Sure Start-type services available to them. The government argues that the move of Children's Centres into established schools, although removing the original vision of community control, will ensure that they do not suffer the short existence of previous projects. This will mean 1700 Children's Centres by March 2008, providing services and linked childcare places, another significant step forward towards the goal of a Children's Centre for every community. The settlement will support 100,000 new childcare places, including in extended schools, and a pilot to extend a free part-time early education place to 6000 2-year-olds in disadvantaged areas.

National differences in curriculum and transitions

The devolved governments of Wales, Scotland and Northern Ireland have shown independence, vision and imagination in their education policy-making, particularly in the Early Years. Rather than following the DfES in pursuing targets and rigorous testing they have taken a rather more relaxed position. It also worth noting here, that these three countries have higher percentages of children and families in economic and social disadvantage than England and are concerned to combat these conditions. This is made clear in the report of Scottish Parliament Select Committee:

> We debated the issues of whether investment in Early Years should be intended to meet the needs of children or of their parents or the wider economy and society. Fundamentally, should Early Years be a focus for public policy and investment for reasons of children's development, or the current and future economic well being of the country? The answer, quite simply, is both.

The Committee goes on to recognise the importance of play for cognitive growth and responds positively to the Scottish Education Department's move to introduce play into Primary 1 (the first year of formal education). The Scottish Committee also stresses the value and importance of high quality Early Years provision for future development (Scottish Parliament 2006).

In a similar manner the National Assembly of Wales, through its debate on *The Learning Country*, produced the following statement on a 'Foundation Phase' for children aged 3–7:

> The early years of a child's life forms the basis for their future development. It is during the early years that we have the opportunity to enhance each child's disposition to learning and to start them on the road to being 'lifelong learners'. The Foundation Phase is a vital **part of the journey which is based on learning through play, active involvement, practical activities and enhances creativity, knowledge, skills and understanding** [our emphasis]
>
> (Welsh Assembly 2003)

This focus on play and activity brings ideas in Wales and Scotland closer to the kinds of provision provided in other areas of Europe. The Welsh assembly prioritises the need for young children to plan and review their own work in order to 'develop positive attitudes to learning and, benefit from educational opportunities later in life and become active citizens within their communities'. It also asserts the importance of a learning continuum from 0 to 7 years. This is synergistic with the position in Scotland and Northern Ireland. An important feature of the position in the devolved governments is respect for parents and communities and a sense that while some parents may need help, it is not the business of the state to prescribe what should go on before children enter Early Years provision.

This is in rather stark contrast with the thrust of central government in England which first set out a curriculum for 0- to 3-year-olds (*Birth to Three Matters*: DfES 2003e) in 2003, the same year Charles Clarke published *Excellence and Enjoyment,* a new primary strategy (DfES 2003a). This emphasis placed on the importance of creativity and enjoyment in learning was been welcomed by those in the teaching profession, especially those who recognised the overlaps between some of its assertions and the principles of the Foundation Stage, for example 'the importance of building children's confidence through success, vivid learning opportunities, collaborative working and engaging the child in his/her learning and problem solving'. Sadly the document continues to emphasise a summative view of excellence, i.e. SATs results. As a consequence the difficulties and confusion faced by many children and their teachers on transfer from the Foundation Stage to Key Stage 1 seem set to continue in England. As our brief reference to Wales and Scotland shows, it does not have to be so; in fact the Welsh have already abandoned Key Stage 1 SATs.

Summary

The features of the contemporary Early Years terrain in the UK lead us to suggest that in order to be confident, knowledgeable, contributors to the field of Early Years, teachers will need to be equipped with a multi-dimensional, interrelated set of knowledges. They will need knowledge of the dynamic relationship between social policy and education alongside knowledge of constructions of childhood, knowledge of alternative curricula in their social and cultural contexts, and most significantly, a powerful insight into and account of the contribution play processes make to cognition and dispositions to learning. These go beyond the standards set out by the Teacher Training Agency in *Training to Teach* (TTA 2002), but it is these enriched insights and understandings which will afford young children of the future the opportunity to grow, play, learn and develop alongside teachers who have an expanded vision and increased sensitivity to the context and meanings of learning and living aged 0–7. Finally, we suggest that all primary teachers need to be aware of the issues discussed in this chapter, so that they can not only build on children's earlier experiences, but also critique policies and provision to ensure their children's future progress.

Reflection

In what ways has this chapter encouraged you to think about the knowledges, skills and attitudes which are important for teachers to possess? Drawing on your reading and experiences of working with young children, identify those which you consider are important for your own practice.

Chapter 4

What makes a pedagogy fit for Key Stage 2?

Martin Ashley and Michael Nicholson

Introduction

In this chapter, we raise questions concerning what makes an appropriate pedagogy for Key Stage 2. These questions are well worth asking since a serious study of child development as a central concern of teacher training has been off the training agenda for some time for English primary teachers. The curious persistence of the generalist class teacher system in English primary schools, in spite of a strong steer to the contrary by a report supported by government ministers and the tabloid press (Alexander et al. 1992) and ongoing OfSTED dissatisfaction with the teaching of foundation subjects, is remarkable (Bell 2003; OfSTED 2005c). If there is such a thing as a distinctive Key Stage 2 pedagogy, it is likely to have something to say about the nature of 7- to 11-year-olds, and the teaching of the whole curriculum.

This chapter will help you to think about the following questions:

* Are Key Stage 2 children developmentally any different from Key Stage 1 or Key Stage 3 children, and does this matter?
* Can one teacher know enough to teach every subject at Key Stage 2?
* What influence may different forms of classroom organisation and school ethos have on children's learning?

We draw on two comparative studies to tease out whether the effective teaching of 7- to 11-year-olds is fundamentally any different from the teaching of 5- to 7-year-olds, or 12- to 14-year-olds. We argue that it is, but that educational discourses and practices in England have been inexplicably reluctant to grasp this nettle.

Theorising the problem

Some may argue that as children grow older there is a progressive shift from teaching as caring for the child, towards teaching as an intellectual activity based on sharing the knowledge and skills of a given subject. We do not suggest that this view is entirely defensible, but to state the obvious, a visitor to a class of 5-year-olds would find a teacher who stayed with the children all day and who engaged in many activities supporting children both emotionally and socially. Visitors to a class of 15-year-olds would find themselves in a lesson of perhaps 40 minutes duration taught by a specialist in the particular subject who disappeared at the end to give a lesson in the same subject to another group of pupils. What needs to be emphasised is the relative lack of pedagogical theorising on this subject that has gone into a National Curriculum supposedly attentive to such matters as progression and continuity.

This is not to say that there is no awareness of the problem. Many school clusters work hard and imaginatively to overcome the problems of Year 6 to Year 7 transfer, but they do so against the tide of the system. During the 1970s and 1980s, there was a brief flourishing in England of the three-tier system (first, middle and upper schools) that was founded in some cases on a coherent attempt to identify a developmental pedagogy with a distinct 9–13 phase (Badock et al. 1972). This began to founder for economic reasons during the late 1980s (it costs more to educate a 10-year-old in a middle school than in a primary school) and was dealt a devastating blow by the 1988 Education Act, which firmly reasserted the principle of 11+ transfer through the introduction of the present Key Stages. It is beyond the scope of this chapter to debate whether reasons any sounder than economic expediency and government ministers' memories of schooldays played much part in this.

What are the problems that now face our schools and might be attributed to lack of relevant pedagogical theory? In secondary schools, teachers complain of constant low level disruption and growing levels of pupil disaffection. In primary schools, the complaint is of the neglect of the foundation subjects. Geography and technology have figured prominently in recent criticism. Music and PE have been perennially difficult. Many of those old enough to remember primary school art in the 1970s are shocked at the decline since literacy and numeracy became the only priorities in both initial teacher training and continuing professional development. Unfortunately, adequate data to validate this 'shock' do not exist.

To begin to theorise this, we need to see that where the problems are predominantly of disruption and disaffection, the issue is that of teachers' knowledge of pupils and how to manage relationships. Where the problems are predominantly of poor attainment or low expectations in a particular subject, the issue is that of teachers' subject knowledge. That, in a nutshell, is the Key Stage 2 pedagogy problem. How do teachers working in the years of middle childhood (which we might more broadly state as between the ages of 8 and 14) develop an adequate knowledge base? These teachers need extensive knowledge of rapidly changing young people, and they need extensive knowledge of ten or more curriculum subjects. In fact, they need a large range of knowledge bases, and much has been written on the subject of what kind of professional knowledge teachers need (Shulman 1986; Alexander et al. 1991; McNamara 1994; Turner-Bisset 1999). These authors agree that the knowledge bases needed are more wide ranging than the simplistic idea of 'knowledge of children' and 'knowledge of subject', and we suggest that you study more of their ideas.

Galton (1995) gives a colourful account of the debates generated at the time of the so called 'three wise men' report (Alexander et al. 1992) which confirms the degree to which the current model of pedagogy in England is the result of political prejudice and a tabloid media driven agenda, a point that is substantiated in Brian Simon's account of the wilful refusal of politicians to recognise that there *is* such a thing as professional knowledge of education (Simon 1994). Quite where the professional knowledge that is specific to middle childhood fits in this void is even more open to conjecture, though Robin Alexander is, perhaps rightly, firmly dismissive of the tendency to create naïve polarities such as '*I teach children*' or '*I teach my subject*' (Alexander 2004).

We cannot answer this complex question in one chapter, but the two case studies that we now offer – of Danish schools and Steiner Waldorf schools in England – should generate enough reflection for you to realise that the concern about a poverty of pedagogical thinking specific to Key Stage 2 is justified. Hopefully, the case studies will inspire you to reflect on your own Key Stage 2 practice and consider how the question of 'teaching children' or 'teaching a subject' might be intelligently and practically progressed.

Activity

Talk to a group of Year 6 children. Discuss with them which aspects of school life they are looking forward to when they enter secondary school in Year 7. What aspects of secondary school life concern them? Do they have any views on the subjects which they will learn and the teachers whom they will meet?

How do you think both primary and secondary schools can prepare children for transition? Discuss with teachers in your school.

Schools in Denmark

Although it is only a few hundred miles away from the eastern shores of England, in Denmark the approach to raising children is rather different from that in England. Inevitably where you have children, teachers and school buildings the similarities of schooling in any country outweigh the differences, but it is those differences that reveal alternative starting points and procedures in what is a common task. It is fascinating that societies and cultures having so much in common can evolve such apparently distinctive approaches to raising children in the formal community institutions we call schools. It should be remembered that the two countries share much of a common history and centuries of social, commercial and political interaction.

To make the most sense of a curriculum experienced by children aged 7 years to 11 years we need to make a short summary of some of the key components of the Danish school system, the schools, the role of the teacher and the relationships between the school, the parents of the children and the community at large. In Denmark children do not attend formalised schooling until the age of 7. Most attend kindergarten, but this is not a statutory obligation. Indeed, there is no statutory schooling in Denmark. At the age of 7 almost all children start their schooling at the 'Folkeskole'. The Folkeskole is a very different institution from both the state primary and secondary schools in England. The differences are many, but principally and most obviously they are as follows.

In the main children attend the Folkeskole from the age of 7 until the age of 16. There is no phase change at the age of 11. In Denmark primary education is the Folkeskole and secondary education is post-16 (but not higher) education. As with many schools in England, the Folkeskolen are comprehensive and neighbourhood in that they draw in nearly all of the children from the local catchment area. The average roll for a Folkeskole is, at the time of writing, a little less than 350 children, and the average class size is currently about 19 children, though this seems set almost certainly to increase. It is noteworthy that the larger age range of the Folkeskole and the dilution of adolescent youngsters by the younger children, together with other elements described below, give a much calmer tone to the Folkeskole compared to the secondary school in England. It also avoids the 'phase change' from primary school to secondary school that younger children can find threatening in the English system. In Denmark there is also an independent sector – about 15 per cent of children attend these independent Frieskoler. These schools receive government funding that covers most of their costs and require the minimum of fees from parents. In effect parental income has no bearing on whether children attend the independent Frieskoler in Denmark.

At the heart of Danish culture and its expression in schools is the desire for consensus and the development of a communitarian ideal. There is a pervasive collaborative tone in Danish government and administration that differs markedly with the more adversarial traditions that exist in England. A key component of this is the way in which the learner, student teacher and teacher have not only the right, but an obligation, to contribute to the content, organisation and method of the teaching and learning which is to take place.

Since 1998, Danish teachers have been trained to teach their four chosen subjects to all forms of the Folkeskole system. Their expertise has traditionally been considered to be, in the main, in the teaching and developing of children. From 2007, however, a new Act of the Danish parliament requires student teachers to study two or three main subjects. They will also have to choose between the teaching of maths and Danish to the first–sixth grade, or the fifth–tenth grade. It will be possible to choose both of these age ranges together as part of the subject portfolio. One of the authors of this chapter has spent many years collaborating with colleagues in Denmark and engaging in research into the 'professional identities' of both Danish teachers and student teachers in training. Although, as in England, the Danish central government lays down a framework for teacher education, the detailed content and procedures are devolved to the individual institutions and the students are expected to play their part in this.

When one of the authors asked a Danish teacher educator to provide the details of a forthcoming programme he was responsible for he remarked, *'That is not possible. I will meet the students and they will tell me their priorities and my job is to go away and design a programme that meets their needs and the regulations.'* This neatly illustrates the degree of involvement expected from all those engaged in schools in Denmark. The 'voice of the learner' is much in evidence throughout the whole of the Danish education system.

Danish student teachers train to be class teachers. There is a direct and linguistically correct translation of class teacher from English into Danish. However, a conceptual translation is something rather different. As described above, the nature of Danish schools is somewhat different from English schools. A similar situation applies with the concept of what it is to be a class teacher or 'klasselaerer'. The klasselaerer is almost invariably the teacher of Danish, so those students who do not choose Danish as a main subject seldom become klasselaerer.

In the ideal model the Danish klasselaerer will be the principal teacher of a group of children from the age of 7 to 16 years of age, teaching them most subjects at the beginning of their school careers and gradually handing over to subject specialists as the children get older. These subject specialists also act as klasselaerer to other groups of children. The klasselaerer will also have oversight of the general intellectual and social development of individual children and the group as a whole.

In this way each pupil group in Denmark has a teacher who has a long-term role as counsellor, encouraging maximum contact between the family and the school. Pupils and parents can relate to a teacher who is entirely responsible for the class's social welfare. Class teachers are always the parents' primary contact with the school and they are required by law to inform parents twice yearly about all aspects of the child's life at school. These meetings are usually carried out with the children present and attendance among parents is said to be almost 100 per cent (Bach and Christensen 1992). The intimate knowledge which class teachers build up about children and their families fosters a great trust and confidence between them which may contribute to their relatively high status.

The klasslaerer's long-term relationship with children provides perspectives on children's development which are not enjoyed by class teachers in England. In addition, criteria for judging children's progress are set entirely from within the school and are a private judgement made between the klasselaerer, the parents and the child. As with schools in England, children's academic progress and intellectual development are assessed, but the thrust of this assessment has traditionally been formative and focused on an holistic approach. Great emphasis is placed on the children's affective and social development, and the contribution the individual makes to the class as a whole. This communitarian approach has followed a key element in Danish society, the attempt to achieve consensus in all areas of public life (Alexander 2000; Osborn et al. 2003). However, the influence of the English and American emphasis on testing is becoming felt in Denmark. From 2007 there are national tests in maths, English, physics and chemistry, biology and geography.

All of the above creates a curriculum both overt and covert that gives the children at the equivalent of Key Stage 2 an experience that is substantially different from that experienced by their counterparts in England.

There is a common National Curriculum in Denmark which includes an obligation to engage in periods of 'Free Class Discussion'. These periods are the equivalent of one lesson a week. This allocation of time is enshrined in the statutory programme that the schools must follow and perhaps exemplifies much of the approach to schooling in Denmark, and as described above also to teacher education. Even from the first grade the children and the klasselaerer and other teachers have to spend time discussing how to approach the forthcoming work of the class. These discussions would include methods of teaching and learning, issues of collaboration between the children and between the children and the klasselaerer, general school issues and relationships between children. The degree of sophistication of the discussion will depend on the age of the children, but at every grade the children are expected to take responsibility for their own contributions. Responding to the voice of the learner is also part of the teaching and learning that takes place in the rest of the curriculum (Denmark 1996a, 1996b).

So the life of the children in Danish schools is different from that experienced by their counterparts in England. The relatively light touch of external statutory direction into the school helps the klasselaerer to shape the learning of the children more to their individual needs, and without the obligation to make assessment public. Indeed, assessment is first and foremost formative in its nature. The parents and the local community do not just have the opportunity to influence the work of the school, but also have a strong social obligation to do so. Finally, through the process of class discussion and through the general tone and *modus operandi* of the school, the children have a significant influence in the way in which their education progresses. It may be the case that this early immersion in the experience of contributing to a quasi-democratic activity leads Danes to greater involvement in elections for local and national governments. The raw data on the proportion of Danes voting at such elections compared with the case in England suggest there may be a connection worth pursuing further.

In Denmark, the devolved process of control over the processes of schooling from central government even as far as individual classes allows, in our view, the creation of a pedagogy that is more appropriate for the needs of individual children, their schools and the communities in which they live. This persistent reflection and adjustment of the 'learning milieu' and, to a lesser extent, the 'instructional system' (Parlett and Hamilton 1977), gives a nimbleness and speed of response to contemporary needs that seems to be lacking in the model in England. The weaker drive for compliance with central directives in Denmark compared to England also allows for, no calls for, a professional commitment to a discourse about educational values by all of the stakeholders there. In England, in our experience there is more conversation about how to achieve compliance with central directives and approval from the inspectorate than about educational values (Nicholson 2004). Moreover, these conversations almost always exclude parents, children and the community at large.

In our view, the power of centralised government policymaking to promote measurements of success in education based almost exclusively on national testing regimes and prescriptive teaching programmes has restricted reflective development of pedagogical debate amongst pupils, students, teachers and even teacher educators. Using Alexander's definition of pedagogy, 'the act of teaching together with its attendant discourse' (Alexander 2004), the emphasis on act and 'the instructional system' so constrains freedom to debate at all levels of the educational community in England, that the development of discourse is both difficult, and at times dangerous.

The Danish tradition of a broader and communitarian basis for policy-making, largely still in keeping with the Grundtvigian ideal of popular enlightenment (folkeoplysning), requires much more reflection and responsibility from both the individual pupil, student, teacher and teacher educator. This is not without disadvantage (Winther-Jensen 2001) and it does attract pressure to change. However, intellectual flexibility and a willingness to continue to be educated does bring economic advantage in a globalising financial climate (Nicholson 1990; Nicholson and Moss 1990). The extent to which such ends may continue to be achieved in Denmark is being questioned: the present Danish government is pursuing a policy of zero increase in taxation with the consequence that in-service and evening classes are becoming increasingly remote possibilities for growing numbers of teachers.

Reflection

From your reading, make a list of the differences which you have identified between the roles of teachers in Denmark and your experiences of teaching in the UK. Use your list and compare your notes with those of colleagues.

What implications are there for learners arising from the differences in your observations of teachers' roles?

The two main areas for discussion in this chapter look at pedagogies and principles of education that bring ideas in from other cultures in Europe, ideas that seem to be consistent with the way children develop and the professional ambitions of educators. We are aware of the dangers of 'cherry picking' ideas from the experiences of others and that to fully understand what goes on in other pedagogies one must engage in prolonged reflection. However, perhaps it is such 'cherry picking' of the latest 'good idea' and the need to 'do something' that has led policymakers to develop the piecemeal and inconsistent curricula that exists not only at Key Stage 2 but throughout the pupils' school experience in England.

The Steiner Waldorf curriculum that we now consider is characterised by an almost complete immunity from these considerations. Policymakers external to the pedagogical communities of the schools have been excluded from the educational development of the schools. The principles of the curriculum and pedagogy were laid down by Steiner himself in a series of lectures to teachers. Steiner Waldorf teachers, whilst building on them, have remained faithful to these principles throughout the history and development of the schools.

Steiner Waldorf schools

The first Steiner Waldorf school was founded in 1919 by the Austrian philosopher Rudolf Steiner (1861–1925) to serve the children of employees at the Waldorf-Astoria cigarette factory in Stuttgart, from whence the name 'Waldorf' originates. The Steiner Waldorf schools are now a world wide movement that constitutes one of the most strongly established alternatives to mainstream schooling. There are 870 schools globally in 60 countries including most European countries, Australia, Canada, Egypt, India, Israel, Japan, Kenya, New Zealand, South Africa, South America and the US. Twenty-three of these schools are in England and range from large, well-established schools catering for the entire 5–18+ age range to small schools of relatively recent foundation employing only two or three full time teachers. The English schools have recently been the subject of a detailed DfES funded study by the author and two colleagues (Woods et al. 2005). This study forms the basis of the comments that are now made.

Steiner's output of scientific and philosophical writing was immense, and covered fields such as agriculture and architecture as well as education. Much of Steiner's work is highly esoteric and grounded in a spiritual-scientific system of thought known as anthroposophy. For this reason, the English schools can be regarded as eccentric or even cult-like. However, our study revealed that all the subjects of the English National Curriculum are taught by means of a coherent pedagogy, greater knowledge of which might benefit maintained schools. Of particular relevance to the present discussion are Steiner's views on child development, class and subject teaching and collegiality.

A detailed and ongoing study of child development is absolutely fundamental to the work of Steiner Waldorf schools and the curriculum has been developed to follow closely the way in which the interests and aptitudes of children change with growth. Steiner teachers receive in-depth education about child development and, importantly, continue the development of this understanding throughout their careers through the ongoing child study that takes place in the schools. Steiner suggested that during what the maintained system currently calls Key Stage 2, children are in an aesthetic phase – a point also made by Howard Gardner but often overlooked in the current enthusiasm for multiple intelligence (Gardner 1973). During the aesthetic phase (7–14) learning through 'feeling' is dominant and all subjects are taught through an emphasis on creative arts that builds on the earlier phase (under 7) of imitation and physical movement ('willing'). Steiner teachers are thus encouraged to be themselves highly proficient in creative art. Two particular skills were exhibited by all the teachers studied – the ability to produce detailed chalk drawings and the ability to narrate and tell stories. Both of these are fundamental to Key Stage 2 pedagogy in Steiner Waldorf schools, which strongly emphasises a very direct form of human contact between teachers and children that needs to be observed to be understood.

Most particularly, Steiner suggested two crucial transition points. During what would be Year 5 in a primary school, 9-year-old children pass through what Steiner teachers refer to as crossing the Rubicon. During their ninth year, children who were previously secure and settled can become rebellious and obstreperous, indulging in 'silly behaviours' such as blowing their recorder upside down or experimenting with miniature handwriting (Carlgren 1972). This is thought to be the result of subconscious questioning of the teacher's authority that is in turn related to a child's dawning appreciation of self and the wider world. The world is no longer the secure place associated with an adult who is admired unquestioningly or food and material comforts that just appear. The response is to call both for new teaching methods that combat testing of adults and cruel teasing of peers, and a particular phase in the curriculum that focuses on how humans make their world secure through activities such as farming and building (Rawson and Richter 2000).

The second crucial Key Stage 2 transition point occurs at around the age of 11 years when the thought processes of the child begin to change again. This time, the security of the aesthetic world view is challenged by the dawning of intellectual thought which is associated during the period 11–14 years with the child's much increased desire to control his or her world. It is sometimes said that the Rubicon is a crisis for the child, but that the dawning of 11-year-old thought is a crisis for the teacher. Children can take on a new phase of rebelliousness and will subconsciously seek out weak teachers to challenge much more overtly (Woods et al. 2005: 77). This must be countered by a different understanding of relationships and the child, and by further progression in the curriculum leading to an emphasis on making and controlling things or, in history for example, to the study of a dominant and controlling race (the Romans).

The response of Steiner pedagogy to issues that will be familiar to all Key Stage 2 teachers is striking and merits further study. Crucial to its operation, however, is the class teacher/subject teacher that operates in Steiner Waldorf schools from ages 7 to 14. Children meet, at the age of 7, the person who is to be their class teacher for the first eight classes until they transfer to the upper school at the age of 14. Unlike the primary generalist, however, the class teacher sees the children for only part of the day. The first two hours of every day are given to the 'main lesson' in which the class teacher works with the children for a study block, typically four or so weeks in length, in which there is an in-depth focus on one particular subject. After the 'main lesson' children receive typically four different subject lessons taught by specialist teachers. These specialists may be upper school teachers, they may be class teachers teaching their own specialism, or they may be visiting specialists. It is the subjects that are often the most problematic in primary schools, music or modern foreign languages, for example, that are most likely to receive such specialist input.

School teachers in the maintained sector are often anxious to know what it is like to have the same children for eight years, perhaps pointing to the possibility that a teacher and child might not get on. The answer to this lies in the intensity with which the issue of relationships is addressed, and the degree of knowledge the teachers are expected to have of their children – both at a personal level and at the level of professional knowledge of child development. The pedagogy of the two-hour main lesson also has no direct comparison in maintained schools. It is not like primary topic work – there is a much clearer subject focus, although cross-curricular links are developed. Neither is it two hours of all the same thing. Whilst maintained schools have developed a focus on pace and working to targets, Steiner Waldorf schools have always had an emphasis on rhythm. The rhythmic structure of main lessons allows for an alternation between quiet book work, teacher exposition, singing, acting and movement and more – all aiming to be in harmony with what are believed to be the natural rhythms of the particular age of children.

Steiner teachers thus do not work in isolation. They share the load of subject specialist and class teaching through daily alternating between main lesson and subject lessons. The coherence for all this work, however, comes from the collegiality of the school. Steiner wrote much on the 'threefold social order' which stressed the need for new forms of social equality and collaboration in the wake of nineteenth-century industrial conditions and the devastation of the First World War. Schools, in this philosophy, were to be 'republican academies' run on collegial rather than hierarchical lines. Present-day Steiner Waldorf schools thus have no headteacher. Instead, staff who have completed satisfactory induction and probation are invited to become members of the Teachers' College, which is the body responsible for the management roles more normally associated with a headteacher – what would be termed 'distributed leadership' (Woods 2005).

The pedagogical significance of this collegiality lies in the weekly pedagogical meetings, initiated by Steiner himself, and copied as a matter of priority in all the schools. These are linked to the practices of child and class study that are undertaken. There is a considerable degree of mutual sharing of pedagogic problems. These are not token gestures, but fundamental to the running of the schools and duly prioritised in teachers' time schedules – a fact that is not unrelated to what is perceived by Steiner teachers as unwelcome levels of bureaucracy and centralist prescription in maintained schools (Woods et al. 2005).

Activity

Imagine that you have no headteacher, no literacy or numeracy strategy, and no guidance from the DfES or OFSTED on how to teach.

* Identify a lesson you have taught which you have not been entirely satisfied with.
* Prepare an input for a 'pedagogical meeting' at which you bring a problem in your own teaching from the lesson to colleagues for open discussion.
* Try to gather a group of colleagues and have this discussion.

In particular, focus on these two questions in planning your input to this meeting:

1 To what degree might your dissatisfaction be due to knowledge of how to manage and care for children? Was there a particular child that was an issue? Was it more to do with interactions between children? Could it

have been anything to do with 'crossing the Rubicon' (9-year-olds) or the dawning of rational thought (11-year-olds)?

2 To what degree might it be due to your subject knowledge? What was the subject? What is your own level of knowledge in that subject (e.g. degree, A level, etc.) and how much further professional training have you received in this subject? How could you be further supported?

Legitimate questions might be asked about whether Steiner's ideas work. How helpful do you think 'pedagogical meetings' would be? In a further analysis of the data gathered for the DfES study, an interesting answer to the question of whether one teacher can know enough to teach all the subjects was given (Ashley 2005). Contrary to a recent polemic by David Hart (Secretary of the National Association of Head Teachers, Hart 2005) in favour of the rapid introduction of specialist teaching into primary schools, the data from the Steiner study suggest caution. No general conclusion could be drawn in favour of either specialists or generalists. However, it was possible to suggest, on the basis of the evidence, that Steiner's ideas on child development merit serious consideration.

Observations of lessons in Steiner Waldorf schools suggest that it is indeed true that children change significantly during their ninth and eleventh years, and that this requires a significant change in teaching style. This finding runs contrary to any assumptions in favour of middle schools that seek to extend the traditional primary ethos upwards. The strongest Key Stage 2 teaching observed in Steiner Waldorf schools was by class teachers (Ashley 2005). Sometimes subject teachers were able to give very good Key Stage 2 lessons, but at other times, subject specialist lessons were weak or even poor due to the teachers having less knowledge and understanding of the pupils than the class teachers.

At Key Stage 3, however, this position was reversed. There were still a number of good, or very good lessons by class teachers up to the age of 14, but the better lessons were more likely to be by the subject specialists. The explanation that was given in the study of Steiner Waldorf schools centred around the operation of Steiner's ideas on child development, particularly the changing nature of teacher authority and how it is perceived by children. The main challenge to a teacher's authority in Key Stage 2 would appear to come from teachers' ability to manage classroom relationships, and it was on this attribute that subject specialists teaching in Key Stage 2 could be weak. At Key Stage 3, however, whilst understanding of young people remained important, challenges to authority increasingly came from pupils' judgements that the teacher did not really know his or her subject. If any generalisation can be made, it is that at Key Stage 2, knowledge of pupils and relationships trumps subject knowledge. It is currently rare to find such consideration of the effects of child development on pedagogy in English maintained schools.

The prospects for Key Stage 2 pedagogy in England

What, then, are the prospects for Key Stage 2 pedagogy in England? There are clearly possibilities in learning through comparative education. Significant ideas are found in both Danish Folkeskolen and Steiner Waldorf schools. These possibilities, however, must be approached with extreme caution. Practice does not readily transfer from one system to another and the notion that there can be any 'cherry picking' from what is fundamentally an holistic system needs to be strongly resisted. Even more caution needs to be exercised with regard to the degree to which English pedagogy (if there is such a thing) is associated with political fashion. Unlike Steiner Waldorf schools, which have evolved slowly and systematically, English primary education has been subject to constant political interference and sometimes wild swings between extreme liberal progressivism (Ellis 1976) and the romanticised version of classical humanism (an emphasis on culture as the 'best that has been thought and known through subjects') that underpinned the so-called *Black Papers* of the same era (Cox and Boyson 1975).

The present Primary National Strategy is founded on what some might regard as a naïve mixture of evidence-based practice, opportunism and idealism (Yates 2004). The research reported in this chapter cautions against bandwagons, and unduly strident calls for wholesale conversion of Key Stage 2 pedagogy to a specialist teaching mode undoubtedly fall into this category. Galton (1995), whilst recognising the serious inadequacies in science teaching that arise from weak subject knowledge (to say nothing of the problems with music and PE), remains glum about the prospects of increased specialisation and rightly, in our view, points out that questions dealing with the way that subject knowledge interacts with knowledge about teaching have been neglected (Galton 1995: 138).

We cannot agree with Galton, however that a better choice may be to avoid the need to specialise at primary level and concentrate on improving motivation and basic skills. Here, surely, Galton hangs himself by his own petard. Is not this call for 'basic skills' precisely the kind of crude 'curriculum as opposed to child' approach favoured in the 'three wise men' report (Alexander et al. 1992) to which Galton so strongly objects? If Galton links this to motivation, then the point must be made that it is precisely the practice of over-teaching the basics that is leading to a plateau in the performance of procedural skills required for success in SATs and possibly even an alarming decline in conceptual understanding in science (Shayer 2006) or a more steady decline in higher level conceptual understanding of literacy and numeracy

(Galton et al. 1999: 168–170). Over-teaching of the basics may be due partly to the effects of SATs and league tables as Galton et al. suggest, but also, we would argue, to the decline in subject advocacy.

Ashley's study of primary schools where the teaching of music is good (Ashley and Lee 2003) suggests that both motivation and learning of the basics are beneficiaries when the intensity of literacy practice is relieved by music (or other artistic/physical activity). Subject advocacy by headteachers who appointed staff to reflect their own values and priorities was significant in this study. These headteachers of effective schools clearly identified themselves as believers in the value of the arts. The Steiner pedagogy that was later observed (Woods et al. 2005) undoubtedly encapsulates this principle to a fine degree. Music and the other arts were advocated by Steiner himself as a pedagogical approach through which the 7–14 age group would learn all subjects, and this advocacy is enshrined in the values and practices of the schools. The ongoing problems of inadequate subject knowledge or practical expertise in music, other performing arts and PE suggest that the idea of a Key Stage 2 pedagogy based on partial specialism cannot be dismissed if these advantages are to become more widespread.

Activity – 'Over-teaching' the basics and a pedagogical experiment

What happens if you introduce arts-based activities within your literacy teaching? Do you feel confident with any of the following activities?

- telling (*not* reading) the children a story;
- leading the children in singing;
- leading the children in rhythmic body movements (e.g. clapping and stamping to learn some number facts);
- demonstrating skills of calligraphy or illustration that children might use to enhance the presentation of their work;
- making up and reciting a poem to celebrate a child's birthday;
- organising a short drama vignette in a foreign language .

These are only suggestions based on the observation of Steiner pedagogy.

Identify at least two similar arts-based activities that you feel confident with at your own level. Find points in your literacy teaching where you could refresh the children's attention level by weaving such activities naturally into the flow of the lesson.

Try this for at least a week and evaluate the effects.

The other main conclusion we would draw from a comparative study of Steiner pedagogy is the emphasis on collegiality. To a degree, this is echoed in Denmark where teachers of the first–seventh grades work as teams to create year plans. Other chapters in this book suggest that there has been a trend towards collegiality in maintained primary schools over the last 20 years. The evidence on this, however, is mixed. Galton (1995), for example, is critical of the pedagogical role of subject co-ordinators heading up whole school planning, suggesting that the climate in which it takes place leads to improvements in 'planning' as a ritual, but little else. Webb and Vulliamy (1996) went as far as to suggest that collegiality in primary schools suffered a significant decline as a result of delegating curriculum responsibility to subject co-ordinators. Apparently agreeing with Galton (op cit) they referred to the replacement of informal networks by committees or planning groups as less collegial in structure and consequently less engaged in pedagogical deliberation.

Collegiality in Steiner Waldorf schools is clearly of quite a different order to anything before or after the introduction of subject co-ordinators in maintained schools (Woods 2006). This is evidenced very directly by the absence of a headteacher, or indeed, at Key Stage 2, subject leaders. The Teacher's College in a Steiner Waldorf school is the main authority on pedagogy and curriculum and this cannot be comparable with the 'delivery model' that has been linked to the transformation of Key Stage 2 teaching from a professional to a technical occupation (Galton et al. 1999). Teachers' loss of feeling of being professionals in control of curriculum and pedagogy that was reported by Pollard et al. (1994) and Croll (1996) was the most frequently cited fear of the Steiner teachers opposed to state funding in Woods et al.'s (2005) study.

We are not ourselves advocating wholesale adoption of Steiner style collegiality here, not least because we are mindful of the indifferent results of English primary schools during the so-called Plowden era (Galton et al. 1999). However, we feel confident in suggesting that the Steiner approach to the three key issues of child development, subject expertise and collegiality merits serious consideration.

What does Danish practice contribute to this debate? The practice in Denmark exhibits features of a living pedagogy. It is a pedagogy that is shared, in the main, throughout Danish society. The purposes of the school curriculum may be seen as measuring and certifying pupil performance (calibration and certification), providing pupils with a range of knowledge and skills (accumulation of knowledge and skills) and contributing to the development of 'good citizens' (social cohesion). There is a constant interplay between these different functions of the curriculum as illustrated in the diagram overleaf.

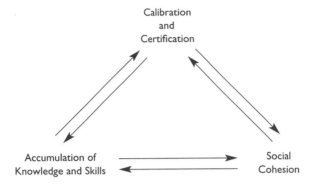

We argue that the curriculum in England is weighted toward the 'Calibration and Certification' of what is learned. This seems to be akin to digging up a plant to see how well the roots are growing. In Danish schools and in the Steiner approach the emphasis is on the 'Accumulation of Knowledge and Skills' and the development of 'Social Cohesion', with the lightest touch on 'Calibration and Certification'. In our view this leads to a pedagogy that places the progress of the child at the centre of schooling. In turn this requires more detailed and complex measurements of progress which are not amenable to the simplicity of cruder approaches to summative testing and league tables.

Summary

In this chapter we have asked you to reflect on some fundamental questions in relation to pedagogy. The case studies illustrate alternatives to the pedagogies already discussed in Chapters 1 to 3. We have considered teachers' roles and responsibilities within both Steiner Waldorf schools and schools in Denmark and noted how different pedagogies are determined by views on the purposes of education and how children best learn. In particular, we have noted that both Steiner and Danish educational ideologies emphasise the accumulation of knowledge and skills and social cohesion more strongly and in contrast to the emphasis placed on measuring attainment in England. The professional knowledge bases of teachers working in these different contexts have been discussed and variations in the expectations of knowledge which teachers need to acquire in order to be effective practitioners are identified.

Reflection

In what ways has this chapter encouraged you to think about your own professional knowledge? What knowledge helps you to plan your work with children?

Review the different aspects of professional knowledge which we have indicated that teachers need to acquire. Which do you think are the most important?

Activity

Imagine you are planning an activity for a group of children. What do you need to know to help you plan and implement the activity? Add further suggestions to those which we make below.

Knowledge of:

- the statutory curriculum requirements;
- the learning needs of individual children in the class;
- the children's prior experiences;
- the learning resources available;
- the strategies which will promote talk;
- the children's interests.

Chapter 5

Current assessment practice
Driving or supporting practice?

Gordon Guest and John Lee

Introduction

Assessment is a key feature of the educational system in England. The introduction of the National Curriculum in 1988 brought with it the requirement for formal assessment at the ages of 7, 11, 14 and 16. Since then a range of different modes of assessment have been developed and assessment used for a variety of purposes.

This chapter will help you to think about the following questions:

- What is assessment and why is it considered important?
- What is the relationship between assessment, learning and teaching?
- How does monitoring, recording and assessment influence practice in primary schools and educational settings?

We begin by reviewing the background to assessment policies since 1988 and indicate some of the issues involved in the way assessment is promoted by policymakers. We look at a range of types of assessment and explore the implications which they have for learners and teachers. Case studies of children working in different classrooms are used to explore features of effective assessment and ways in which teachers use assessment to support learning. Dialogue between teachers and pupils is analysed. In discussing monitoring and assessment in primary schools we analyse issues relating to target setting in terms of both schools' and children's performance.

Background

The report of the Task Group Assessment and Testing (DES 1988) began with the statement 'at the heart of education is assessment', which is in startling contrast to Plowden's comment which placed the child at the centre of education (Central Advisory Council for Education 1967). The report's statement signalled a major ideological change from a focus on the child to a focus on the content of schooling and its assessment. It also made assessment seem benign, a part of the processes of teaching and learning. A closer examination of what is happening in England, however, shows an emphasis on measuring outcomes which test knowledge retention. The desire of central policymakers is to measure the quality of schooling and to compare schools and, ultimately, individual teachers by the use of statistical data. The panoply of examinations and tests that have been visited on primary schools since 1988 is evidence of this. Year on year league tables comparing the performance of schools are published and only reluctantly has government withdrawn the public comparison of Key Stage 1 results. The use of assessment data to make comparisons has some merit but only in a limited way, as we will show. What we want to do from here on in is to examine the nature of assessment and how it may be used to improve the quality of learning and the effectiveness of teaching.

What is often forgotten about assessment is that it is a power relationship and there is a necessary asymmetry between the assessed and the assessor. We also forget that as term it has only a fairly recent history of ubiquitous use in educational discourse. It is as it were 'a new kid on the block'. Lee and Withers (1988) discussed the way in which the term 'assessment' could be seen as a disguise. The term has connotations of friendliness, a sort of soft quality very different from the tough connotations that are associated with the word 'testing'. Testing, they argued, reveals the power relationship between the tester and tested. It almost invariably encompasses the purpose of testing. For example the old 11+ tests were there to sift and sort children into groups so that they could be placed in the old tripartite system. No matter how hard educationists or psychologists tried to claim that the testing was neutral, parents, children, school teachers and local politicians were in no doubt of the nature and purpose of the test. The phrases 'failed the 11+' or 'passed the 11+' were common currency.

When the National Curriculum came into being the term 'assessment' rather than 'testing' was attached to it. The Task Group on Assessment and Testing (TGAT) first proposed Standard Assessment Tasks (SATs), claiming that these summative assessments could be constructed in such a way that they were almost exactly the same as the teaching and learning which went on in primary classrooms. The TGAT Report indicated that the average performance expectation of an 11-year-old was level 4 (DES 1988: para 108; Black 1998). Pollard et al. (1994) report that teachers engaged in the very first SATs were at pains to hide from the children the purposes of the tasks and to protect the children from the naked power of assessment.

The problem the primary teacher faces is making use of assessment to enhance and encourage learning in a context in which assessment is imposed on both pupils and teachers and its results used to make invidious comparisons between individuals and institutions. Stobart and Gipps (1997) make an interesting conceptual distinction about assessment by considering what its explicit use is. They refer to the kinds of assessment such as SATs or GCSEs as 'assessment of learning'. What is being prioritised is measuring what pupils and students know against specified standards. A further way to think about this is to consider reading tests used in schools whereby tests were used to identify children's competence as readers. Traditionally children's scores are expressed as a comparison between their chronological age and their reading age. Their reading age is used as a marker of individual level of reading or special needs.

While 'assessment of learning' is useful for some purposes, Stobart and Gipps also argue that 'assessment for learning' is important in the day-to-day life of the classroom. They describe 'assessment for learning' as essentially formative, undertaken as teaching and learning occur in the classroom and used by teachers and learners to improve learning.

Reflection

Consider the different ways in which your performance in different subjects and skills has been assessed. Which ways would you describe as 'assessment of learning' and which ways would incorporate 'assessment for learning'? How useful did you find the different ways of assessment for your learning? How did they make you feel?

Making assessment work for learners

The ongoing work of Black, Wiliam and colleagues (Black and Wiliam 1988; Black et al. 2002, 2003) insist that assessment is central to the learning and teaching cycle and that good formative assessment raises achievement. They present a range of descriptions of assessment which are related directly to the purposes to which assessment is put. Assessment is described in terms of the functions it might serve, namely diagnostic, formative, summative and evaluative.

Any one of these functions can be brought to bear on the assessment of learners' practical skills, thinking skills, knowledge, values and feelings. When listed as above they appear as distinct and separate. In actual fact teachers very often mix these different assessment functions; they are not purists. Alexander (2004) suggests that this is a particularly English phenomenon, and stems from the limited English lexicon related to pedagogy.

The subject element, *didaktika* in Russian, *la didactique* in France, *die Didaktik* in Germany, subdivides variously into, for example, *allgemeine Didaktik* and *Fachdidaktik* (general and specialist subject didactics) in Germany, *didactiques des disciplines* and *transpositions didactiques*, or *savoir savant* and *savoir enseigné* (scholarly and taught knowledge) in France

(Alexander 2004: 8)

In Russia, Germany and France the type of assessment is clearly linked to specific elements easily identified, so assessment functions are less confused, whereas in England by using the word 'assessment' as an umbrella term with many variations it is often not clear what meaning the term has. For example in recent years, particularly in Key Stage 2, teachers have used summative assessment – SATs results – to plan for progression and development.

Black (1998) argues that in England there are five assessment systems in place. First a range of tests used for diagnostic and selection processes. Second the national SAT assessments at 7, 11 and 14. Third public examinations such as GCSEs, fourthly vocational assessments and the fifth group are informal assessments. Teachers are expected to know and be able to use these assessment types appropriately.

Research has shown that both primary and secondary teachers mix types of assessment and in doing so, may not be using assessment data effectively, particularly formative assessment (Torrance and Pryor 2002; Black et al. 2003). If we are to link assessment to learning then we need to think carefully about policy and practice. The Qualifications and Curriculum Authority (QCA) has proposed the term Assessment for Learning (AfL) and describes the characteristics of AfL in the following way:

> Assessment for learning involves using assessment in the classroom to raise pupils' achievement. It is based on the idea that pupils will improve most if they understand the aim of their learning, where they are in relation to this aim and how they can achieve the aim (or close the gap in their knowledge).
>
> (QCA 2006)

This leads QCA to identify good practice in this manner:

- sharing learning goals with pupils;
- helping pupils know and recognise the standards to aim for;
- providing feedback that helps pupils to identify how to improve;
- believing that every pupil can improve in comparison with previous achievements;
- both the teacher and pupils reviewing and reflecting on pupils' performance and progress;
- pupils learning self-assessment techniques to discover areas they need to improve;
- recognising that both motivation and self-esteem, crucial for effective learning and progress, can be increased by effective assessment techniques.

Activity

Make a list of the different types of assessment undertaken which you have observed in schools for different subjects, topics or themes. Use the table as a guide, but you may want to add additional information.

	English	Reading	Mathematics	Science	ICT	Creativity	Physical Skills	Citizenship
Assessment types								

Which types of assessment do you think best support children's learning across these different areas?

QCA also suggests that the above points can and should be used as a checklist to test the quality of teaching and learning. Classroom teachers will reflect on their own practice in the light of the list and change it accordingly (QCA 2006).

The Assessment Reform Group (2002) draws on similar principles and activities for using assessment to promote learning.

- Assessment for learning should be part of effective planning of teaching and learning.
- Assessment for learning should focus on how students learn.
- Assessment for learning should be recognised as central to classroom practice.
- Assessment for learning should be regarded as a key professional skill for teachers.
- Assessment for learning should be sensitive and constructive because any assessment has an emotional impact.
- Assessment should take account of the importance of learner motivation.
- Assessment for learning should promote commitment to learning goals and a shared understanding of the criteria by which they are assessed.
- Learners should receive constructive guidance about how to improve.
- Assessment for learning should develop learners' capacity for self-assessment so that they can become reflective and self-managing.
- Assessment for learning should recognise the full range of achievements of all learners.

In summary, therefore, we draw attention to the importance of effective questioning techniques and the value of feedback, both oral and in written form to guide pupils' future learning. We note the importance of teachers and pupils sharing learning goals and teachers working with the pupils to develop a sort of learning map.

Examples of assessment in practice

It will be helpful here to look at two examples, the first being from Key Stage 2 and the second from a Nursery class.

Key Stage 2

A Year 5 class of 34 pupils in an inner city school was involved in a science lesson for the whole afternoon. The lesson had four distinct parts: an introduction, a lengthy practical, an interim plenary, and finally a writing up session. The children were organised into ability groups which were expected to be self-supporting. They were studying materials and their properties.

During this session summative assessment was not used. The emphasis was on formative assessment involving diagnostic and behavioural assessment.

The children responded well to questions raised by the teacher and their peers. The teacher often waited a long time to allow the children to think and structure their answers. She also asked children to explain particular points that caused confusion to the class or an individual. They were encouraged to be self-critical and to suggest alternative viewpoints.

The teacher identified one group that was uncertain and, as the class moved to the practical activities, the teacher spent some more time with this group. She had identified a particular difficulty these children were experiencing and was able to discuss it with them.

The children responded enthusiastically to the practical work, although the limited amount of resources for some activities prevented all children from having hands on experience. At this point the children were responsible for their own learning, through the carefully structured tasks. The teacher also repeatedly used specific science vocabulary and pointed children to the appropriate vocabulary rather than everyday utterances, which might have reinforced scientific misconceptions. The children were given time to think and to work out their explanations, which is a key element of formative assessment identified by Black et al. (2002). Throughout this period there was explanation between children about the experiment and the results. Individuals from other groups were sometimes called over to observe a result or help explain what was going on. The teacher remained alert to children as she moved around the class, and at other times remained stationary so that children were able to come to her.

The interim plenary enabled children to feed back their results and conclusions orally. They were encouraged to explain and use scientific vocabulary. When a child was not sure, rather than intervening the teacher asked other specific children if they could help the child. The teacher facilitated a discussion between peers so that peer explanation clarified the issue, which the teacher summarised if there was a need. The children were continually drawn into the cycle of explaining the science and reminded that assessment was about their ability to explain this clearly. The teacher used this process to register mentally whether the groups had done what was expected and could explain it scientifically. The children were supported by vocabulary being written on the board as children talked.

The lesson concluded with the children writing a report with diagrams about the activity, the focus being on the results and the information they had gathered. The science books were collected in for marking, although the teacher had looked at work in progress and made comments about the pupils' written work during the lesson.

The teacher marked the children's work, making notes or ticks in their own assessment file and particularly noted if the children were recording significant things which needed following up. The written feedback given to the pupils reinforced the discussion that had occurred during the activity.

The written feedback offered the pupils advice on their use of scientific vocabulary and explained how they should document science practical work.

The constructive feedback provided through the written comments in pupils' books was time consuming. The teacher was quite clear in her comments to children and her written and oral comments were linked. She was working from the principle that the more clearly children could explain the science they did in class the more it helped them organise their ideas. This organisation of their ideas was then reflected in the written work which they completed. This science lesson was notable in several ways. The teacher used open questioning; time was given to children to explain and peers were encouraged to give answers rather than the teacher. A further aspect was that the teacher recognised and continually informed the children that 'science' was different from other subjects and needed working at in a particular way. Children were thus encouraged to recognise that learning in science needed to address subject specific knowledge and the skills of processing that knowledge. In this way learning became more meaningful with the possibility of greater retention in the long-term memory.

The Nursery

This second example comes from a Nursery class. The children were playing outside with a range of equipment: big toys; two water tables and drainpipes; a sand tray and some big building bricks. The children were engaged with the activities and they all knew where to start. Some children were happy to stay with activities for long periods of time whilst others moved on from activity to activity. The teacher observed this and re-directed children as she thought appropriate. She gave both supportive answers to children and raised questions, for example she asked one child 'Is it easier to scoot with this foot (touching the left foot) or this foot (touching the right foot)? and encouraged the child to try using both left and right feet.

At other times the children were asked if they could repeat an activity or try doing it in a different way. But for much of the time the teacher was a silent observer watching and listening to the children and then intervening with a series of questions, which provided more focus to the activity. A significant intervention was with a particular boy at the water table. He had discovered that if he poured water into plastic guttering and lifted it up the water ran down. The teacher indicated to the other adults that they were to leave this child involved in that activity and not to move him on. As each new group of children came to the water table he took delight in demonstrating and explaining his new discovery, regularly prompted by the teacher, 'Danny tell Alison what you have found out'. Through providing time and frequently asking him to explain to others, Danny was able to refine his explanations. Sometimes other children would just nod and watch; at other times they would ask questions. Danny demonstrated that it did not matter which end of the guttering he held up; the water always ran down. As he showed other children what was happening, Danny's explanations became clearer and more concise. Danny was entirely unconcerned with the other activities and persisted with repeatedly pouring the water until the water table was empty. The teacher used a variety of questions and prompts, '*Can you show me that again? – Well does it always do that?*' to encourage Danny to keep thinking even when sometimes he made no verbal reply but continued with the pouring process.

We see in this situation the child taking control of the learning experience and the child's responsibility is explicitly acknowledged by the teacher. Her questioning and prompts provided Danny with positive feedback and also encouraged him to reflect and explain what he was learning as he was engaged in this activity. Later she talked at length, to the author, about Danny's abilities and skills and why on this occasion she let him develop the activity in the way he did. At the end of the session the teacher made notes about the children's activities looking in particular at skill development, and persistence, but focused on making a more detailed commentary about Danny to remind her later of what had transpired.

Analysis of examples of assessment in practice

Black and Wiliam (1998) suggest an essential element of assessment is dialogue. 'The dialogue between pupils and a teacher should be thoughtful, reflective, focused to evoke and explore understanding, and conducted so that all pupils have an opportunity to think and express their ideas' (Black and Wiliam 1998: 12). Vygotsky (1978) argues that learning takes place through social interaction. Each of the case studies illustrates how children are engaging with each other and the teacher; learning is not an isolated activity.

These two case studies are examples of 'good dialogue', but they also indicate other strategies for assessment, including the importance of detailed observation. There was a similarity in purpose between the two teaching activities in the way that the teacher used assessment even though the activities took place with different age groups. The significant difference is that the Nursery children are not yet at a stage where they can record through writing what they have done. They may of course make their own representations and the teacher will encourage them to do so. In the case of the Year 5 class, children were asked to record but this met with resistance from some pupils. They were doing or had done the activity; they had talked about it and so saw little real purpose in writing. This example exemplifies the challenges in moving from formative to summative assessment modes within a single learning activity; some children were unwilling to repeat work which they felt they had already completed, in order to receive a mark. Gradings obtained from summative comments may also affect ways in which some children respond to formative feedback in that they interpret teacher's comments not as advice, but as some judgement on their work.

Reflection

Reflect on ways you have observed teachers using dialogue to assess children's learning. In what ways have you noticed that teachers support and extend children's thinking through their questioning and conversations with children?

Further issues surrounding the purpose of assessment

We must now turn to the problem that assessment brings for the primary teacher in the twenty-first century. The range of purposes for assessment and the types and methods of application have grown substantially in the last two decades. As we noted earlier, the challenge arises from the lack of clarity concerning the purpose of assessment in education. Black and Wiliam (1998) have argued that assessment which does not support learning is not assessment, but a form of testing and this is almost always problematic. Such testing was often a way of maintaining social and educational divisions; calling it assessment as Lee and Withers (1988) argue rather softens the blow and makes testing seem neutral. Goldstein suggests that assessment through such tests has several purposes:

> To certify or qualify individuals by discriminating amongst them: for example on the basis of a test, examination or teacher grading (e.g. those who have passed a driving test and those who have not). For making inferences about the functioning of institutions, enterprises or systems
> (Goldstein and Lewis 1996: 2)

We would argue that there are both moral and political issues to be debated concerning these purposes, and suggest however that these views on assessment have dominated and have effectively driven out formative modes. Despite politicians' arguments to the contrary, in many respects the Key Stage 2 SATs for children at age 11 have reinforced this discrimination between those achieving well and those failing. SATs are an interesting example of high stakes testing in that they are high stakes for schools and for politicians but not for the children. Unfortunately there is now some anecdotal evidence that certain parents are seeing these tests as high stakes for their children and this has led to a plethora of published materials aimed at 'getting the children through'. In reality SATs are there to measure the performance of schools and teachers and to produce evidence of improving standards. However, undue concentration on SATs scores may have the effect of de-motivating some children who did not engage with the learning required to achieve high scores. As G.F. Madaus in Stobart and Gipps (1997: 5–6) argues:

> While testing is seen historically as a relatively objective way of adjusting the system, the negative impact eventually outweighs any benefit and when test results are used for important social decisions, the changes in the teaching system brought about by such a use can be both substantial and corrupting.

Target setting

Successive governments have employed assessment data as a means of judging schools' performance and setting targets for future development. For example, recent targets have included:

- 50 per cent of all pupils nationally should achieve level 4+ and 35 per cent should achieve level 5+ in English and mathematics in 2004.
- All LEAs should have at least 78 per cent of their pupils achieving level 4 in English and mathematics by 2004

(DfES 2006a)

The SATs scores for Year 6 pupils are analysed in detail. Responses to individual questions are correlated; the QCA then produces a short review of this information in the autumn. This is to enable schools to see which questions pupils responded well on and which questions caused problems. The intention is that the problem areas are then addressed by schools in their teaching. This is one form of target setting – identifying questions and question types that cause difficulty for children and then teaching them to successfully answer the question.

To encourage this, each year primary schools are allocated a budget for 'booster classes'. This is additional money to pay for extra teaching for Year 6 pupils to aid them to answer questions successfully and reach the government target of 90 per cent of Year 6 pupils reaching Level 4 in English, mathematics and science. It is helpful to recall that originally TGAT saw Level 4 as the average and anticipated a normative distribution across levels 2, 3, 4 and 5. This performance expectation is now skewed so that all pupils should reach the average.

Primary schools are expected to examine their own performance in SATs at Year 6 and Year 2 and the optional Year 4 SATs and with advice from the LEA begin to determine their school institutional targets. Where a primary school regularly has 90 per cent or more children achieving level 4 they have some flexibility. Where a school is consistently achieving only 46 per cent of pupils gaining level 4, the targets become harder and more rigid. However, in one instance a school achieving high SATs scores was told their targets should be 100 per cent of pupils gaining level 5 in English and mathematics. This clearly makes nonsense of SATs providing a reliable and valid measure of achievement. Wiliam (2001a, 2001b) and Black (Black and Wiliam 1988; Black et al. 2002, 2003) have written extensively on issues of validity and reliability, and the unreliability of SATs as performance indicators. Thus schools develop targets for pupils based on performance in three subjects, English, mathematics and science, and in a large measure the assessment evidence is test based rather than teacher assessment based.

Each primary school uses a package of statistics, formerly known as the Performance and Assessment report (PANDA) and the Pupil Achievement Tracker (PAT), now replaced by RAISE Online. These statistics, together with Pupil Level Annual Schools' Census (PLASC) returns, enable head-teachers and assessment co-ordinators to explore in depth their school's performance. The software allows manipulation of variables to give value added performance, account for the numbers of children on free school dinners and so forth. Using this data, each school develops school-based targets and individual class targets. Class teachers will be informed of their class targets and discuss strategies they may use to reach them. These targets relate to institutional performance in comparison to centrally imposed expectations. The Primary National Strategy contains guidance on target setting related to the school, curricula and the pupil. Local Authority Inspectors and Advisers and OfSTED monitor school performance. Richards (2001) questions the reliability of PANDA data, the process of benchmarking, that is of comparing schools, and the expectation that the data allow for accurate year-on-year comparisons. Nonetheless, OfSTED and the DfES remain committed to using these data as performance indicators.

Within the classroom, however, teachers identify targets for individual children in a number of ways. They may make explicit the class-based targets or, as the Primary National Strategy calls them, curricula targets for English, mathematics and science, arising from statistical data. Alternatively teachers may take a step back, looking at where the child actually is and judging what they need to do to improve, for example can they analyse sources in history? design a fair test in science? do a forward roll in PE? Teachers use acronyms such as WALT – What Are We Learning Today – to make learning objectives clear to children, and WILT – What I Learned Today – to encourage pupils to be active in self-assessment. Targets used in this way relate to children's actual performance, how they improve, and how they know what they have done. This is known as ipsative assessment. In such instances, the targets relate to the individual and their achievement rather than explicit curriculum levels. The Primary National Strategy refers to this as pupil target setting. Pupils will have targets explained to them and with older children these will be written down. Often the targets are arrived at through discussion between the teacher and the child.

Reflection

Reflect on your own teaching or on observations which you have made. How are learning intentions shared with children? Think of an activity which you would like children to do. What are your learning intentions? How would you share them with children? What success criteria would you identify to assess whether your intentions had been achieved successfully?

In one school children write their targets into the back of their English or mathematics books. Pupils are encouraged to look at their targets frequently and be active in identifying when they have met them. In another primary school, all the Key Stage 2 children have a targets book. All the targets from any area of the curriculum are written into this book and as they are achieved new targets are set. The targets book allows for targets to be set in areas such as art and PE as well as mathematics and English. The setting and completion of targets is seen as a collaborative process rather than the teacher just telling the child what they must do. This process is time consuming; involving pupil and teacher discussion, but it is this interaction as a part of the AfL process that does improve achievement. Indeed these actions correspond with the QCA suggestions for Assessment for Learning (QCA 2006).

An ongoing problem with this highly interactive formative assessment undertaken by class teachers is the value given to it. Whilst it guides and directs pupils' learning, identifies pupils' performance and suggests the National Curriculum level reached, teacher assessments do not count towards the SAT score data. This may explain why in some instances use of AfL materials and strategies has not had the high level of teacher involvement that was expected. The two processes of setting targets, one from statistical SAT data and the other from holistic ipsative assessment, are not seen as equal.

It is interesting to observe variations in how schools are able to respond to target setting. Schools which consistently achieve high scores in SATs appear to have the confidence and flexibility to be more creative in target setting with children. They are confident to have oral only lessons, to vary the curriculum and teaching delivery styles. One can speculate that perhaps it is this variation and flexibility that contributes towards higher achievement. In contrast, some schools with low SAT performance have adopted a more rigid curriculum; pupil targets are much more orientated towards institutional performance and there is less flexibility in teaching styles. In one such school all of Year 6 begin taking practice SAT papers in November for the May SATs. The pupils sit in the hall in desks in rows in exam conditions. It is not surprising that such pressure may lead to pupil resentment and reinforce poor performance.

Black et al. (2003) emphasise that when teachers are given confidence to make assessment decisions within a formative assessment programme learning improves, and contrast this to more limited outcomes arising from assessment of learning.

Reflection

Formative assessment:

- involves teachers having clear learning intentions;
- involves teachers in having clear success criteria;
- involves letting children know the learning intention and separates this from the activity instructions;
- involves children assessing their own work;
- involves guidance on future learning.

Reflect on an activity which you have undertaken or observed with a group of children. Evaluate the activity to see whether some or all of the above assessment points were used in that assessment activity.

Assessment and the future

Memory is an important feature in learning. Teaching for tests often encourages rote learning. With rote learning, learners master facts which they can then recall in the test situation. Pupils may become very efficient at this form of memorisation, but facts learned in this way may be quickly forgotten.

Whilst there might be occasions when rote learning could be useful, learners also need to create their own conceptual frameworks and understand what they have learned. The challenge for teachers and pupils arises in being able to select appropriate knowledges to meet new situations. Simply 'knowing that' will not help in using knowledge to solve problems or even to create new knowledge. For example in design and technology a group of Year 5 children made a range of vehicles from Lego Technic. They then rolled these down a ramp to see how far they travelled. Initially the children had great difficulty in measuring using metre rules and tape measures. They had learned about measuring in mathematics but had rarely had the chance to apply measuring in real life settings. They needed the teacher to remind them of their work in mathematics and to make connections with their prior learning experiences. In this activity children were using both 'knowledge that' as well as 'knowledge how'.

Cognitive psychology and perhaps even common sense supports the view that understanding something involves creating links within the mind that make sense and can be drawn upon in different situations. Creating connections between things and identifying patterns is highly significant. We argue that in order to facilitate this, teachers need not just to test what children know, but also to use information about what and how they know, to move them forward in their learning.

Summary

In this chapter we have identified some of the tensions relating to 'assessment for learning' and 'assessment of learning'. The principles of learner involvement and individual motivation do not sit comfortably with parallel summative assessments, particularly testing. The UK National Assessment Agency (NAA) is piloting a range of frequent progress tests in several subjects. The aim is that the initial pencil and paper tests will be replaced with online tests. It is not yet clear whether these tests will be serial summative tests or formative activities to assist the teacher. Primary teachers in the twenty-first century have to develop the kind of professionalism that enables them to resist and reject those pressures that lead to a total focus on outcomes rather than on processes of assessment. Consequently teachers will need be aware that learning involves social interactions not just with the teacher, but also child with child, and to be aware of a range of different types of assessment to use in the classroom. This point is summarised by Shirley Clarke (2001: 2):

> I believe we need to simplify the argument (between formative and summative assessment) in order to get on with developing classroom strategies which help children to learn. My definition of the two types of assessment, through a gardening analogy, hopefully adds to the continuing understanding of purposes of assessment:
>
> If we think of our children as plants . . . summative assessment of the plants is the process of simply measuring them. The measurements might be interesting to compare and analyse, but in themselves do not affect the growth of the plants. Formative assessment, on the other hand, is the garden equivalent of feeding and watering the plants – directly affecting their growth.
>
> Formative assessment describes processes of teaching and learning, whereas summative assessment takes place after the teaching and learning.

The challenge for class teachers is to become familiar with the range of assessment opportunities and to use them appropriately to meet the needs of children within the classroom and to ensure their progress.

Reflection

In what ways has this chapter encouraged you to think about the different purposes and methods of assessment? To what extent do you think assessment should drive practice in school and what is its function in supporting and extending children's learning? Share your ideas with others – is there a consensus on the role of assessment?

Chapter 6

Developing inclusive school communities

Helen Mulholland and Jane Tarr

Introduction

In this chapter we explore the concept of an inclusive school community where all children learn and are supported if required, by a range of adults. Such an organisational context recognises its responsibility to the community it serves and empowers members of the community to work within the learning environment to provide quality teaching and learning for all children.

This chapter will help you to think about the following questions:

- What does an inclusive school community look like?
- What are the roles of the different members of the community and how may they support each other and learners within the school community?
- What knowledge and skills do teachers require to support inclusive school communities?

We draw on case studies to enhance your understanding of the complex nature of including a broad range of adults within a learning environment by describing many different ways in which these adults may be involved. Beginning teachers need to take account of the potential contribution of different adults, bearing in mind the nature of the learners, the parents, the local community and the children's services available to them in the locality of the school.

What is an inclusive school community?

Recent emphasis upon inclusion as a concept in education probably rests in part on its consonance with the wider notion of inclusivity in society – of a society in which each member has a stake. This concept of inclusiveness necessarily requires recognition of mutual obligations and expectations between the community and institutions such as schools, in such a way that these institutions are reminded of their responsibilities and public duties

(Thomas et al. 1998). In turn this implies that the policy and practice of an inclusive school should be to encompass curricular and social principles and practices that are recognised within the local and regional community.

An inclusive school community is one where all children are accepted; all pupils are valued as part of the community and their educational needs are able to be met within the overall framework of the school. The process which 'inclusion' describes concerns a broader range of children than, for instance, those with physical impairments and difficulties with learning at school, and a broader range of school practices. Whilst the term 'functional integration' concerned itself with the practical placement of a child with special educational needs within a mainstream school, the term 'inclusion' encompasses all those who experience disadvantage arising from any number of differences (Slee 1996; Thomas et al. 1998). This wider meaning for inclusive education, which emphasises the comprehensiveness of schools, is involved with ensuring that all students have opportunities to engage in the same educational processes. An inclusive community is concerned with, 'providing the chance to share in the common wealth of the school and its culture' (Thomas et al. 1998: 9).

Since 1997 the Labour government has sought to introduce a new form of socialism that places responsibility for everyone with everyone, in effect a 'stakeholder' society (Plender 1997), where the role of intermediate institutions such as schools, hospitals, and colleges is enhanced and reinforced. The relationship between such institutions and the community that they serve becomes fundamental to the progress and success of the public service provision. Consequently a clear articulation of responsibilities and public duties is required that recognises and acknowledges the value of the 'stakeholder', the 'client', and seeks to promote the institution's cultural mores to foster their participation and partnership.

There have been considerable developments in policy and legislation to encourage schools to become more inclusive communities. A major aspect of this process is the enhanced focus on listening to children and young people and encouraging their participation in decision making about 'matters affecting them' (United Nations Convention of the Rights of the Child Article: UNCRC 1989). This has led to the Code of Practice for Children with Special Educational Needs (DfES 2001) providing a whole chapter on 'pupil participation' in order to ensure that children and young people are involved in negotiations around their individual education planning process. The integration of public services provision for children is proving to be a difficult process and various strategies have been taken. The Sure Start initiative for 0- to 5-year-olds (DfEE 2000) and the Children's Fund for 5- to 13-year-olds (2004) drew the voluntary and community sector together with public service providers and enabled funds to be spent directly on children and their families following a widespread consultation process. Further consultation with children and their families took place under the auspices of *Every Child*

Matters (2003–6; see www.dfes.gov.uk/consultations/conArchive.cfm), which is resulting in a wave of policy initiatives representing the greatest change in children's services since the creation of the welfare state after the Second World War. *Every Child Matters: Next Steps for Children* emphasises how everyone working with children has a responsibility to ensure that the following five outcomes are met: 'Be healthy, stay safe, enjoy and achieve, make a positive contribution and achieve economic well being' (DfES 2004a: 25).

The implications for joint agency working practices are key for these outcomes to be met, hence the emphasis on a more integrated approach to schooling. The government document *Excellence and Enjoyment: A Strategy for Primary Schools* (DfES 2003a) outlined initial proposals for extended schooling which currently are proposed for every school by 2011. These are controversial proposals, but if all schools are to be fully inclusive, the extended school model is an interesting way forward. Such a model seeks to include provision from all agencies working with children and families within one location in a similar manner to the Sure Start Centres for Early Years. Another model is the Children's Centre or Family Centre, where a range of different services can be available for families in accessible locations. The primary school is one of the local buildings where communities might gather and children's services be provided. Available space is clearly a key issue, but the range of support available for the teacher could be greatly enhanced to enable a wider range of children to be included within the mainstream setting.

The concern for this chapter is primary schools and teachers working therein, whose main role is to ensure the highest attainment and educational development of children and young people. In order to clarify the implications for schools in moving towards a more inclusive practice, we first need to reflect upon who would be involved.

Who can contribute to building an inclusive school community?

There are numerous models for inclusive school communities arising from the variety of practice within different locations. For example, a rural community is more likely to form social interactions around their school such as dances, sports events, film showings, entertainment, spaces for the nurse to hold clinics and so on, particularly if the school is the only shared building in the community. Whilst created to serve children, the school may provide space for groups to meet in the evenings, events to take place at weekends, grounds to be used outside school times and employment for members of the community. Schools have developed in this way for decades. Current policy is encouraging schools to provide for a wider range of children, resulting in the need for a wider range of persons being involved in the daily process of schooling. The following instances of who might be included is not intended as a definitive list, but provide opportunities to reflect on some examples.

A primary school community includes children and young people potentially from a wide range of cultures, religious beliefs and abilities. This is dependent upon the position of the school and its admissions policy which cannot always accept everyone for often complex reasons. The parents, carers and wider families of children attending the school form part of the school community and potentially have great impact on children's learning. The school staff themselves are an integral part of the day-to-day school community and can include teachers, teaching assistants, learning support assistants, learning mentors, school meals supervisory assistants, cleaners, administrative support, financial officers and governors. There are also those who may not be based within the school itself but who visit the school regularly and work with the children and staff. These might include educational psychologists; curriculum advisers; support teachers; health practitioners – therapists and nurses; social service practitioners – community workers, social workers, family link workers; religious leaders, and people from various organisations or bodies volunteering to work with young children in schools.

There is growing evidence that an inclusive school community can produce 'academic and social gains for the children in those schools' (Grainger 2003: 31). To ensure that educationalists facilitate the maximum benefit for learners from this wide range of persons included within an inclusive school community, it is necessary to explore the possibilities for each group. For this purpose each group is taken in turn, opportunities are explored and scope for further investigation provided.

Children and young people

The main players within the school context are of course the children and young people for whom the institution is created. These members of the community if they are to be fully recognised will need to be listened to with their views and interests reflected in the organisation and management of the school. The following presents some examples of children learning within an inclusive school community:

- children involved with their school councils;
- children within a special school involved in writing their own behaviour policy;
- children representing their local community in discussions with local planners about the new playground;
- children from a special school visiting their neighbouring primary school for sessions with a drama company;
- a boy with Asperger syndrome building relationships within a reception class;

- refugee children linking with 'buddies' to support their initial days in school.

Joe, a pupil with Down syndrome, transferred to a new primary school with half time support from a specialist teacher and half time from a learning support assistant (LSA). It soon became apparent to the specialist teacher that Joe was very dependent on his LSA and tasks set by the class teacher were often unsuitable for him. Joe was becoming more and more reluctant to try things for himself and was also displaying some disruptive behaviour at times. An opportunity arose for Joe to experience a different kind of learning. The specialist teacher suggested that Joe do some cross-curricular project-based work. It was decided that Joe would bake a cake for the class. He chose the recipe, wrote out a shopping list, selected and paid for the ingredients in the local shop and then made the cake with minimal adult help. The event was recorded in a book written in Joe's own words and illustrated with his own photographs. Not only was he very involved and pleased with his achievements, but also the LSA and other children were amazed at how much Joe had been able to do for himself.

Joe's disruptive behaviour was actually a way of trying to make his voice heard. He was not engaging with the curriculum on offer because it did not make sense to him. When he was given the opportunity to make his voice heard and take real control over his learning, Joe was able to gain a real sense of achievement. The LSA saw what Joe had achieved and began to re-assess the way she had been supporting him. The challenge for the specialist teacher was to find a way to allow everyone working with Joe to share their views and work towards giving him space to operate as a more independent learner. This was particularly challenging for his mother, who had clear views on what she wanted for him.

Children can be constructed as a disempowered group within society, placed in a dependent relationship to adults and parents. The power relations that exist between adults and children reiterate the view that childhood is a discrete category of human life. Four models of childhood coined by Jenkins (1993) present the child in different positions as possessions, as subjects, as participants in society and as citizens of society. These four models provide insight into how we as adults relate to children and understand their status as developing adults; further explication of these models can be found in Tarr (2000). In relation to children who have additional support requirements these constructions are even more pertinent. They emphasise the Freudian perspective of the adult's role in the protection of children, which can be exaggerated.

Protection is mostly accompanied by exclusion in one way or the other; protection may be suggested even when it is not strictly necessary for the sake of the children, but rather to protect adults or the adult social orders against disturbances from the presence of children. This is exactly the point at which protection threatens to slide into unwarranted dominance (Qvortrup, J., cited in James and Prout 1990: 87).

To move to a position where children are listened to and held as important and valued members of society, rather than subjugated, requires a reconceptualisation of our model of childhood and recognition of children's productive contribution through listening to their views and allowing their participation in decision making. Parents have a vital role to play in developing a level of autonomy and independence for their children.

Reflection

Reflect upon interactions which you have had with children and identify opportunities you were able to create for children to share their viewpoints, ideas and thoughts about their social and educational experiences. How might you as an educationalist provide further opportunities to actively and persistently listen to the voices of children?

Parents and carers

The adults closest to children are their parents or carers. These people know their children very well as individuals and their insight into their child's temperament can be very valuable for anyone working with the child within a social group throughout the day. Whilst the relationship between parent/carer and child is very different to that of the class teacher and child or learning supporter and child, we would argue that there is considerable knowledge and insight held by the parents/carers that can, if encouraged, be shared to the educational benefit of the child.

Moreover, parents/carers may also be encouraged to feel an integral part of the school community as the following examples show:

- Sarah's mum was a strident woman determined to achieve the best for her child, who was profoundly deaf. She led parent support groups in the community and often knew more than the teaching staff about issues concerning the deaf community. The school responded by inviting her to stand on the governing body, work as a school meals supervisory assistant, make resources for school and join trips with the children when required.

- Laura's father visited her school to talk about his work as a car mechanic.
- A grandmother shared her collection of postcards and talked about her past.
- Parents belonging to different cultural groups were invited to share their insights in class.

A nursery school had displayed a poster showing the word welcome in a number of different scripts in the entrance hall for some time. One day a Chinese speaking parent asked one of the teachers if he could make a tape with some of the other parents of the greetings written onto the poster. He thought that this would be a good way of getting all the children to have a chance to learn to say some of the greetings. The teacher enabled the parents to make the tape on their own. The result was most impressive with a large range of languages being recorded and many parents being involved.

The teacher was not only able to listen to a parent's voice, but also by standing back and entrusting the community was able to empower them to produce a very special resource that enhanced the curriculum in school. This example of parental inclusion supported the school staff in developing children's individual identity and celebrating the range of cultures within the school. It is important that school staff encourage involvement from all parents and carers at some time and not just those who are the most enthusiastic. Some parents and carers may feel more confident about coming to events such as sports days, rather than attending more formal meetings such as parents' evenings.

A report conducted by a pan-European body (OECD 1997) into relations between schools and their communities identified a widespread movement to involve parents, though the practice varied in different cultural and political situations. This study related solely to parental involvement in education whilst the issues around children with additional support requirements also crosses into health and social services. The report made an analysis of parental involvement with schools and indicated the following aspects, which are important to reflect upon in this wider frame. These relate to enhancing the democratic process through parental engagement in learning contracts; increasing accountability through parental involvement in governing bodies; parental choice of which school to attend; approaches to tackling disadvantage through provision of family learning projects; addressing specific social problems through provision of parenting classes; and enhancing the school's resources through fundraising events. A cultural analysis identified that parents valued communication with the school because for them it was educative and enhanced their own influence on raising their child's achievement. Moreover, this was a process through which the school provided support for them. Working with parents is a valuable yet challenging process to engage with.

Activity

Parents are a source of knowledge and information about the children with whom you work in school. It can be challenging to find the most suitable mode of communication for different parents. List all the modes of communication you know about and use in your life and clarify the strengths and challenges for using each of them to communicate with parents in the professional arena, for example mobile telephone and texting.

Classroom support staff

There is a range of new roles developing to enable all children to be included within the mainstream classroom. Such roles have been developed to support teachers, to support learners and to enable teaching and learning to take place without disruption. A few examples are mentioned here. The role of the *learning support assistant* (LSA) is usually to ensure that an individual child accesses learning as much as possible. LSAs work very closely with one child on an individual basis, within groups and in whole-class situations. An inclusive school community will ensure that such support staff are involved in all school decision making as they are often the voice of the learner with difficulties and changes could ensure the greater independence of the child. An *inclusion worker* could be performing the same task for a child visiting from a special school. Again, the involvement of the inclusion worker in all school processes is vital if their knowledge and skill is to be shared across school staff. A *teaching assistant* (TA) focuses more on the teaching process, supporting the teacher in differentiating the curriculum to suit all learners, organising and managing groups in the classroom. A *learning mentor* has a role in supporting the learner who displays behavioural difficulties. Learning mentors aim to enhance learners' understanding their own approaches to learning and to enable them to develop strategies to cope within the classroom environment. It is helpful to all involved if clear roles, job specifications and expectations are recorded so that everyone is aware of their different responsibilities for children's learning. Some ways in which classroom support staff may be employed are outlined below.

- All support staff's work is included on a timetable displayed in the classroom for staff and children to see.
- Opportunities are created for support staff to talk with teachers within an inclusive staff room.
- Support staff build relationships with the community through parental contact.
- Social skills classes and peer mediation are introduced by support staff.
- A learning support assistant works with other professionals and feeds back to the teacher at the end of each day or learning session.
- A learning mentor works with a group of children who display challenging behaviours.
- An inclusion worker brings one child from the local special school to join the mainstream class on an afternoon each week.

Adebayo, a learning support assistant, worked with Simon. Simon had been identified as having Asperger syndrome and sometimes his behaviour was particularly challenging. Adebayo had formed a very positive relationship with Simon and helped him to develop his confidence. Adebayo had become so interested in this work that he had sought to inform himself about Asperger syndrome. Moreover, he had become particularly expert at working with Simon and understanding his needs. The class teacher encouraged Adebayo to share his knowledge and strategies at a lunch time meeting.

The class teacher had sought to empower Adebayo, the LSA, by allowing him to develop his own expertise. This could have been done more formally by making provision for Adebayo to attend courses in school time. She encouraged Adebayo to share his expertise within the larger staff group. Sensitivity to the timing of such an event is important as often classroom support staff are only paid for the specific hours worked in the classroom. The challenge for the teacher is to be able to manage other adults working within the classroom and to develop a collaborative and effective team. There are skills required for this which are further developed in a text on team building (Vincett et al. 2005).

School support staff

The additional adults working within an inclusive school can be many and various. We have included a separate administrative section. Here we include those who support the whole school for example the *school meals supervisory staff, the caretaker, the cleaners* and *any grounds persons.* Some examples in which these people may support the school include:

- A school meals supervisor supported the Healthy School initiative for children.
- A caretaker made good links into the local community and encouraged parents into school.
- Parents working as cleaners developed their understanding of the goals of the school.
- Opportunities were provided for local community members to gain employment through working within school operating a regular book exchange fair.
- A member of the grounds team planted a herb garden as a sensory stimulus for the children.

An inner city special school for children with a variety of learning needs decided to review its behaviour policy. The head felt that it was important for all staff and pupils to be involved in the decision making process and to have ownership of the policy. It was also decided that all the adults working in the school should be involved, including the caretaker and school meals supervisory assistants. Everyone met together in the school hall and each class sat in a circle to listen to each others' views and share ideas. The adults were free to join a class group. It was very difficult to get everyone together at the same time, but the headteacher solved the logistical problems by arranging for some temporary staff to cover the duties of the caretaker, administrative officer and canteen supervisor. All staff were very pleased to be involved in such important policy decisions and the caretaker and lunchtime supervisors were able to highlight issues and make suggestions that none of the teaching staff had thought about.

The school was able to overcome common difficulties in making sure that all members of the school community were involved in an important decision making process by allocating funding for temporary staff cover. Not only were all the adults able to contribute their ideas and have their voices heard, but also the subsequent implementation of the policy appeared to be more successful because everyone had ownership of it. It also provided opportunities for the children to discuss issues with adults working in the school in different ways. Support staff can often feel excluded and that their views are less important than those of the teaching staff. We argue that an inclusive school community values everyone's contributions and ensures that it has a genuine whole school approach to dealing with many issues.

Activity

As a developing teacher you have a wealth of knowledge and information about teaching and learning. Your support staff develop equally important knowledge. You will wish to share knowledge and information as you work together in the learning environment. List all the support staff in a specific context and clarify which aspects of your knowledge might be necessary for you to share with them. Engage in a discussion with support staff to understand their knowledge of children.

Administrative staff

The administrative support required in a school is growing and can today include a wide range of different people providing different aspects of administrative support. In the past the *school secretary* frequently covered all roles but as schools have developed, administrative staff may also include a *bursar, financial officer, fund raising person* and *filing clerks*. These adults form a valuable part of the school community and their involvement with children's learning will impact upon their motivation and commitment to the work they do in support of the school community. Some examples of administrative staff's contributions include:

- A finance officer was employed to apply for funds to local companies.
- A school secretary also takes small groups of children for sports coaching.
- A bursar was involved in making bids to trusts for additional funds to support a counselling service within the school.

Governors and community members

School governors have a specific responsibility in the management of the school and as such can encourage or discourage the involvement of others in the school. In most cases school governors are also members of the local community, thus providing a different perspective and a valuable resource for the imaginative teacher. The following are examples of ways in which governors and community members might be included within the school community:

- A chair of governors visits school regularly to support other staff members supervising children and young people in the playground.

- Community members can provide a valuable link into specific cultural groups within the local community.
- Specific governors share their professional skills in the classrooms.
- Class groups visit local businesses and organisations with governor links.
- There is liaison with community members working in supplementary schools.
- Cultural and religious leaders visit and host school pupils.
- A local vet visits a school to talk about working with animals.
- Local artistes contribute to school experiences.
- Old people are visited by children.
- A local health centre holds displays of children's work.
- Children sing in a local shopping centre.

The chair of governors was a keen chess player and volunteered to run an after-school club. This was fairly popular and she got to know a number of the children. However, at a staff meeting a newly qualified teacher suggested that it might be a good idea if the governors could work with a wider range of children, so she suggested that they be invited into school to join the children in the playground for games on a regular basis. The newly qualified teacher offered to organise this and liaised with the governors to draw up a rota and to devise some activities that they could introduce. Not only were the governors more directly involved with the children, but there was also an improvement in behaviour during playtimes.

Schools often need to think of creative ways to involve governors who may have limited time to be involved in school life. Class teachers may often have little contact with governors who do in fact have considerable influence over important school policy decisions. Effective communication between governors and all members of a school community is a challenge that needs to be reflected upon and tackled.

Rose had an allotment in the same street as an inner-city school. She was passionate about her hobby and was particularly proud of the fact that she could grow so much of the same produce she had known as a child in Jamaica. She knew many of the children and their families and also some of the school support staff. One of the teaching assistants suggested that a Year 2 class might like to visit Rose's allotment as part of their project on food. Rose was able to share her passion with the children, many of whom were fascinated by the variety of plants and vegetables.

By acting upon the teaching assistant's suggestion the class teacher was able to engage a member of the community in an educational activity. Moreover, because the context was beyond that of the classroom, it was less daunting for the community member than coming into school to talk to the children. Although some children were not familiar with the produce, other children were proud of the fact that they knew about it because it was part of their own cultural heritage. The teacher then extended the project by inviting other community members in to cook dishes enjoyed by a range of different cultural groups. Together these community members worked with the children to make a recipe book which was offered for sale in the local library. This enabled the school/community partnership to celebrate the link in creating a useful product – the recipe book.

Activity

Find out what social or educational activities for children and their families take place in the local community surrounding your school. How might you incorporate contact with a community member into your teaching? How might you build professional relationships with members of the local community? What contribution might they bring to enrich children's learning?

Health practitioners

In an inclusive school community there are likely to be children who require some medical support from time to time, or regular therapeutic interventions to support their physical and mental development. There is a wide range of health practitioners whose role is specifically to work with children and young people. If such practitioners are able to work within the school context they may well find children more receptive and it could also minimise the travelling that families have to engage in to access such provision. As educationalists the knowledge and expertise of health practitioners could be very helpful in maintaining children's motivation and capacity to learn. Some examples of ways in which health practitioners have worked in schools with teachers follow:

- A physiotherapist working with individual children discussed with teachers the development of a PE curriculum to support the children more directly within the whole class.
- A joint health and education funded project enabled three speech therapists to work within specific schools with small groups of children, teachers and parents.

- A dental hygienist and nurse visited a Nursery to present a puppet play about caring for your teeth.
- A dietician from a local hospital helped children to make a video about healthy eating as part of a topic on food they were doing in the classroom.
- A school provided a room in school to use as a clinic for the local community.
- A school nurse talked to a mother and toddler group in a parents' room within school.
- A physiotherapist ran a Pilates class for the local community and school staff in the school hall.
- An occupational therapist introduced art activities to children and adults in an after-school club.

Ann was a speech therapist working with a number of children in several primary schools. She was surprised by the fact that her work varied so much from school to school. One inclusive school that she visited had a headteacher who was keen that she work alongside teachers in the classrooms, modelling her strategies for them to incorporate into their own teaching. There was virtually no withdrawal of children and all pupils saw Ann not just as a health care professional from outside, but as someone who was part of the staff of their school. Ann was very keen on drama and offered to take a leading part in producing the school play. She knew that the welcome that she was given by all the staff of the school made it easier for her to give extra time and support to them.

This speech therapist was clearly keen to work with children and was willing to do this when the headteacher was welcoming and teachers enthusiastic for her to be involved. This demonstrates that although schools can make opportunities for professionals from other disciplines to make their voices heard, this is much more likely to be successful if it is done in an imaginative and welcoming manner. The *Every Child Matters* (DfES 2004a) agenda has provided the impetus for health practitioners to work more closely with educationalists to support children and young people. Teachers concerned about their children's behaviour may wish to consider advice from counsellors and mental health workers who could enhance teachers' understanding of emotional development and mental health.

Social service professionals

Social services are currently undergoing much systemic change; in many local authorities they have merged provision with education services to form children's services. There are children's trusts being created in a few parts of the country where the primary focus is children and young people including workers from health, education and social services. Within this area of work there are also many people who might receive funding from the Children's Fund or from local children's charities such as Barnardos, NCH or The Children's Society. Such workers are frequently from a social work background although their workplace could be part of the voluntary sector. The roles are described in a variety of ways but include *community care workers, play workers, youth workers, family link workers, social workers* and *foster carers*. A few examples of ways in which they work follow:

- A community care worker supported a family in ensuring that the children got to school each day, and worked with teachers in helping to ensure that the success could continue once her input stopped.
- Youth workers operating after school worked with children outside in the community to ensure they did not get into trouble; they also provided school support in working with children at lunchtimes.
- Every other weekend one child goes to a family link worker, who talks with the class teacher on a Friday; this enables her to understand the child's needs more easily.
- The social worker is encouraged to attend annual reviews, making discussions much easier.
- The voluntary sector supported families in babysitting, thus reducing pressure on families.

The pastoral support worker is a highly valued member of the school team as he engages with the children in a different way from teachers. Whilst attending all staff meetings to understand the working of the school, his main responsibility is to the children, building trusting relations with them. He takes responsibilities, helps with playground duty, and attends assemblies. He is a member of staff. He takes children out to have conversations with them, to challenge them, to play games with them, to have a cup of tea with them. One of his roles is to get children back into the classroom comfortably whilst not actually teaching them. He picks up a lot, particularly at playtime and lunchtime, lessening the need for teachers to have to talk to upset children which takes up teaching time. The pastoral support worker has been very useful in preparing children to learn.

The inclusion of the pastoral care worker was beneficial for teachers and children in this school and was achieved through funding from the Children's Fund. Imaginative teachers can analyse aspects of the school day and see that some of their work is far more about social concerns. There are other professionals working within social services who could support educationalists in understanding such issues and potentially find other professionals with whom the school or the class teacher might work. Such support for children and families can be very valuable.

Activity

Begin to build a folder of all the health and social care professionals you meet during your work with children. Attempt to clarify the nature of each person's work, their title and role and whether they work in statutory services or for the voluntary sector. Create a notice board within your educational setting that provides information about the broad network of people working for children and their families that might be useful to others.

Educational advisers/practitioners

In many areas there has been a reduction in the numbers of education support staff available to schools from the local education authority. In most cases schools have had funding devolved to them and they are now free to buy the services back from the local authority. It is therefore useful for teachers to understand the nature of such services so they are able to gather understanding of what support may be available. The most commonly used professional in this position is the *educational psychologist* whose role is developing from support and assessment of individual children to an advisor for all staff in working with different children. Schools also might access the *behaviour support teams*, or *special needs support teachers* and *learning supporters* to help and advise in working with a broad range of children. Such professionals can be crucial when developing a more inclusive community so it is important to be able to understand their different roles and functions. The range of people involved in this area is extensive and will vary according to each location, a few examples follow:

*   A LEA literary adviser is invited to a parent workshop.
*   An educational psychologist collaborates with a class teacher on a research project about the use of home/school laptops.
*   A behaviour support team member and school special educational needs co-ordinator share ideas with the local community police officer.
*   A specialist music teacher and children join community musicians in a performance in the local hall.

Maria, the inclusion adviser in a local education authority, was concerned that the Primary National Strategy Framework for Teaching Mathematics was not leading to inclusion of all pupils. Invited by a primary school she was able to work with a class teacher, the mathematics curriculum leader and learning support assistant to select rich mathematical activities which made sense to all the children and allowed them all to participate at their own levels. She encouraged them to follow their own lines of enquiry, develop their own problem solving strategies and to work together collaboratively. Maria worked very closely with the teacher and the learning support assistant in order that they understood the new approach. To ensure that parents understood she ran a series of workshops which included them alongside the wider community. She invited a number of people in to talk about and demonstrate the mathematics that they used in their everyday lives. Those invited included the manager of a local Chinese takeaway, some officers from the local fire station, a health visitor and one pupil's grandfather who was a carpenter.

Maria had clear views about the development of an inclusive school community and sought to achieve it in a number of ways. She realised that an inclusive curriculum entailed developing a range of teaching and learning strategies. In this context she set a range of mathematical activities in contexts which made sense to the children and involved members of the local community.

Issues for the beginning class teacher

The process of engaging in building an inclusive school community that is able to support a full range of children with different learning needs is indeed a challenge for the beginning teacher. We draw attention to a number of issues which contribute towards a fully inclusive school community. A major issue is the importance of understanding the context where one is working. This includes knowing the children in your class and the social community within which they live, alongside being aware of the strengths that lie in the school where you are working. A further important aspect is the capacity to think flexibly about the teaching and learning of the curriculum within the classroom. There may be specific children for whom learning is difficult and who require additional support from another adult. It is important for the teacher to consider what expertise is required of that additional adult, particularly if they are to facilitate the learning for the child in the mainstream classroom. A visit to or a visitor from outside the school might contribute to children's understanding of any topic or learning process. Teachers will need to reflect and plan how such a process might take place to develop high quality teaching and learning for all children which also has the potential to enhance learners' motivation.

Teachers may also seek advice from a range of different professionals and recognise that it is useful to be able to frame their questions carefully in order to obtain useful knowledge. This chapter has clarified the nature of other professionals' involvement in educational processes in order to encourage the beginning teacher to enhance the teaching and learning process through wider involvement of others. The education of young children is a challenging process and the more people we can involve, the more opportunities we have for stimulating and motivating that learning. Teachers who work with other professionals will find it useful to consider the following:

- management of other adults in and around the classroom;
- facilitation of collaborative learning environments in/outside the classroom;
- interpersonal relationships, communication skills;
- capacity to define clear roles and responsibilities for self and others;
- building and maintaining a broad network of contact;
- enhancement of one's knowledge and understanding of the community served by the school;
- adopting a learning approach to your teaching, seeking support from others both within and outside of school.

Summary

This chapter explores the concept of an inclusive school community which enables all children to belong and to learn within it. It applies to all children of all abilities, all cultures and all levels of spoken English. There are professionals working within children's services who support children in a wide range of different ways. If schools are to maintain the level of support necessary for children to enjoy and achieve in school, then involvement with other professionals is vital. This process of inter-professional collaboration is not easy and will inevitably be a 'complex and fluctuating interplay of conflict and submission, acceptance and resistance, contestation and negotiation' (Vincent 1997: 276). However, it is this dynamic process which provides new and exciting ways forward. Skrtic cites the example of many experts involved in the NASA project to get a man onto the Moon. The Apollo Project employed a range of professionals but did not use their expertise separately 'division of labor and co-ordination of work were premised on collaboration and mutual adjustment, respectively' (Skrtic 1995: 204). The project involved much contestation and interplay, but the sum of the parts was greater than the individuals and the project was successful.

In relation to the building of an inclusive school community, the right to take part is not always acknowledged. All those discussed within this chapter

– children, parents, educationalists, health practitioners, social care workers, support staff, administrative staff – need to recognise their contribution to the educational achievement of children and to feel valued and listened to by those working in schools. Teachers have a very important contribution to make to this inter-professional working practice which will support all children and adults within the inclusive school community.

Reflection

In what ways has this chapter encouraged you to consider the different adults/communities with whom teachers need to engage? In terms of your own development, reflect on your own conversational competence. Being able to chat and converse with all people from different cultures, religions, ages, abilities, gender is one of the most valuable skills required if you are to part of an inclusive community. Interacting with those you find challenging or difficult is important. Record your evaluation of such interactions and be prepared to develop skills for effective conversational competence.

Chapter 7

Space for learning?

*Sue Hughes, Mandy Lee
and Juliet Edmonds*

Introduction

The introduction of the Primary National Strategy was hoped by many to signal the dawn of a new era for primary education, one that gives due prominence to children and their learning. However, there is still evidence that many schools are hesitant to take risks and are continuing to follow a highly prescriptive curriculum based on the National Literacy and Numeracy Strategies and the QCA Schemes of Work.

This chapter will help you to think about the following questions:

- What happens when teachers loosen their grip on the prescriptive curriculum to give children space for developing their own learning?
- How may ICT contribute in fostering children's independent thought and activity?
- In what ways does collaboration in the context of ICT provide fruitful learning opportunities for children?

We review government policy in relation to ICT and draw on research which analyses the impact which ICT may have on children's learning. Examples of children working creatively with PowerPoint and Roamers are used to explore the issues and challenges which arise when opportunities are provided for more exploratory and open-ended learning. We focus on the importance of organising the classroom to support purposeful talk and draw on children's own comments to illustrate how their respond to more open-ended activities.

Increasing use of ICT in the classroom does not demand a particular pedagogical approach. However, teachers who are keen to support pupil empowerment may find a particular benefit in incorporating ICT; ICT lends itself to a more exploratory, playful approach to learning.

Teachers who favour ICT are likely to have well-developed ICT skills and to see ICT as an important tool for learning and instruction. They are also likely to value collaborative working, enquiry and decision making by pupils. Teachers who have reservations about using ICT are likely to exercise a high degree of direction and to prefer pupils to work individually

(Moseley et al. 1999: 97)

Activity

What would you like to achieve through using ICT in the classroom? Make a list of the ways in which you have observed teachers and children using ICT in the classroom.

	Teacher use	Children use
At school		
Out of school		

The current context and ICT in primary schools

The background to the Primary National Strategy is explored more fully in Chapters 2 and 8. In this chapter we remind the reader that the foreword to *Excellence and Enjoyment: A Strategy for Primary Schools* makes some important statements such as: 'Children learn better when they are excited and engaged', 'there will be different sparks that make it vivid and real for different children' and that schools 'themselves will take responsibility for making what they do better all the time' (DfES 2003a). Schools' freedoms to take charge of their curriculum to meet the needs and interests of their children are re-iterated in the range of resources currently emanating from the Primary National Strategy.

Government policy has demonstrated a firm commitment to ICT in education in the last decade – as a National Curriculum subject, to support teaching and learning and to support professional and administrative functions. Initiatives have included setting up the National Grid for Learning, the New Opportunities Fund (NOF) programme of in-service training for teachers and the ICT in schools initiative. This last initiative has included a number of projects including the laptops for teachers scheme and most recently, funding for interactive whiteboards (OfSTED 2005b).

The aim of enhancing the experience and attainment of learners at all levels through the use of ICT is a key policy priority. It is argued that ICT will lead to:

> . . . improved educational outcomes, with higher standards of attainment and the acquisition of important skills such as digital and visual literacy. It should also help to make learning more differentiated and customised to individual needs, and deliver a more engaging, exciting and enjoyable learning process that encourages better learning outcomes, including greater autonomy and emotional resilience . . .
>
> (DFES 2003b: 7)

The British Educational Communications and Technology Agency (BECTA), in their *Review 2005: Evidence on the Progress of ICT in Education*, leads with the assertion that:

> It is now reasonable, and indeed necessary, to expect that by the end of the next five years there will be effective, embedded and systemic ICT practice which has transformed educational opportunities and achievements for all our students and educators
>
> (BECTA 2005)

This notion of 'transformation' appears across many reports on ICT in education but what this transformation might look like in practice is harder to draw out. Many projects have exploited the potential of ICT to provide opportunities for creative, exploratory learning experiences which reflect the more imaginative, adaptive approach invited by the Primary National Strategy.

Futurelab, an organisation which researches and coordinates innovation in educational technology, describes a number of initiatives which use technology to promote creativity and collaboration. In Futurelab's handbook, Facer and Williamson (2004) report on the use of Kahootz to provide tools for 3D multimedia story-telling and KidStory, which emphasises collaboration through enacting stories and creating different forms of representing a story. BECTA's Creativity in Digital Media Awards showcase a fabulous range of inspirational work which can only have been absorbing and challenging in equal measure for the children who created them. It is also easy to see how the Year 3 project to make digital image narratives based on Anthony Browne's *The Tunnel* described in *More than Words 2* (QCA 2005) would have been similarly engaging for the pupils involved.

Researchers examining the nature of educational change in the form of technological innovation have been particularly interested in the motivational impact on learners. The study by Passey et al. (2003) found a positive motivational effect which extended to behaviour inside and even outside school, as well as on learning. Critical to the aim of enhancing learning for *all* pupils was the evidence that appropriate use of ICT, 'helped to motivate pupils who were disaffected with traditional forms of learning'. They also found that ICT had a particularly positive effect on boys' learning as it helped them to work in a more persistent way (a pattern more commonly attributed to the way girls work) rather than a 'burst' pattern. Interestingly, when the Passey study asked pupils for their recommendations on the use of ICT, one of their suggestions was that they would like ICT to be used to 'make things harder'.

Recent inspection findings also remark on the potential for ICT in motivating and engaging children. In their evaluation of the Primary National Strategy, OfSTED comment that:

Where ICT is used effectively, pupils:

- show improved attitudes to learning through the interactive nature and visual appeal of computers and interactive whiteboards
- are excited by the wider range of resources available to them
- find the use of ICT a helpful way to share ideas and techniques
- gain independence and confidence in their learning . . .
- are motivated and consequently produce work with greater effort and often superior quality

(OfSTED 2005b: 20)

Reflection

Identify an experience where you felt the use of ICT increased children's engagement in learning.

What made it effective?

We turn now to consider some examples of ways in which ICT may provide opportunities for children to have greater involvement in their learning and engagement in exploratory activities. We recognise the importance of talk and analyse classroom interactions within some of the themes emerging from QCA's set of discussion papers, *New Perspectives on Spoken Language in the Classroom* (QCA 2003), In particular we consider the opportunities of creating spaces for talk to occur; ways in which children use talk for learning and instances of exploratory and extended interactions.

In order to explore the issues and challenges which arise when providing more exploratory, open-ended learning opportunities we carried out some work in a primary school in the outskirts of Bristol. The work involved engaging children in ICT activities using applications with which they were unfamiliar; the Year 1/2 group explored Roamers and the Year 3/4 group worked with PowerPoint. In each case study we worked with a small group first in order to observe them more closely, and then with the whole class.

What happens when children choose? Children in Years 3 and 4 working with PowerPoint

In the PowerPoint sessions children were invited to choose both whom they worked with and what they created. These freedoms were unusual for the children; in their normal activity the class teacher commented that she would have determined both the groupings and the nature of the slide show to be produced.

The children's enjoyment of these sessions was evident; they felt ownership of their learning and relished the freedom to make independent choices. The majority of the children chose to work in friendship groups, which for this activity was highly constructive: the children had shared interests and experiences on which to draw, they felt comfortable in sharing and discussing tasks, and in tackling problems encountered during the session. In these sessions learners were talking and thinking together. They were 'inter-thinking' which Dawes describes as, 'thinking collectively', and involving 'people combining their mental resources to enable them to solve problems, or to plan and carry out actions together' (Dawes 2002: 126). Such inter-action is crucial for children's development as independent learners and Dawes notes the contribution which children's competence in speaking and listening makes to their progress across all curriculum areas. In particular, Dawes asserts that ICT may provide many opportunities for such communi-cation to take place.

However, findings from projects such as RATTLS (Raising Achievement through Thinking with Language Skills) clearly point to the necessity of teaching children how to talk together. The role of the adult in such learning is critical; with teacher involvement children can establish 'ground rules' for talk and develop strategies for using talk effectively for learning. The majority of the children in this study did engage constructively in 'interthinking'. Where this aspect of the learning is valued and made explicit then this type of activity has great potential for enabling children to develop as articulate and autonomous learners.

The importance of teaching talk is clearly communicated both in the National Curriculum (DfEE and QCA 1999). The speaking and listening guidance for Key Stages 1 and 2 (DfES 2003d) provides clear objectives for this aspect of learning but it is clear from research and inspection evidence that such collaboration is still limited. According to Galton et al. (1980), when groupings were analysed in the primary classroom, little collaborative learning existed. Children were often grouped together but worked on separate tasks. Galton found that although the children were placed in groups for 56 per cent of the time they were involved in collaborative tasks only 9 per cent of the time. As Crook puts it, 'It is as if the seating has been socialised into collaboration, while the pupils have not' (Crook 1994: 239). It is clear from Alexander's work (2005) that this situation is still much in evidence today.

Making decisions using PowerPoint

The range of content chosen by the children was wide. Many of them chose to base their shows on personal interests, animals, the *Lord of the Rings*. One pair, a girl from Year 3 and a girl from Year 4, wrote their whole presentation about their friendship, inspired by this unique opportunity to choose their own groupings. One of their slides read: '*This is Freya on the computer. She never gets to go with Hannah. Except for now.*'

As the children's composition was not directed by teacher instruction or constrained by explicit learning objectives, the children were able to make their own choices, one of which was how much attention to give to images and words in the creation of their work. Perhaps we should be unsurprised if a little disappointed that the children actually relied a great deal on words; visual features of texts have traditionally received limited attention in the teaching of reading and writing in primary classrooms. However, as Eve Bearne observes, children 'think multidimensionally' and 'transformations in communications mean that the landscape of literacy seems altered out of all recognition' (Bearne 2005: 16).

Whilst standardised testing of literacy continues to prioritise 'written' texts, research such as the More than Words project carried out by the United Kingdom Literacy Association in conjunction with QCA, and the resulting guidance for schools, *More Than Words: Multimodal Texts in the Classroom* (QCA 2004a), would indicate that there is a growing recognition that:

> The wide availability of texts with pictures, diagrams and print means that written composition will include elements of design and decisions about layout. Presentational software and databases extend possibilities for composition. Mixed-mode texts can be constructed on paper, but digital technology, with its facility for importing pictures and manipulating text, means that presentation of writing can be more varied, involving design features that paper-based writing does not allow. There are issues of how such texts can be taught and assessed as well as what getting better at multimodal writing involves
>
> (QCA 2004a)

In both the small group session and in the follow-up session with the whole class, the vast majority of children produced work which included a significant amount of written work. However, their shows included much more than just words. They did a great deal more than just roam clip art collections and even time spent on this involved a great deal of thoughtful discussion and use of the search facility. Only one pair of boys (in the whole class session) produced a very small quantity of written work but they both seemed confident and articulate and they spent a great deal of time on task in discussion. They spent much of their time finding, discussing and selecting images for their slide show. This approach concurs with research which indicates that boys draw more on 'their popular, cultural, multimodal and multimedia experience' than girls, who 'tend to written texts as models' (Bearne 2003: 1). However, Bearne concludes that both boys and girls need to be given opportunities to compose in a 'range of modes and media' and suggests that this may be developed, ' by explicit discussion of variations in the structures, purposes and effects of popular cultural texts as well as book texts' (Bearne 2003: 2).

Playful learning

When the PowerPoint group was asked about what they thought of the session they all started talking at once in a very enthusiastic way. They said it was *'Fun'*, *'It was really great'*, *'You could do anything you like.'*

Later, when they were asked if there was anything about the session that they didn't like they responded as follows:

Jamie: *I've never done anything like that with computers before.*
Harry: *I've messed around before on the computer once.*
Researcher: *Were you messing around? It didn't look like messing around.*
Harry: *No, I messed around but I did noises with it.*

On further questioning it seemed that the noises Harry referred to were to do with a previous experience of using PowerPoint.

Harry's choice of language is interesting. He distinguishes between elements of his own activity: he did *'noises with it'* as well as *'messing around'*. It is easy to empathise with Harry's lack of vocabulary to describe his experimentation with unfamiliar software: when exploring what a new program can do, many keys will be pressed, and processes initiated that will challenge the 'learner'. Harry's use of exploratory language is interesting also in that it exemplifies the sort of exploratory talk that researchers such as Tharp and Gallimore (1988), Eke and Lee (2004) and Mercer (2000) view as critical to learning.

Although the children do not, as yet, have the language to (re)present their actions, they are clearly demonstrating their understanding of the value of 'noises' to a multimodal text. Had the task been set by the class teacher, it is unlikely that sound would have been included in the brief. The children would have been asked to produce a presentation based on their current topic consisting of a set number of slides, thus limiting opportunities for children to be creative and take ownership of their learning.

The open nature and organisation of the task encouraged children to make their own choices, to problem solve the activity and determine their product. During the PowerPoint session, Harry and the other children had the opportunity and time to play and experiment with the software, as well as complete the task, something they felt they had little time to do normally.

What happens when children choose? Children in Year 1 working with a Roamer

Working together

In contrast to the friendship groups established in the PowerPoint sessions, groups for the Roamer activity were determined by the teacher due to practical considerations. The children were given a short demonstration of how to make the Roamer move forwards, backwards and turn. They were then simply invited to play.

In the Roamer activity, one of the groups worked well and talked together to decide what they wanted to do and how they would collaborate to achieve this. Alex explained: '*What we have been doing is how to take it in turns to have a go. I do CM and the arrows and Lewis does the numbers and Megan does the Go*'. This sounded a bit limiting for his partner Megan and they were asked if they were going to swap jobs. Interestingly, Megan, who began rather quietly in the group, later managed to assert herself more and programmed the Roamer to do what she wanted it to do. The three children in this group maintained their individual goals for the Roamer but were able to work effectively together to achieve these.

The other Roamer group found it more difficult to work together. This group was dominated by a boy who really wanted to just try out his ideas and even when he was asked to let the others have a go, he hovered over the Roamer pointing at buttons and telling the other two children what to press! This scenario demonstrates the problems with groupings where the power is held by one or two individuals rather than shared by a group or where children have assigned themselves specific roles in the task. As Dawes cautions, 'Group work is disrupted and learning falls away, if children who do not know how to talk constructively to one another revert to socializing, demanding, asserting, ordering, disrupting – or to silence' (Dawes 2002: 128). These younger children were less experienced in talking and listening to each other with a collaborative purpose. Combined with the fact that this experience of working with control technology was new to the group, the Roamer sessions may have constituted a relatively high-risk activity for the learners. However, they did enjoy the session and worked hard to achieve their goals.

The Roamer group also enjoyed the freedom to choose what to do with the Roamer, but they provided themselves with considerable challenge as the things they wanted to do with the Roamer were quite advanced. The initial introduction to the Roamer was only concerned with which buttons to press to move it forwards, backwards and to turn. The children were then curious about what the other buttons did, including the sound buttons. It emerged that the children were only moderately interested in moving the Roamer around the room. Once they got started both groups became really interested in high numbers – they wanted to get the Roamer to turn, but this soon expanded to using very high numbers to move the Roamer forwards. They were also very keen to make the Roamer 'sing'! One child, Lewis, even suggested '*If we could get, um, two knives, and we put four wheels on the knives and we tell it to go forward and it would be like a train!*'

The children in these sessions were clearly challenged by the practicalities of working with control technology. However, they responded positively and maintained engagement. Lewis's desire to transform the Roamer into a train demonstrated his desire to incorporate this new artefact into his imaginative play; this might also be said of those who wanted to make it 'sing'. Rather than being intimidated by the technology, the children were happy to challenge themselves, wanting to experiment with high numbers and complex commands.

Whilst it is clear that the children in these sessions would benefit from planned teacher intervention, what also emerged was their willingness to persevere with the challenge, to extend their understanding, in order to achieve their planned goals.

Issues arising from our work in school

We anticipated that many children would enjoy having the freedom to decide what they wanted to work on during the sessions – what we had not anticipated was quite *how* exciting this would be for them. In both the PowerPoint and Roamer sessions children were given the opportunity to engage in undirected learning with the teacher acting as facilitator. In both contexts, the children responded positively to the challenge. The children were enthusiastic and interested. They were able to draw on what they already knew and used their personal interests to direct their learning rather than follow the explicit direction of the teacher.

Such undirected activity is critical; it allows us to reconstruct our own understanding and provides the space and opportunity to discover what is possible. Through play we learn to be flexible and innovative in our thinking. Play is an opportunity to try out different possibilities to combine elements of a problem in novel ways (Bruner et al. 1976).

It is also interesting to note that most children demonstrate great perseverance with such challenges: this is evident from the amount of time children and many adults will devote to mastering a new game or new piece of software in their 'leisure' time. For the children engaged in the Roamer activity such 'playful learning' was fun, however the older children were conscious of the difference between this type of activity and the more directed learning in which they are normally engaged. Harry seemed to equate this free exploration of a new application with 'messing around', which may suggest that he places little value on play-based activities. What may feel like time wasting, or indeed 'messing around', forms an essential part of the learning process. As David Whitebread points out:

> What is now well established amongst developmental psychologists and well understood by teachers of young children, however, is that play is one of the most effective mediums for children's learning. . . .. Bruner's and other research has demonstrated that, for children and for adults, initially being given open-ended, exploratory and 'playful' tasks enhances problem–solving capability far more effectively than being introduced to an new area with carefully broken down, 'closed' tasks
>
> (Whitebread 1997: 29–30)

Throughout these sessions, children were engaged in high levels of inter-action. Alexander (2005) argues such learning talk is critical not only for successful learning in schools but also for the rest of children's lives. If children are provided with a curriculum that offers only structured activities that lead them to reach a stated outcome of which they are already capable, what opportunities will they have for reaching new understandings? Wegerif (2005) supports Alexander's view and suggests, there is a need for opportunities for 'creativity in talk'; spaces where children can engage in 'playful talk', which he suggests 'may well be central to the aim of improving the quality of thinking and learning in classrooms'.

In both groups the children chose to take greater risks and greater learning challenges (the creation of multimodal texts, working with high numbers and singing Roamers for example) than would have been presented in a more teacher-directed activity. Such open-ended activities provide teachers with opportunities to learn about what children can do and want to do. Without a predefined outcome, it seems that children are more willing to take greater risks.

Further support for this view that children need more opportunities for personal exploration and discovery in learning is found in the research carried out by Bet McCallum (McCallum 2000). Her survey of research work on assessment for learning, published as a key resource on the QCA website concludes that teachers need to be 'flexible in their planning and lose some of the "must cover" anxiety instilled by over rigorous and constraining planning sheets'. More opportunities for open-ended learning are advocated and the importance of teacher interaction with children to gain insights into their learning is emphasised.

For teachers to plan a curriculum that builds on what learners already know, teachers need to create more opportunities for children to communicate what they know. Children need to engage in enjoyable and valuable experiences in which they feel free to take risks and to realise for themselves the true extent of their existing knowledge and understanding.

Reflection

What are the challenges for you in providing opportunities for children to make choices about their own learning?

The role of the teacher

We draw attention to Chapter 1 which discusses the nature of classroom discourse and the extent to which teachers control the talk in their classrooms. Alexander (2005) also reports on the predominance of what he calls 'recitation script' emanating from closed teacher questions. He argues that such questions demand:

> . . . brief recall answers and minimal feedback which requires children to report someone else's thinking rather than to think for themselves, and to be judged on their accuracy or compliance in doing so (Tharp and Gallimore 1988). This script is remarkably resistant to efforts to transform it. 'When recitation starts', notes Martin Nystrand (Nystrand et al. 1997: 6), 'remembering and guessing supplant thinking.'
>
> (Alexander 2005: 2)

However, as we can see from the plethora of research and inspection evidence, there is an increasing awareness of the need for greater space and voice for learners to be heard. Consequently the teachers' role in creating interactive opportunities for this to occur becomes very important. If children are to maximise these opportunities then they do need help in learning how to talk and how to listen and a vital part of the teacher's role is to facilitate this learning. ICT provides an ideal context for such learning to take place.

> The teacher's role in harnessing the technology to the aims of the talk focused classroom is therefore crucial . . . A classroom community is the unique construction of its component teacher(s) and learners, and in this lies its strength. The ability of learning communities to pool experience,

ideas and intentions, and to come to joint solutions through talk is a powerful means to get things done

(Dawes 2002: 131)

In order to develop their voice, children also need space in which to develop and explore their ideas with others and to participate in exciting and engaging learning. The PowerPoint group was clearly eager to take ownership of their learning. When initially asked for their ideas on how the session should be managed for the rest of their class the researcher asked, *'Tell me what to do with my lesson'*. *'But it's our lesson!'* answered Alex!

The use of ICT seems to encourage pupils to work more independently of the teacher and more collaboratively with their peers (Cox et al. 2003). In a study on primary school children's awareness of the links between ICT and the way they learn at school, Goodison (2002) relates extracts from the following interview with Kieran who is 7 years old:

Teacher: Right, what about you Kieran, when did you start learning about computers?

Kieran: At first, when I before, I couldn't remember when I did but how I learned was I saw my brother do it and I saw everyone else do it and I learned from them and I learned mostly from my brother. He told me how to copy and paste and stuff.

Teacher: He told you how to use PowerPoint as well, didn't he? And that was very useful.

Kieran: Yes, my sister told me how to do PowerPoint.

Teacher: Did she?

Kieran: Yes.

Teacher: That was very useful wasn't it? Because who did you tell then?

Kieran: You, the whole class.

(Goodison 2002: 286)

So whose lesson is it and how do teachers feel about this degree of pupil self-direction? Gibson (2001) argues that although ICT tends to be evaluated in terms of the contribution which it makes to student-centred learning, in fact most teachers prefer a more teacher-centred approach. Children are not given opportunities to direct their own learning, and for this to occur some teachers will need to make 'radical changes to the way they teach'. Although schools and teachers have been encouraged, through the Primary National Strategy, to develop more creative and flexible curricula which really engage and involve learners, this may be very challenging to achieve across the board.

The need for teachers to find the balance between over-prescription on the one hand or leaving pupils without the benefit of structured support based on ongoing assessment of their learning needs on the other remains as keen as ever. In their review of research literature on ICT and pedagogy, Cox et al. (2003: 25) note that:

> . . . one of the key benefits of these new technologies, the possibility of greater control of the learning process by the pupils, can become disadvantageous if it results in the absence of structure. Laurillard (1998) reported that learners working on interactive media with no clear narrative structure tend to be unfocused.

Consequently, we need to constantly monitor the amount of structure we provide. And the amount and nature of this support should depend on ongoing assessment of the learners' current level of understanding. Teachers need to recognise that when children are allowed to choose, they will also need structure to help balance the children's natural curiosity, children's need to challenge themselves, and their own interests with the requirements of the curriculum. Such learning and teaching requires changes to curriculum management and classroom organisation and benefits from a whole school commitment to this approach.

Despite their enjoyment of the activity, the PowerPoint group thought that, for the whole-class session, the short initial teaching section should be kept the same, but that the rest of the class should not be allowed to choose what to do. When the researcher pointed out that they had really enjoyed the choosing, Meggie suggested '*Why don't you tell them sort of what not to do, only part of it?*' Meggie may have been unsure about whether others could be trusted to manage such a self-directed activity, but she may have been expressing a need for choice but within a more structured session – she may have wanted more teaching.

Some basic instruction was given at the start of each of the two activities discussed. This was probably sufficient for the older group using PowerPoint, but more structure would have been helpful for the Year 1 and 2 group who were using the Roamer. A more structured lesson which still allowed the children to take some responsibility during the first session would also have provided support and scaffold planned by the teacher to enable all learners to develop personal engagement, curiosity, skills and knowledge. For example in this initial lesson we could begin by asking them to set up their own route to move the Roamer through. As these children gained experience and knowledge through these shared and scaffolded experiences they would be able to take an increasing role in discussing and determining future learning challenges, and not 'waste their time chasing intellectual red herrings or wandering up alleys that the teacher knows full well are blind' (Mercer 1993: 36).

Mercer argues that teachers need to provide sufficient support to develop children's independence. In this respect 'the teacher's task is to increase progressively the learner's autonomy, not (as in radically child-centred approaches) to assume its prior existence, or (as on unreflective teacher-directed approaches) to stifle it through excessive levels of social control' (Mercer 1993: 8). In relation to ICT such approaches might include planning joint tasks and ensuring all children have opportunities to engage in different roles; encouraging children to manage their time and work effectively and supporting them in making links with their prior learning.

Summary

This chapter explores the dilemmas currently facing teachers in schools and how ICT-based activities lend themselves to the sort of creative learning and teaching promoted in the Primary National Strategy. Findings from the HMI subject report on ICT in primary schools and the 2004 ICT in Schools report (OfSTED 2006a, 2004c) indicate that an increasing number of schools and teachers are covering the ICT curriculum in a satisfactory way, but that many schools are failing to use ICT to support cross-curricular work.

This may change rapidly – some of the initiatives are still very recent, most notably the interactive whiteboard programme, and it is possible that the impact will be considerable. However, in many schools the use of ICT needs to be more firmly embedded across the curriculum (BECTA 2005).

We have illustrated in this chapter how teachers need to consider creating opportunities for children to use ICT creatively. There is much evidence to support the importance of making learning vivid and challenging and to involve children as partners in their own learning. We believe that ICT provides great opportunities for children to take ownership of their own learning, to make connections with experiences beyond school and to develop effective strategies and dispositions for current and future learning. This may require great courage from teachers and schools to exchange ways of working based on the current 'must cover' anxiety' in favour of more effective approaches. These approaches may require great skill from teachers to plan and scaffold children's learning; however, the challenge is there if we wish to take it and the quickening pace of technological use in the classroom could be the perfect catalyst.

Reflection

In what ways has this chapter encouraged you to consider the contexts where ICT may be employed to engage children in purposeful activities across a full range of curriculum areas. What spaces and opportunities do you need to plan for children to realise their learning potential? What balance does there need to between freedom and structure?

Chapter 8

What has happened to curriculum breadth and balance in primary schools?

Penelope Harnett and Maria Vinney

Introduction

Curriculum breadth and balance became a statutory requirement within the 1988 Education Reform Act. Within the primary curriculum however, varying degrees of attention have been focused on these aspects of the curriculum as different governments have changed the scope of the curriculum within the last decades.

This chapter will help you to think about the following questions:

- What does a broad and balanced curriculum really look like?
- How do teachers view the curriculum?
- What are children's views and experiences of curriculum breadth and balance?

We begin by exploring the development of a broad and balanced curriculum in the past decades and assess how it has been influenced by changing government policy. In terms of implementation we discuss how teachers view the curriculum and ways in which they plan for curriculum breadth. We examine how different schools are planning to enrich the curriculum to meet their children's needs and interests. Finally, we draw on children's views to evaluate the curriculum and to explore their understandings of ways in which they learn.

Background

The notion of curriculum breadth has its antecedents in the work of progressive educationalists in the early twentieth century who reacted against the utilitarian elementary school curriculum provided in the earlier stages of compulsory schooling. The limited opportunities afforded by such schooling were criticised and alternative views outlined in the Hadow Report (Board of Education 1931). Children's active involvement in their learning and the importance of a range of learning experiences were emphasised and the Report advocates 'that schools needed, to broaden their aims until it might now be said that they have to teach children how to live' (Board of Education 1931: 92). Child-centred theories of education continued to be influential in Britain after the Second World War, and were enshrined within the Plowden Report. Its dictum, 'at the heart of education lies the child', placed in the foreground the needs and interests of children, 'to be themselves and to develop in the way and at the pace appropriate to them' (Central Advisory Council for Education 1967: 187) – a view which is still in evidence in the Framework for the Foundation Stage, where children's active investigations of their world are valued (DfES 2003c).

However, this liberal tradition, within primary education in particular, has had many critics. For example, Dearden (1968) questions whether children's interactions are all educationally valuable. Are there some aspects of society/ learning which all children need to experience? The creation of a balance between the transmission of shared cultural heritages and children's own independence and individual interpretations of their learning experiences were some of the tensions debated throughout the 1980s. HMI published a series of curriculum documents which attempted to draw together key issues within the debate. In *The Curriculum from 5–16*, HMI view the curriculum in broad terms, noting that the curriculum comprises all activities which promote, 'the intellectual, personal, social and physical development of pupils', and that this development occurs both in the formal programme of lessons as well as the more 'informal' programme of extra-curricular activities and values which the school promotes through its ethos (DES 1985: para 11).

HMI emphasise the importance of developing breadth and a 'wholeness' for children's experiences as they discuss different forms of curriculum organisation including topic work and single subject teaching. Children's active involvement in their learning – 'the development of lively and enquiring minds' – is acknowledged and HMI also draw attention to the need for an established core of worthwhile and educationally valuable experiences, which are described within areas of experience and elements of learning.

The areas incorporate aesthetic and creative, human and social, linguistic and literary, mathematical, moral, physical, scientific, spiritual and techno-logical experiences. These are broad groupings of experience, not necessarily linked with traditional subject boundaries, but which are all important for children's learning and development. Alongside the areas of experience, the elements of learning provide an analytical tool for determining the content of the curriculum in terms of knowledge, concepts, skills and attitudes.

HMI advocate the importance of a broad, balanced and relevant curri-culum and this informed some of the thinking behind the National Curricu-lum which was introduced following 1988 Education Reform Act. The preamble to the Act emphasises a broad and balanced curriculum to prepare children for adult life, which was translated into a range of curriculum subjects. Enshrined within the notion of a broad and balanced curriculum is the entitlement of all children to receive an education which is more extensive than the narrow skills-based curriculum of early compulsory education.

Activity

Obtain a weekly timetable of lessons from a school/setting where you have taught. List all the different lessons and activities which the children have during the week.

Look at the areas of learning and experience drawn from *The Curriculum from 5–16* (DES 1985):

- aesthetic and creative
- human and social
- linguistic and literary
- mathematical
- moral
- physical
- scientific
- spiritual
- technological.

Where do you think these areas might be covered in your current timetable? Are there any areas missing on your timetable? Do some areas occur across different lessons and activities?

Try and construct a weekly timetable based on the areas of learning and experience. Is it similar/different to your current timetable? Write down your views on some of the observations which you have made.

Interpreting breadth and balance within the primary curriculum

In contrast to HMI's proposals for a range of areas of experience and elements of learning in *The Curriculum from 5–16* (DES 1985), the Education Reform Act linked curriculum breadth with traditional subject areas. Within primary schools children have a statutory right to learn nine subjects (soon to become ten when modern foreign languages are introduced in 2010). These subjects were created by subject working groups working independently of each other to translate key features of each subject within a programme of study. Since the subject groups worked largely in isolation from each other, when the programmes of study for each subject were published there was little evidence of an integrated vision for children's learning experiences and how links between different subjects may be developed.

In the early 1990s as primary schools strove to implement the statutory requirements to teach all nine subjects, it would appear that children did experience greater breadth in their experience of the curriculum. Despite the rhetoric of child-centred theories of education, the curriculum in many schools had remained very narrow with an undue concentration on maths and English (DES 1978). Learning in many other subjects varied greatly. For example, prior to the National Curriculum children's experience of history was very patchy: HMI conclude that history was underemphasised in two out of three infant classes and that it was underemphasised or not taught in half their sample of junior schools (DES 1989). In this respect, the introduction of the National Curriculum did give children access to a broader range of curriculum subjects.

The imposition of a broad subject-focused curriculum presented great challenges for teachers in their curriculum organisation. Fitting (or squeezing) everything in was a real concern (Campbell and Neill 1991, 1992; Webb 1993). At first primary teachers tried to map the new subjects onto the existing topics which they taught. However, excessive content within the Programmes of Study for each subject made this a very complex task, and HMI very shortly began to urge the need for careful curriculum planning (OfSTED 1993, 1995). Difficulties were acknowledged within the discussion paper, *Curriculum Organisation and Classroom Practice in Primary Schools*, which argues that 'there is clear evidence to show that much topic work has led to fragmentary and superficial teaching and learning' (Alexander et al. 1992: para 3.4), and advocates the need for separate subject teaching to ensure all aspects of the curriculum are covered effectively.

The extent and depth to which children were able to experience a broad curriculum was short-lived. Sir Ron Dearing in his curriculum review of the initial National Curriculum comments on the perceived problems in its design.

> The architects of the first subject curricula designed what for them, as subject specialists for the most part, was an ideal and comprehensive curriculum for each subject. Not until this was put into practice in classrooms did it become obvious that the combined weight of all the subject curricula was simply too great to be manageable.
>
> (SCAA 1994: I)

We have here, the notion that some restrictions must be placed on breadth if the curriculum is to be successfully implemented.

The Dearing Review of the curriculum still maintained a commitment to a broad range of subjects, but reduced the content of different subject areas within their programmes of study. The commitment to curriculum breadth has also been retained in Curriculum 2000 which re-echoing the Education Reform Act, states within its values, aims and purposes that schools should provide a balanced and broadly based curriculum that:

- promotes the spiritual, moral, cultural, mental and physical development of pupils at the school and of society
- prepares pupils at the school for the opportunities, responsibilities and experiences of adult life.

(DfEE and QCA 1999: 12)

More recently, the Primary National Strategy continues to promote the importance of a broad range of experiences for children. 'Essential tools for learning' are important, but the Strategy also states, '. . . primary education is about children experiencing the joy of discovery, solving problems, being creative in writing, art, music, developing their self-confidence as learners and maturing socially and emotionally' (DfES 2003a: 4).

However, whilst during the last decades there has remained a commitment to curriculum breadth, it might be argued that the curriculum has had varying degrees of balance. What does a balanced curriculum look like? Does it mean that all subjects should be given equal weighting in terms of curriculum time and the allocation of resources? What is the status of different curriculum areas within a balanced curriculum? Inevitably this raises questions of values: different subject leaders may have views on how balanced the curriculum is according to the priority relating to their own curriculum subject; others may evaluate balance in terms of SATS results – is there a balance between children's (greater) experiences of the core and their (lesser) experiences of foundation subjects? Balance may be evaluated in terms of providing opportunities for children to experience different learning styles and in promoting children's attitudes, enjoyment and willingness to engage with varied activities.

More recently, many primary teachers might argue that a balanced curriculum disappeared following the introduction of the Literacy and Numeracy Strategies in 1998 and 1999 (DfEE 1998, 1999a). With over half the timetable time being devoted to these Strategies, the remaining foundation subjects were only able to be squeezed in. The status of the foundation subjects was further eroded between February 1998 and September 2000 with the suspension of the statutory requirements to teach them, and the relaxation of the requirements to inspect non-core subjects.

Here the demand for higher standards in literacy and numeracy to be achieved through specific teaching strategies was seen to be more important than the notion of a broad and balanced curriculum. Although there was an outcry from different subject associations and some members of the teaching profession, OfSTED inspections ensured that most primary schools began to follow the Literacy and Numeracy Strategies closely. The advice from the Qualifications and Curriculum Authority in their publication, *Maintaining*

Breadth and Balance at Key Stages 1 and 2 (QCA 1998) showing how a broad and balanced curriculum could be maintained by combining, adapting or reducing curriculum content was not widely followed.

Curriculum 2000 restored the statutory obligation for all schools to teach the full range of the foundation subjects, but has balance really been achieved? Data from section 10 OfSTED reports reveal that in 2000 and 2001, problems of coverage were particularly marked in design technology, art, music, geography and religious education. Such views were endorsed by the external evaluation of the Strategies undertaken by the University of Toronto who report headteachers' concerns about the Strategies squeezing out other, 'crucial programmes of experience' (Earl et al. 2001).

Lack of curriculum balance features in Her Majesty's Chief Inspector's (HMCI) report in 2002 which records the focus on raising standards in English and maths is exerting 'considerable pressure on the teaching of other subjects'. However, HMCI also draws attention to the minority of schools which are still able to provide a broad curriculum and high standards and notes, 'often, in such schools, high standards are achieved across the full curriculum' (OfSTED 2003b).

The Primary National Strategy (DfES 2003a) outlines a range of features of outstanding primary schools which include, the provision of a 'rich, broad and balanced curriculum'. The appearance of this new adjective to describe the curriculum may seem puzzling and one could question the extra ingredient which 'rich' contributes to a broad and balanced curriculum. This richness is also in evidence in the way that the Strategy outlines teachers' responsibilities to take control of their curriculum, and, 'think actively about how they would like to develop and enrich the experience they offer their children'.

Selection of the word, 'experience' encompasses a broader notion of learning than that included within terms such as subject or curriculum. This is further emphasised in the Strategy's advice to schools to, 'provide a broad range of worthwhile curricular opportunities that caters for the interests, aptitudes and particular needs of all pupils, and it is interesting to note here that the curriculum is now described in terms of opportunities rather than subject areas. Two decades ago, HMI (DES 1985) was arguing for a similar approach to educational planning.

Activity

Shadow a child in a class where you are working. Write down all the experiences and activities which the child undertakes during the week. Do you think that your child is offered a broad and balanced range of opportunities? In what ways could you extend their opportunities further?

The Primary National Strategy offers greater freedom for schools and teachers to determine their curriculum. However, there are concerns that many teachers are uncertain how to respond to this freedom. In his annual report for 2003–2004, HMCI comments that although the Primary Strategy has been regarded positively, schools 'have been cautious in acting on it', and that 'few schools have made substantial changes to develop the distinctive character of their schools in response to *Excellence and Enjoyment*' (OfSTED 2005a).

Teachers' reluctance to embrace some of the new freedoms in curriculum decision making may stem from the continued demands for accountability and target setting which stifle creative approaches to planning and teaching. As we discussed in Chapter 2, research indicates that the formulaic pedagogy of the Strategies has also sapped teachers' confidence in developing their own approaches to teaching. However, there is evidence to suggest that these fresh opportunities are more attuned to primary school teachers' views on the curriculum and beliefs about primary education. As teachers gain greater confidence in their professional judgements, they will begin to plan more creatively to take into account their children's individual needs and interests. We now turn to consider teachers' perceptions of breadth and balance and discuss some examples of how their beliefs are influencing their curriculum planning and decision making.

Teachers' perceptions of breadth and balance

Research suggests that primary school teachers have a broad conception of their roles within schools; they look beyond individual subject areas to consider children's overall well being (Pollard et al. 1994, Osborn et al. 1997, 2000; Sturman et al. 2004, 2005). In a study which explored the aims of primary school teachers (Harnett and Newman 2002), the highest percentage of responses from primary teachers was accorded to aims relating to help children fulfil their potential. Children's potential is generally regarded as being beyond the narrow confines of academic potential and is often elaborated with comments from teachers such as:

> *'to fulfil their potential academically, socially and emotionally'*
>
> *'individual potential, be it academic, artistic or practical'*
>
> *'potential academically, socially, morally and culturally'*

These statements reveal that teachers' views of potential extend to cover a range of achievements, and this impacts on how they conceive their role. For example, one teacher explained that she *'strongly believed in developing the "whole child" . . . finding their own talents, even it it's not numeracy or literacy!'* Another teacher acknowledged, *'it's important that they have a rounded education, including both core and foundation subjects. As all children/people have their strengths and weaknesses in subjects and it's important everyone finds something they're good at.'*

Teachers therefore do demonstrate some commitment to a broad curriculum and range of experiences. This has been a long standing aim of primary school teachers and there is some consistency of teachers' beliefs over a long period of time. Ashton et al. (1975) identify teachers' key priorities as children's personal development, social and moral development and basic skills. Incorporated within personal development are children's positive attitudes to school, self-confidence and the development of children's individuality. Many teachers also refer to meeting the needs of the whole child, although Ashton foreshadows later developments in criticising this notion as lacking precision.

Teachers in Harnett and Newman's research emphasise the importance of children's happiness and enjoyment in learning. These factors are important in Ashton's study and also emerge as important in other studies, although there is some evidence to suggest that teachers' priorities for this area decline as children move higher up in Key Stage 2 (Osborn et al. 2000: 110).

Harnett and Newman note that teachers are highly committed to the notion that the development of self-esteem and confidence are linked with children's motivation to learn. Several teachers emphasise the importance of creating a safe and secure environment and ensuring that children were happy at school. *'I try to enthuse the children and get them to be excited about their learning. I would like them to be active learners so I need to make them interested (a tricky task) at times.'*

Teachers particularly value the social nature of learning. Fostering personal and social skills and positive classroom relationships all rank highly amongst their responses. Positive relationships embrace a number of aspects; the ability to relate to others, to work collaboratively and to respect different beliefs and values are all emphasised. *'Social skills are something that also influence my teaching. Manners, respect for each other, being able to work collaboratively with others even if they're not your best friend.' 'I try to get the children to respect and value each other and listen to each other. Tolerance of others' views, beliefs, etc. – very important.'*

The above comments were made by teachers in 2001–2002 when evidence from both HMI and the evaluation of the Strategies indicates that in many schools curricular opportunities were narrowing. Despite this, the research appears to suggest that teachers do look more broadly at the range of opportunities which they are able to offer children, although they might feel constrained in doing this. In this respect, the Primary National Strategy may offer teachers greater scope, although many teachers might need support in developing more creative approaches to the curriculum and to embracing experiences beyond the confines of different subject areas. Indeed, the evaluation of the impact of the Primary National Strategy in primary schools in 2004–2005 indicated that although the Strategy's emphasis on freedom and greater flexibility had been generally welcomed, the daily literacy and mathematics lessons remained intact and that schools had addressed change ' with caution' (OfSTED 2005b).

Reflection

List the three most important aims which guide your work as a teacher. Share your aims with others. Do you share similar aims?

Talk with teachers about their educational aims. In what ways are they similar/different from your views?

We now turn to consider ways in which teachers are developing creative ways towards planning their curriculum in line with their own values and educational aims in the following case studies.

Teachers' responses to breadth and balance: creative approaches to curriculum planning

The value the Strategy attaches to the importance of making learning enjoyable for children was a key feature in one school's approach to planning their curriculum using an arts-based model. The arrival of a new headteacher at the school prompted a whole staff meeting where a mind map was created centred around 'What our children need'. All staff contributed their thoughts and ideas about where the focus for time and energy should be spent in order to improve the quality of the learning experience for children in the school. As the mind map grew, it soon became apparent that issues around low self-esteem and confidence, amongst not only the children but staff and parents as well, were a key concern. These issues needed to be addressed to excite people in their learning and to re-energise and motivate them. The staff took a long hard look at what they were teaching and how. There was an awareness that this process had to be about the whole school community, and it had to make learning relevant and start from where the children were.

There were many challenges within the learning community: the school was in an area of high deprivation with just over half of the children at the school entitled to free school meals and a similar percentage on the Special Educational Needs Code of Practice due to their significant levels of emotional, learning or behavioural needs – often a combination of these. Children appeared to be turned off by learning, they found it uninspiring and irrelevant and therefore, seemed unwilling and unable to persevere or engage. Teaching staff appeared to be worn down – they felt they were working hard but not really making progress. They were committed to supporting the children, but staff felt caught up in a culture of control and compliance. Relentless attempts to move the school away from the lowest position in the county league tables had resulted in the school being part of every government initiative available to raise attainment – mainly focused on more literacy and more numeracy. This approach had however, generally failed to have the desired impact and something more radical was clearly needed.

Learning opportunities which increased children's access to a range of arts experiences across the curriculum were created throughout the school. Support and encouragement were provided by the school governors and the local education authority who agreed to monitor progress rigorously by carrying out evaluation visits every six weeks.

The journey began with a whole-school drumming day which involved all 200 children in key skills such as listening, co-operating and counting. The impact of the learning that took place on the day was discussed with the children and related to their learning as a whole: How did it feel to be part of a large group, all working together on something? How important was it not to give up even when it got hard? And so on.

Every time a unit of work was planned staff found ways to enhance the children's learning in each class. For example, they worked alongside Indian dancers as part of their geography focus on a contrasting locality; performed with story tellers in literacy; re-enacted Sir Walter Raleigh's return with the help of a local drama company as part of their exploration of Tudor times; modelled and danced their way down the catwalk in the outfits they had made for design technology, and so on. With each experience the children's confidence and self-esteem grew.

As well as inviting people in, the children also went out into the community, for example making visits to see *Stomp!* – a production in which everyday objects are used to make music. They dressed in role as Victorian school children for a day at a real Victorian school and visited a local art gallery to create their own Matisse-style collages. The expectation was that all the children, from Reception to Year 6, would go out on an enrichment visit as part of their learning each term and rather than being used as simply an exciting experience, the visits were used as a springboard for learning across the curriculum back at school.

Alongside this were all kinds of whole-school events which helped raise self-confidence and reinforced the notion of a 'learning community' which involved all the school, children, staff and increasingly, parents. There were, for the first time in this school, Christmas shows, art exhibitions and focus weeks which concentrated the whole school on one aspect of learning such as poetry. A particular highlight, which was to become an established part of the school calendar, was an 'in house' version of 'Stars in their Eyes' where children (and staff) dressed up and performed as their favourite pop star or group. This proved so successful that parents and carers requested their own event and a community version was consequently organised. This in turn, led on to the school successfully bidding for additional funding for 'Family Learning' which enabled weekly workshops to be offered for parents and carers in areas such as silk painting, cookery and wood work and culminated in Whizzy Week – a varied programme of activities in every class aimed at encouraging parents and carers to come into school and learn alongside their children.

As they prepared for their SATs, Year 5 and 6 children worked with a theatre company for an intense and thought-provoking week where they wrote the script and the songs, made the props and the costumes for an all-singing, all-dancing performance on the Friday night. All the ideas came from the children themselves and proved to be a powerful, vibrant example of learning at its best which helped to reinforce the underlying principles the school were trying to communicate. This was a real challenge and there were times during the week when it seemed the show would never come together – but it did and proved a huge success. Children learned how important it was to think positively; to believe you can and you will achieve. They recognised that they needed to be brave and to be prepared to take risks in their learning at times. The value of collaboration, supporting each other and learning from each others' skills was also experienced.

Children also learned the true meaning of words like perseverance and resilience that week and, together with their parents, felt a huge sense of achievement and pride. The week marked a change in their attitudes and responses to learning across the curriculum. This was particularly true for the children with special educational needs, many of whom helped give an all action presentation about their special week to a large group of head-teachers and county advisers who had heard what the school was attempting to do and wanted to know more.

Two years following the adoption of these learning opportunities, the school received national recognition for its promotion of the arts in education and was presented with a Silver Artsmark Award by the Arts Council. Attainment across the curriculum continued to rise and the education authority, in one of their frequent evaluation visits, confirmed that the ethos and learning culture within the school had undergone a transformation. It could truly be called a learning community with children, staff and parents actively engaged in learning, which was now firmly at the top of the list. Staff also began to take control of their own professional learning, seeking out research to inform their practice and the school joined a research group linked with other schools to explore what it means to be a 'Vibrant School'.

An alternative approach to curriculum planning was adopted by another school to incorporate children's interests and staff expertise. In contrast to the school above, this school already had strong links with the community and parents. Formal assessment indicators were strong and a recent OfSTED visit confirmed that it was indeed a successful school with a rich, stimulating and creative curriculum.

Staff, however, were concerned about curriculum balance. The balance of time allocation for different curricular areas had become seriously 'skewed' despite the fact that staff had worked hard the previous year to integrate and blend certain areas such as humanities and science. Staff had audited instances where curriculum subjects overlapped, yet together with their children were still reporting stress caused by lack of time to develop skills and ideas. The staff were generally confident and enthusiastic about their roles and yet there was the feeling that many of the good things, such as project work that had been part of the school, had been squeezed out of the curriculum with the introduction of the National Literacy and Numeracy Strategies in the late 1990s.

Like many schools, teachers wanted to follow their professional instincts and plan projects or contexts for learning, which encouraged children to make connections and develop their thinking. As long as projects are demanding and well informed, they are clearly relevant to adult life in the twenty-first century and have the ability to seize children's imagination and persuade them to want to keep learning beyond the confines of the classroom. This kind of joined up thinking seemed to make such sense from the children's point of view and yet it had become one of the casualties in recent years. Teachers at the school wanted to return to this way of working but were keen to ensure the projects they planned would involve clearly defined content and outcomes and were more rigorous than the 'topics' of old.

Staff had already made attempts to rationalise and establish priorities within their curriculum and had increased time allocations for some subjects such as PE. However, there was still a feeling that there was too great an emphasis on knowledge content and that more attention needed to be paid to the development of key skills, attitudes and values. The curriculum was viewed as fragmented; children had a range of experiences throughout the day, but were rarely given the opportunity to reflect, make choices or plan future learning for themselves – let alone finish anything.

Staff thought carefully about the opportunities which the school needed to provide for children. They agreed that school needed to be somewhere children could:

- have fun!
- continue to have a rich and creative curriculum with the time to explore ideas and concepts in depth;
- know and understand how learning takes place;
- apply this knowledge to themselves as learners;
- be motivated and take responsibility for their own development in all areas;

- not be afraid to try new things, make mistakes and sometimes fail;
- know what to do if they do fail;
- take from and also give support to others;
- make decisions based on consideration and understanding of all the relevant factors;
- solve problems, using a logical sequence of thinking skills;
- work as a team or independently, whichever is best;
- learn from all sorts of experiences, and people – not just the teacher in the classroom;
- have some say in what and how they learn.

The school began this process by deciding to timetable one day each week where staff and children could specifically develop opportunities to meet these criteria. They wanted these criteria to permeate the entire curriculum throughout the week, and identifying a specific day was judged as an effective way to introduce this change. An agreement was made to review progress and effectiveness regularly – and Freaky Fridays were born!

Freaky Fridays were devised to stimulate both the adults in the school as well as the children, so that both might thrive through creative opportunities. Freaky Fridays provide different opportunities for grouping children throughout the school. There are free choice, mixed age Interest Groups which run for half-term blocks and which are staffed by teachers, teaching assistants, parents and members of the community. The aim of these Interest Groups is to offer as wide a choice as possible and to cater for the children's multiple intelligences, allowing them to play to their strengths or to develop new skills in areas which might be less familiar to them. No attempt is made to influence children's choice of Interest Group. In addition, there are Home Group sessions which focus on activities such as problem solving, philosophy, current affairs, debating, thinking skills or anything that children, parents or teachers may suggest.

There are more age specific activities; Key Stage 2 children are involved in learning to learn activities and also in learning French. At Key Stage 1 children have opportunities for dance, drama or paired challenges. Key Stage 2 children have time to develop their own self-initiated research and present their work. There are also fortnightly celebration of achievement days during Freaky times and half-termly special days when the whole school has a theme or goes on a trip together. For example, Poetry Day, UNICEF Day, Languages Day, and Theatre Day.

Almost three years later, the impact of Freaky Fridays has been carefully monitored and evaluated in a variety of ways, including child-based, parental and staff questionnaires. There is much evidence to support that both children and adults have greatly enjoyed the Interest Groups. They have responded very positively to doing something different; working with different children and adults and having greater freedom and time. Parents have been very supportive of the process and clearly appreciated the effort taken at the beginning of the project to inform them about the reasons for trying to do something different and to reassure them that it would be carefully monitored. Many parents have become involved as helpers and some have offered their talents and taken responsibility for a group, as have members of the local community.

However, whilst staff have thoroughly enjoyed the days, they have found that some of their Interest Groups have taken a lot of time and energy in gathering resources, planning activities and liaising with helpers. Staff also feel that running Interest Groups every Friday could result in extra pressure being put on time to cover the rest of the curriculum. It was therefore decided to move to a model where Freaky Fridays take place every other term so the school works in this way for about six weeks and then has a break. The Interest Groups have been organised into a two-year cycle as many children said that there was more than one activity they would have liked to have chosen and it has not always been possible to give children their first choice as group sizes have needed to be balanced.

The Home Group sessions have been less successful as staff have been tempted to use them for finishing off curriculum work rather than exploring thinking skills or problem solving. In order to promote these skills, the school is in the process of trialling opportunities for staff to swap classes and plan an activity for a different age group, which appears to be working well. Over half the children, in the self-evaluations they write for their annual reports, have commented positively on Freaky Fridays. It has, it seems, become a well established and much looked forward to, part of the curriculum.

The two case studies described above illustrate some of the creative ways in which schools are responding to curriculum breadth and balance. In the arts-based model, the curriculum was broadened to incorporate a whole range of activities and children's sense of achievement and levels of attainment increased. This example which indicates that a broad curriculum may contribute towards higher standards is supported by HMI's conclusions in *The Curriculum in Successful Primary Schools* (OfSTED 2002b). In the past some schools with children who have low levels of attainment have focused their teaching more exclusively on the core subjects. However, there is limited evidence that repeated teaching of the core and consequent narrowing of the curriculum necessarily raises children's level of achievement long term.

The second case study describes one school's approach to developing curriculum balance through Freaky Fridays. In this example, teachers are looking beyond the prescribed curriculum to consider learning opportunities which will develop all children's potential. Perceptions of their children's potential are in accord with earlier research on primary school teachers' views of their roles (Pollard et al. 1994; Osborn et al. 1997; Harnett and Newman 2002; Sturman 2004, 2005).

The case studies are revealing in that they demonstrate examples of real inclusive learning communities which we explore more fully in Chapter 6, where the contributions of different community members including children, teachers and parents are described.

Activity

Try thinking outside the box! Imagine that you had to plan a themed day for whole school/setting. What sort of activities and experiences would you include for the children? How would you organise the day? How would you justify your choice of activities and organisation to other members of staff and parents?

So far the chapter has considered curriculum breadth and balance in terms of government and teachers' organisation of the curriculum. The chapter now turns to consider the sense which children make of the curriculum and how they respond to varied learning opportunities.

Achieving breadth and balance within schools

The following case studies illustrate how children's learning may be enriched when opportunities are planned to provide children with broad educational experiences which might not necessarily relate to defined curriculum subject boundaries, but also take into account the processes of learning and children's attitudes and motivation.

Every year students plan work for Foundation Stage and Year 1 children when they visit the Faculty of Education at the University of the West of England. The students use a range of stimulus materials to encourage children to think about 'special places' and encourage the children to design and build their own. Children have been remarkably creative in the places which they have created. Cold places, the seaside, jungles, planets, travel agents, forests and caravans have all been designed and built. As children build their 'special places', they demonstrate a range of knowledge about different places, climate and its effect on people and vegetation; building materials; different ways of life and recognition of what different people think is important or special. Here children draw on much of their existing knowledge and understanding of the world. Stories, trips to the shops and park, holidays, films and TV all contribute to children's ideas of different places and a curriculum which ignores these experiences outside school provides limited opportunities for enriching children's learning. In this respect, children's learning in creating these 'special places' provides examples of child-centred traditions which can be traced back to policies stated in the Plowden Report (Central Advisory Council for Education 1967) and the Hadow Report (Board of Education 1931).

Although the finished outcomes of their work were impressive, it was the children's engagement with the activity which provided much fruitful learning. Children became absorbed in different aspects of their building; they played together and alongside each other and the control which they exercised over their own play led to many unforeseen and exciting experiences. Children planned and communicated their ideas; they demonstrated remarkable skills and ingenuity in assembling different materials and joining them together.

This emphasis on children's active learning and engagement in decision making about their learning underpins research about powerful and effective learning. The Effective Lifelong Learning Inventory (ELLI) identifies seven dimensions of learning power important for successful learning – Learning Relationships, Changing, Meaning Making, Creativity, Critical Curiosity, Resilience, Strategic Awareness (Deakin Crick 2006). *Learning Relationships* recognise the importance of children developing effective partnerships in learning with their peers, teachers and other people and *Changing* involves children gaining confidence in their learning over a period of time and identifying different strengths which they need to draw on. Effective learning is characterised by children *Meaning Making* and seeing connections between their existing knowledge and the world outside the classroom. This requires a sense of *Creativity* and *Critical Curiosity*. As children learn they need to be *Resilient,* recognise that they will face challenges and that they need to persevere. *Strategic Awareness* is also important to encourage children to become responsible for their own learning and to develop a toolkit of strategies to help them learn.

Providing opportunities for children to develop understanding of ways in which they learn are important for effective learning. Deakin Crick (2006) argues that creating the right classroom environment is important for powerful learning and identifies teachers' important roles in helping children to explain their beliefs about learning and what is important for them. In this respect, organising time in the classroom to encourage self-evaluation and reflection on learning is important as well as teachers modelling language to help children talk about their learning.

Reflection

Look at the different dimensions of learning identified by Deakin Crick
(2006). Which of these do you think are most important for your own
learning?

- learning relationships
- changing
- meaning making
- creativity
- critical curiosity
- resilience
- strategic awareness

Which dimensions would you like to develop with children whom you are
teaching? In what ways do you think you could encourage children to
develop their awareness of them?

Year 5 children were able to talk about their learning as they worked with
trainee teachers to create a performance of *Noye's Fludde* by Benjamin
Britten in Bristol Cathedral. Children made different animal masks at the
university; they rehearsed their different parts at school and participated in
a joint performance in the cathedral. Responses from children reveal that
they do recognise the importance of such experiences. One child explained,
'*It's fun. When things are fun you listen more – you learn more if you are
enjoying it – you pay more attention.*' This view was re-iterated by another
child, '*when I am trying to learn, I don't learn very well, but when I'm not,
I learn better. What matters is that you want to do it . . . I wanted to do this
. . . .*'

When the children were asked what they felt they had learned, they
identified many unexpected learning experiences, '*I liked singing the second
song, "Soon the evening shadows prevail". I like the old words, how they
sound, how they fit together like poetry.*' Another child commented, '*I enjoy
learning new languages. It is Greek – no, Latin – it means "peace be with
you".*' Interest in language was also expressed by another child, who
described how much music they had learned – '*high notes, low notes, beats
when to come in, songs, how to come in. Kyrie – it's a different language –
it's fun. Singing helps you learn language.*'

These comments remind us of the impact of different experiences on
individual learners, and that too great a focus on pre-specified learning
objectives is not always helpful, since it is unlikely that teachers would have
included all the items which these children felt they had learned within their

planning objectives Teachers may have identified the importance of singing within the activity, but would they necessarily have identified the different dimensions to singing which the children commented on?

Children's comments emphasise the value which they attach to the learning processes itself.

We learned how to be brave – perform in front of thousands. At school you might learn to be brave. How to show off. Sometimes it's a bad thing to show off, but in a play it's not. The director wants you to be a character, like the character of the animal. You have to use your imagination.

Children also recognised the importance of teamwork. '*We had to work together to make the performance. We needed to watch what others were doing so that we could find spaces to do our dance*', and that decisions had to be made, '*I wanted to make the tiger's face look furry, so I tried sponge printing. I think it would have been better if I had had some furry material.*'

In these comments, children demonstrate that, given the opportunity, they are able to reflect on the learning experiences offered and to articulate clearly the learning involved and its value to them as individuals in very broad terms. These examples reveal the rich learning which may occur when children have a broad range of experiences. Planning for such a range of experiences within the curriculum will be a challenge for schools in the future.

Summary

In the nineteenth century a better educated workforce was valued for its contribution to the economy, and this is still recognised by the government today. In 1998 David Blunkett as Secretary of State for Education commented that the best economic policy we have is education. Education, however, has to respond to rapidly changing needs and flexible workforces. A narrow, restrictive curriculum might not be the best means to address unforeseen demands of the future. On the other hand, a broader curriculum which enthuses children for their learning and values the experience which they bring might serve as a stronger foundation, 'for the responsibilities and experiences of adult life'.

The effectiveness of a restricted curriculum is possibly more easy to measure with simple tests constructed to test children's learning and in a society obsessed with accountability and target setting this may seem attractive. Increasing percentages of children attaining level 4 in maths and literacy provide governments with justifications for their policies of testing and inspection. Broader curriculum experiences, however, are less easy to evaluate within instrumental testing, since they involve consideration of a whole range of learning processes, not all of which may be measured.

However, the comments from children above do reveal the very real need to take their perspectives and experiences into account. A broad curriculum provides opportunities for them to take ownership and make sense of their own learning and not remain passive receptors of the curriculum. The Primary National Strategy enables teachers to build on experiences of preceding decades and to have the freedom to develop their own approaches towards curriculum breadth and balance which places the learner at the centre of the curriculum and also considers educational experiences beyond the confines of traditional subjects.

We may return to Plowden's dictum with the rejoinder, at the heart of education lies the child, learning through a broadly based and balanced curriculum.

Reflection

In what ways has this chapter encouraged you to think about how the curriculum is planned and organised in schools/settings? List some reasons why ensuring curriculum breadth and balance are important. Identify ways in which schools may organise their curriculum to ensure children have a broad and balanced range of experiences.

Acknowledgement

The authors would like to acknowledge the contribution of Elizabeth Newman to the data collection in this chapter.

Chapter 9

Children's futures, our futures

Educating citizens for the twenty-first century

Alison Bailey and Steve Barnes

Introduction

In this chapter we recognise education's important contribution to developing children's social and cultural knowledge and understanding to equip them for their future roles as world citizens.

The chapter will help you to think about the following questions:

- What do children need to know in order to become effective global citizens?
- How can education help children grow socially, emotionally, culturally and spiritually?
- How may children be encouraged to think about alternative futures for themselves and their world?

We draw on case studies of working with children in a range of contexts to explore their views and different understandings of their world. In particular, we emphasise the importance of children developing their own points of view and identifying issues which are important to them. Knowledge and understanding of different places, the environment, peoples, societies and issues are all important features of an education system which prepares children for future challenges.

Becoming effective global citizens

A major theme in the writings of the American educator, John Dewey, almost a century ago was that education should educate children to be the problem-solvers of tomorrow. Dewey (1916) explored the range of knowledge, skills and understanding which it would be necessary for children to acquire in order to understand the issues which would face them as citizens in a modern and changing world. Recent events such as the Asian Tsunami on Boxing Day 2004, Hurricane Katrina impacting on the Gulf States of the USA in August 2005 and frequent reports in the media of wars, famine, drought,

Third World debt, energy depletion and questions of sustainability, remind us of the enormity of the problems facing humanity at the beginning of the twenty-first century.

Moore (1982: 45), developing Dewey's ideas, believes that schools should not be 'set apart from' the rest of life for this 'would be to divorce education from the real business of life, which is living, and so would defeat the purpose of education, which is individual growth'. Healthy growth requires an environment in which we are able to express and develop our own ideas in an interested and receptive climate and to show respect for the opinions of others. This individual growth is relative to our social, cultural and environmental settings and is essential for our sense of worth and value. Pupils should be encouraged to develop an awareness of personal feelings. Education, therefore, must promote a democratic ethos within a range of learning environments. We must remember that 'it is not merely a matter of what (content) we teach, but how we teach (teaching style and classroom relationships) which is fundamental to helping children in their spiritual, moral, social and cultural development' (Bailey and Kimber 2001: 27).

Promoting healthy growth: social and emotional well being

Traditionally within the UK, schools have shown regard for pupil development beyond the subject curriculum. This was formalised in Curriculum 2000 with the introduction of the non-statutory Framework for personal, social and health education (PSHE) and citizenship at Key Stages 1 and 2 and the statutory Programmes of Study for Key Stages 3 and 4. The education of the whole child is being increasingly acknowledged at a national and political level. The five outcomes of *Every Child Matters* set children's development within a wider context (DfES 2004a).

QCA's (2007) Working Draft, *A Big Picture of the Curriculum*, builds on the *Every Child Matters* outcomes and suggests that our future primary curriculum must more fully emphasise the development of the whole child, creating 'successful learners', 'confident individuals' and 'responsible citizens who make a positive contribution to society' (QCA 2007).

The social and emotional aspects of learning and their impact on children's lives are currently receiving more recognition. For example, the *Times'* Education Correspondent, Alexandra Blair comments that 'children will be encouraged to "explore their emotions" in school and learn about manners, respect and good behaviour in a bid to raise attendance and improve learning' (28 November 2005: Blair 2005b). This follows on from a successful pilot study of an 'emotional intelligence toolkit' in a few primary schools where 'serious incidents' and exclusions fell as a result of children being encouraged to develop 'emotional literacy' and a greater awareness of their inner feelings and of good behaviour. Batmanghelidjh (2004) the Chief Executive of Kids

Company, suggests that by looking after children's 'emotional and social needs, we will contribute to health, education and crime targets.'

Activity

Read the paragraph below in which the DfES (2003a) describes the 'outstanding primary school' and assess your own primary school against the criteria.

In these schools children are engaged by learning that develops and stretches them and excites their imagination. They enjoy the richness of their learning – not just learning different things, but learning in many different ways: out-of-doors, through play, in small groups, through art, music and sport, from each other, from adults other than teachers, before school, after school, with their parents and grandparents, formally and informally, by listening, by watching and by doing. They develop socially and emotionally. They take pride in their learning and want to do well.

(DfES 2003a :9)

Write down some actions which you and teachers might be able to take in order to enhance the whole school approach to learning. You might find it useful to refer to Chapters 6 and 8 as you complete this activity.

Developing political literacy

As pupils mature, they should be given an increasing range of experiences which engender a secure emotional intelligence, and which increase their understanding of cultural, social, political and economic issues. We advocate that they should be encouraged to question opinions and points of view, to take part in discussions and decision making exercises about issues which affect their lives. In this way, children socially construct their learning and are encouraged to accept the responsibilities associated with being active citizens in society. Throughout this process children are developing their 'political literacy'. Political literacy incorporates knowledge, the understanding of alternative viewpoints, the ability to articulate opinions and to make judgements based on sound evidence and reasoning. An active citizen must, of necessity, be politically literate.

Political literacy involves giving children access to a balanced range of views and opinions, developing their skills in being able to choose from alternative points of view and to allow them to voice their opinions. This must be a far cry from dogmatism and indoctrination. The effective teacher will always be vigilant about issues such as stereotyping, bias, prejudice and partial truth.

It is not enough to engage only in constructed situations and minor problem solving. Children are motivated through being presented with real issues involving real people and through being allowed the opportunities to take positive and meaningful action, ideally in matters which directly impact upon their own lives. In this respect, as McElroy argues, 'Teachers may thus avoid being unwittingly pushed into always handling trivial or politically safe issues. For if we do we may as well give up any attempt to improve our students' political literacy' (McElroy 1988: 42).

The National Curriculum Guidelines for PSHE and citizenship recognise the various roles a child may play as an individual coping with and responding to the demands of their own experiences across a range of scales. It states that children 'learn about the wider world and the interdependence of communities within it; they develop a sense of social justice and moral responsibility and begin to understand that their own choices and behaviour can affect local, national or global issues' (DfEE and QCA 1999).

Schools must embrace the view that we now live in a global village and impress upon children that individual and local decisions may have worldwide repercussions. The notion of the global citizen and the concepts of human rights and responsibilities should be an intrinsic part of every child's education. Indeed, the Citizenship Framework in many ways mirrors the rights for children set out in the United Nations' Convention on the Rights of the Child to which the UK was a signatory in 1991.

Aspects of citizenship such as care for each other, for the local community and for the environment contribute to education for sustainable development (ESD). This involves encouraging children to take responsibility for their actions. Active participation may, for example, take the form of developing a school environmental policy and then implementing it or debating a local issue such as whether speed bumps would help slow the traffic passing the school gates or considering the proposed development of a shopping centre, with groups of children taking on different roles. Research into Key Stage 2 children's knowledge of global warming and pollution led Dearden (2005: 11) to conclude that we should, 'reconsider our priorities within the curriculum to make the environment and sustainable development a key component'. This view is endorsed by HMCI David Bell (2005: 4), who states how important it is that 'the adults of tomorrow understand the management of risk, appreciate diversity, are aware of environmental issues, promote sustainability and respect human rights and social inclusion'.

Constructing children's knowledge and understanding of the world

Geography and other humanities subjects can make a significant contribution to children's developing understanding. Smeaton (2000: 1) argues that geographical education 'gives children a fuller, more rounded, structured opportunity to view, perceive, understand and respond to the world in which we live today'. Geography and the humanities subjects are important not just in the knowledge base they provide, but also in their concern for the individual and the respect they promote for all peoples, cultures and beliefs and for the environment, which accords with the aims and objectives of citizenship education.

By their very nature, the humanities have long utilised a wide range of teaching and learning styles through open-ended discussion and questioning. Children's voices and opinions form an integral part of this approach as they grow towards being independent thinkers and active citizens. Equally essential to the teaching of the humanities are fieldwork and enquiry, which provide opportunities for children to work together and to co-operate as they plan, collect data and analyse their findings. A local area investigation, for example, might involve primary school children looking at the built and natural environment and how it has changed over time. Fieldwork might be complemented by interviews with residents who can offer explanations from different perspectives across generations. Children will be able to identify that the same place may be viewed as special or significant in varying degrees by different people who hold different values. Such projects in the local area can help children and schools to be part of their local community.

Moving further afield, as children study more distant places the National Curriculum programmes of study for geography states children may:

> . . . encounter different societies and cultures. This helps them to realise how nations rely on each other. It can inspire them to think about their own place in the world, their values, and their rights and responsibilities to other people and the environment
>
> (DfEE and QCA 1999: 108)

Teachers and teacher educators have expressed concern over the past decade at the narrowing subject base of the National Curriculum and Penelope Harnett and Maria Vinney explore elsewhere in this book how curriculum breadth and balance have been challenged. Coupled with this view is the recognition of a need for more creativity in the curriculum. For example, Robinson (1999) calls for a major restructuring of the National Curriculum and urgent action to stem the decline in teaching and learning in the arts and humanities.

Excellence and Enjoyment: A Strategy for Primary Schools (DfES 2003a) begins to address these concerns, although an ambivalence still prevails about how serious the government's commitment to 'breadth and balance' really is. Alexander (2004), commenting on some of the inconsistencies and 'non-sequiturs' in the Primary National Strategy, notes how it talks of 'children's entitlement to a broad and balanced set of learning experiences' while at the same time stipulating that at least 50 per cent of teaching time is set aside for literacy and numeracy. This requirement, considered alongside the fact that the number of foundation subjects is actually increasing (with the addition of PSHE, citizenship and a modern foreign language), means that less and less time is available for each of the foundation subjects. With teaching time for the humanities being squeezed, teachers become less confident about using 'enquiry-based teaching strategies' (Catling et al. 2003: 15), an approach which has been shown to encourage high quality pupil learning. The reality is that OfSTED (2004a) noted that schools with the best standards of literacy and numeracy achieved these through the wider curriculum, as children and teachers had a 'meaningful context' for applying, reinforcing and extending the basics.

In many schools, however, OfSTED note that the foundation subjects suffer from insufficient time and resourcing. The foundation subjects are poorly provided for in terms of teachers' in-service training. The net result is a decrease in the number of subject leaders who have sufficient background knowledge to lead confidently and encourage the growth of such subjects as geography or history in their schools.

When planning the curriculum, teachers take into account not only the multiple intelligences of children and their individual learning identities, but also their cultural and social background and the experiences which children bring to school. The humanities have long been seen as a major contributor to the development of the whole child. Kimber et al. observe: 'The distinctive features of the humanities as an area of learning is that they enable young children to develop an understanding of their own place and identity within the world in which they are growing up' (1995: 6). By their very nature, humanities subjects utilise the full range of learning style approaches and offer opportunities for differentiation between visual, auditory and kinaesthetic learners, allowing all children to make valuable contributions.

An understanding of place

As human beings our sense of our own worth and our security depend upon our knowledge and understanding of how we relate to other people and the places in which we and they live. The study of place therefore must be a central part of each child's education.

Place is recognised as fundamental to the study of geography and is important from the Foundation Stage onwards. The Geographical Association (2003) emphasises this in their position statement on the Foundation Stage, recognising the importance of laying foundations for children's understanding of the world in order that they may develop as global citizens. Our understanding of place is always mediated by our perceptions of 'the worthwhile', by which we mean the things that are valued from our personal and social histories and cultural heritage. Matthews' (1992) model of children's environmental cognition calls this the 'lens of experience' through which we interpret our environment. It is important therefore for children to recognise similarities and differences between places and peoples both within their home background setting and in more distant localities. The study of a distant locality should not simply be about children assimilating knowledge. More importantly it should allow children to develop a sense of what it might be like to live in that place so that they develop an understanding of, and empathy with, the lives of people within that place.

For example, children in a Year 4 class in an inner city junior school in Bristol were investigating ways of using the internet to raise global awareness when learning about distant places. While children were comparing aspects of their lives with those of children in parts of India from some pre-selected websites, the teacher observed that 'the boys were particularly impressed with the discussions about cricket they found on one of the websites' (Nolan 2006: 18). Discovering that children in India played cricket and finding similarities with their own lives gave them a greater appreciation of people from distant places. They discovered the growing problems of child labour in India on some websites and 'became fascinated with this and started to empathise' (Nolan 2006: 17). Holden (2003: 204) suggests that 'a study of a distant locality in geography might be extended to include activities on fair trade, looking at the controversial issues of fair prices and child labour'. When the children themselves have unearthed an issue for discussion it may well lead to deeper learning because of their interest and involvement.

What issues should children be exploring in the primary years?

Learning which has a real bearing on the lives of children is often learning of the highest quality. It is important to discuss with the children the issues which most concern them and which most impact upon their understanding of the world. The maturity of children's reasoning and their responses to these issues will often demonstrate the high level of their knowledge and the sensitivity of their thought processes. Equally, we may be confounded by their misconceptions, bias and 'tabloid' attitudes. Weldon (2004: 205) recognises that, 'without intervention, infants are liable to accept uncritically the bias and discrimination they see around them'. Teaching through issues has great strengths and, so long as the teacher assumes the role of wise guide and facilitator rather than that of arbiter of truth, children will gain much in terms of knowledge, self-awareness and cooperative skills.

Activity – Identifying important issues

With your class or your peer group:

• discuss the issues which most concern them;

• group these as they arise into local, national and global (some will overlap and a Venn diagram might be more appropriate);

• discuss with the group where they heard about these issues (e.g. media/ news items, discussions with friends/family) and why the issues are of interest to them.

Use the lists as a starting point for developing curriculum themes.

Discuss with the group what could be done to address these issues.

Hands-on participant activities have the greatest positive impact on motivation. It is worthwhile to remember the motto from the Rio Earth Summit Conference (United Nations Commission on Sustainable Development 1992: Agenda 21), 'Act locally think globally'. The school should be seen as a microcosm of global relationships, socially, culturally, economically and environmentally. Giving children direct local experience of tackling issues will give them a sound base upon which to build their understanding of the broader contexts.

> The Citizenship programme of study encourages pupils to take part in a wide range of activities and experiences across and beyond the curriculum, contributing fully to the life of their school and communities. In doing so, they learn to recognise their own worth, work well with others and become increasingly responsible for their own learning
>
> (DfEE and QCA 1999: 136)

Exploring children's needs and concerns

To enable children to become participative, active and informed citizens of the future, we need to understand both their needs and their concerns. We must address the problems arising from the limitation of their perceptual and actual horizons. The following quotation succinctly outlines the challenge facing us:

> We expect education to help young people to build lives that have meaning and purpose in a future we can scarcely predict. The burning question, for everyone involved, and increasingly that is everyone, is how is this to be done? And what kind of education is needed?
>
> (DfEE 1999b: 18)

Hicks and Holden (1995) found that children's hopes for the future of their local area were mirrored by their fears. Their concerns related largely to 'the environment, personal safety and quality of life' (Hicks 1998: 266). In preparing pupils for adult life we might, for example, ask pupils:

- to list some of the things that they like and dislike about their local area;
- to identify individually three hopes they have for the future of their local area;
- then to identify individually three fears they have about the future of their local area.

(Hicks 1998: 266)

Hicks goes on to suggest ways in which this could be broadened to consider global futures.

Below we consider a range of activities, structures and processes which empower people to make a difference to the quality of their own lives and to the lives of others. Projects which attempt to extend and to enrich children's understanding of the world in which they and others live, so broadening their horizons and extending their aspirations, will be discussed. It is not only children, but adults also who can be constrained by their experiences and their socio-economic backgrounds and cultures. We therefore also consider teachers' perceptions and teachers' horizons.

Discussing choices – water in Ghana

Across the UK, several dioceses have strengthened their ties with local communities by inviting school children to participate in themed days in their cathedrals. For example, the Bristol diocese invites children from its wide geographical area to come into the Cathedral and be involved in a range of educational activities. One such opportunity is for Year 6 children from all schools within the diocese, who represent a wide range of beliefs and cultures, to join together to reflect on their anxieties and hopes as they prepare to move on to their secondary schools. For many this will be the first time they have entered the physical centre of the diocese and some experience a sense of awe and wonder at the scale of the building. There has been positive feedback from the children about sharing experiences and growing in understanding about what it means to be a member of a broad community.

The theme for the Education Days for Year 6 children recently was 'Hopes and Dreams'. In one workshop the learning intentions were for children to develop knowledge and understanding of a locality in a less economically developed country and of the lives and activities of people living there (DfEE and QCA 1999). The children were asked what they would buy if they were given £15. CDs, computer games and sweets featured in their responses. This opening question immediately interested the children, as they all had experience of making similar choices in their everyday lives.

The children were then offered a drink of water. Clean water was poured from a bottle for the first few children, but when this bottle was used up, the next drink poured was murky, dirty water, clearly not to be drunk. After many expressions of *'urgh'* and *'that's revolting'* the point was made that in some parts of the world clean drinking water is not available and that £15 from each member of the community would ensure a clean, safe water supply. This practical activity brought home to the children the contrast between their everyday decisions and the kind of decisions which other children in other places are forced to make.

Moving on from this practical, kinaesthetic learning activity, the children then watched the Water Aid video *Buckets of Water* (Water Aid 1998). This is an excellent, visual and audio resource for helping children to develop an understanding of, and empathy with, the lives of children living in a rural part of Ghana. As most teachers are aware, it is important to avoid stereotyping and bias when studying any locality. Three different villages at different stages of development in terms of their water supply are illustrated. In one village, Christina spends her day walking miles to reach a dirty pool of water from which she collects the family's water and carries it back home again. In Akolgo's village, a hand pump has been installed and he is able to collect the water quickly, allowing him to go to school and have time to play with his friends. In a third village, a well is nearly complete. The children are able to see how the participation and actions of individuals make a significant difference to the quality of life within the community.

After the video the children were given the opportunity to reflect on their hopes and dreams for Christina's village. The posters they produced in groups reflected their developing understanding of the plight of Christina and the limited choices available to her. All children recognised the hard work involved in getting the most basic of resources, water, and many appreciated how lucky they were to be able to attend school.

The workshop activities allowed for a range of learning styles (visual, auditory and kinaesthetic). It also drew upon children's existing experience in order for them to empathise with the experience of others living in different circumstances. It gave them a chance to think about their values and to consider problems faced by people throughout the world.

As children worked through the activities they were following the non-statutory guidelines for PSHE and citizenship at Key Stage 2, 'reflecting on spiritual, moral, social and cultural issues, and using their imagination to understand other peoples' experiences' (DfEE and QCA 1999: 139, 2e).

Making personal choices

Central to the notion of citizenship is the ability of individuals to make informed choices. The culture and economic class from which we come will limit choices in one of the most important areas of our lives, namely in our employment. In the case study above, the children fully recognised that Christina did not have a choice; she had to spend the day collecting water for her own and her family's survival.

Whatever our home background, our choices in important areas of life may be limited. The knowledge of possible jobs and professions open to us is often restricted to the knowledge of the jobs of our family and friends or from information gleaned from the media. Whilst academically bright children from low income families may have little support to draw from when considering their future potential, practically inclined children from white-collar professional homes may have equal difficulties in finding information about (or approval of) employment which suits their potential and inclination. Cultural tunnel vision affects what we know and how we understand. It is a major factor in creating our individual set of values.

Recent government initiatives have been introduced to help to reduce the gap in life chances of different sectors of our society. For example Connexions, aimed at the 13–19 age groups, offers information and advice needed to 'make the decisions and choices in your life', which it takes to include health and relationships, careers and work, learning and money, housing, rights, free time and travel. The Aimhigher campaign supported by the DES is especially aimed at encouraging young people from 'families with no tradition of higher education' to think about its benefits and opportunities.

The number of permanent exclusions from schools continues to rise year on year. These exclusions reveal that it is clear that the education system is failing many children. There is an urgent need to be creative and plan a curriculum for all which addresses both current and future needs and aspirations of all our pupils. Education should be perceived in its widest sense, the partnership between schools and communities, and perhaps the recognition that for some pupils alternative forms of education are more beneficial.

A survey of Year 6 children from a range of schools in inner city and suburban Bristol was undertaken to discover what their ambitions for employment were. The findings are summarised in Table 1.

Of the 123 children interviewed, 72 wanted either to be professional sports personalities, pop stars, dancers, actors, or 'to be rich and famous'. Only 25 children (i.e. approximately one-fifth) aspired to a career involving professional training. Of these, 6 wanted to be a vet or veterinary nurse, some recognising the influence of television programmes such as *Animal Hospital* and *Vets in Practice*.

Table 1 Ambitions of Year 6 children

Ambition	No. of children
Sport, e.g. be a football player, rugby player, skateboarder	43
Be rich and famous	8
Pop star, singer, dancer, actor/actress	21
Work with animals	8 (6 vets)
Hairdresser	8
Mechanic, builder, carpenter	5
Gardener	1
Bank cashier	1
Theme park designer	1
Artist	2
Car designer	1
Teacher or Nursery teacher	5
Police force or fire fighter	5
Nurse	2
Computer programmer	2
Pilot	1
Site engineer	1
Palaeontologist	1
Doctor	2
Lawyer	2
Archaeologist	1
Architect	2
Total	**123**

This survey reflects the restricted range of career paths of children of this age and on which they may make decisions which could profoundly affect their future life chances. It is apparent that some children have limited aspiration; the next case study shows one school's attempt to extend children's aspirations.

The primary school Futures Club

In this case study we outline how children from one primary school were supported in making choices about their futures. The school has a mixed catchment area and a large proportion of its pupils come from low income families. The town where the school is situated has a long history of manufacturing, ranging from the production of woollen goods to light engineering. Many children in the school come from families, generations of whom have been mill or factory workers. There have been periodic slumps in the town's economic fortunes. Since the 1970s there has been a general depression in the town – factories closing and the slow process of realignment of commerce taking place. The town is about to undergo further significant changes and development which will change its character and the nature of employment.

The headteacher of the school was concerned with extending the opportunities available to his pupils and supported the development of an after-school club which looked at other people's jobs. The aims of the club are:

1   to give children a knowledge and taste of a wide range of employment opportunities outside their normal experience.
2   to develop from this an understanding of the ways in which society works and the interdependence of different occupations and the decision making process.

The club operates in two ways, first by inviting in speakers who not only describe their jobs but also try to convey to the children the ways in which aspects of their work impact upon society and people. For example, a physiotherapist gave the children the opportunity to try to manage simple tasks whilst using Zimmer frames. By the end of the session the children's questioning and responses clearly indicated a new found empathy with the disabled and elderly. Other visitors have included people from banking to film stunt training, from motor journalism to motor bike mechanic and from industrial sales to nature reserve warden.

Second, the children have visited a range of employment sites including a graphic design studio, a university and a fire station.

The club has now successfully run for two years and has received the prestigious Gold Medal from the regional Pathways Education Industry Links. During the Gold Medal award ceremony a local mayor asked, '*What does the Futures Club do?*' Without any prompting or rehearsing, a child with some learning difficulties responded, '*It gives us aspirations for when we grow up.*'

Prior to her involvement in the Futures Club this child had a very limited view of the range of possible jobs open to her. The use of the word 'aspirations' in context clearly illustrates that this child is now more fully appreciative of her own potential and is aware that she can set her sights higher than she had before. Children's self-esteem grew. This was apparent in the growing confidence and sophistication with which children questioned later speakers at the club.

Activity – Children's dreams

Note the different occupations which children are exposed to through the media. What effect do you think this exposure might have on their aspirations?

Spend some time talking to children about how they see their futures. Is there a gap between their probable and possible futures?

Expanding teachers' horizons

In order to be truly reflective practitioners, teachers must have a good understanding of where and how their identity and values were shaped. It is worthwhile for teachers to take the time to reflect upon their own values and upon the principles which they employ to govern and sustain their life styles and actions. Unless we understand ourselves we have little chance of understanding the needs and expectations of the children we teach. We all need good role models and positive experiences if we are to develop healthy expectations of ourselves, of other people and of our possible and probable life chances.

Reflection

Who or what have been the major influences in your life and in what way did they influence you?

How did you arrive at the major decisions which have affected your life course – such as choice of career or place to live?

Activity

Think about your own probable and possible futures over (a) the next 5 years and (b) the next 10 years. Share your ideas with a small group.

Additionally, we need to present to children a range of positive role models with whom they can identify. Opportunities to expand both our own and children's horizons are important to permit a better understanding of the similarities and differences, problems and complexities of the lives of people both near to us and far from us.

To extend the perspectives of all teaching and learning support workers in the Primary School Futures Club, the staff shadowed people in various jobs in industry. The intention was to broaden the experience of staff so that they became more aware of the range of future opportunities open to their pupils. It was also hoped that as a side benefit the dialogue between educators and people in the 'real world' would establish much common ground, shared experience and an appreciation of each others' skills and visions. For example, placements were arranged at the BBC, the local museum, banks, organic gardeners, a professional rugby club and with a number of other interesting employments.

In addition to broadening the knowledge base of the children and the staff, the primary school, in line with many other schools, also sought to give the children a range of opportunities to engage in real decision making through forming a School Council. This can be a useful forum for children to take part in active citizenship, making choices about real issues in a democratic setting. After a meeting of the School's Council, one boy commented to his teacher, that, although he enjoyed taking part in the debates, he felt that it was a pity that only other children in the school could hear their points of view. Others agreed with him and an interesting discussion followed about empowerment and ways in which people could get their voices heard. The teacher challenged the children to 'get themselves published' so that they could reach a wider audience. This led to a project entitled 'Let the Children Speak', which is described below.

Let the children speak

During a literacy hour session, while studying journalistic reporting, children discussed the various media outlets through which they could potentially publish their work and ideas. This fitted in with the broader intentions of the literacy hour and was also in line with the aims of the Futures Club, namely to widen horizons and engage the pupils more fully as active citizens.

As a result, fifteen children ultimately had work published in the Local Gazette and in various newspapers and journals. An anthology of children's poetry, *Once upon a Rhyme* (Young Writers 2004) has also been published and includes poems from the children in this school. Titles such as 'Tomorrow', 'Team Spirit', 'The Way Things Always Go' and 'I Have Freedom' illustrate the liberating effect the Futures Club has had on many of the children. The following lines, written by an 11-year-old girl, sum up the maturing awareness of the children: *'It feels like time is a dream, the freedom I have, the independence is the best thing about me.'*

Examples from this primary school illustrate how children's knowledge and understanding can be broadened through working with others, both pupils and adults. The children developed and explored a range of skills and values within the school and the wider community. This has led them to a more secure and confident sense of self-worth. They are now far more enthusiastic about the range of life chances open to them.

Children planning their curriculum

Listening to Children (L2C) is a collaborative research-based project (Barratt et al. 2005) which considered children's perspectives on the local environment through working with 10- to 12-year-olds in a secondary school and one of its primary feeder schools. A key objective was to explore opportunities for change in the school curriculum such that it reflected and was sensitive to pupils' everyday experiences of and in their local community. The project was also concerned that the findings established a creative partnership in local community development.

The project was in two phases. Phase 1 involved setting up a democratic management and research team which included pupils and gathered information from parents, teachers and pupils. In Phase 2 the project team set up an Environmental Curriculum Council which planned and tried out new lessons and presented their findings at a Children's Conference to a panel which included a wide range of local community representatives. Overall the pupils were very positive about the project. They felt their views had been listened to and as a consequence the curriculum had been modified to address their concerns for the locality. In some cases, teachers who lived outside the area relied on the children's expertise to develop their empathy with the real concerns of the community. Many children grew in confidence as a result of having been listened to. Being respected in this way was empowering for them.

These examples represent ways in which some schools and educators are attempting to make a difference. Further suggestions for children and communities working together are discussed in Chapters 6 and 8.

Summary

Such activities require imagination, effort and enthusiasm rather than expensive resources. Education should open doors for all pupils. The task of the teacher 'is to help pupils gain entry into a commonwealth of knowledge and skills, to hand on to them something which others already possess' (Stenhouse 1975: 6). We must be ambitious for their learning and for their futures.

Overall, education should be aiming to ensure that children are both knowledgeable and have the skills to participate fully as active citizens in order to make balanced judgements about their own futures and about local, national and global issues. Working with primary age children it is apparent that they have a real interest in and curiosity about such issues. What better future than one in which children have been educated so that they are able to create a sustainable and desirable world environment for the mutual benefit of all?

Reflection

In what ways has this chapter encouraged you to think about educating future citizens?

Drawing on your own experience and reading, begin to identify some of the key knowledge, understandings and skills which you consider would be important to develop with children as future citizens. What opportunities would you provide to enable the children's voices to be heard?

Chapter 10

Facing the future

The primary teacher in the twenty-first century

John Lee and Christine Macfarlane

Introduction

In this chapter we examine the development of primary school teaching into a profession and argue that the status of a profession was the desire of teachers from the establishment of mass education in the nineteenth century. Current challenges to the established profession brought about by the workforce reforms of the twenty-first century are then explored.

This chapter will help you to think about the following questions:

- How have primary teachers sought to define themselves as professionals and why?
- What are some of the implications for professional identities implicit within recent workforce reforms?
- How do you view your own professional identity and status?

Defining professionalism

R. S. Peters (1966) in his classic book *Ethics and Education* offers what we see as the classic definition of what is meant by the term teaching as a profession. He argues that while to the 'ordinary man being the member of profession means earning a salary rather than a wage', in fact profession means more than this. He states, rightly in our view, that members of a profession share common tasks and have specialist knowledge. Professionalism is characterised by lengthy training and by the need for members to keep in touch with the development of knowledge beyond their initial training. In Peters' view true professionalism means not just a trained person but an educated person. In addition, each profession shares ethical principles and the breaking of those principles can and should lead to a case of professional misconduct and the possibility of disbarment. The 'traditional' professions of medicine, the law and clergy have the independence and autonomy to judge their own members. It is this professional autonomy that we see as crucial in the development of teaching as a profession.

A brief history

Recent changes in legislation governing the way teachers work may be the most important for the profession since the establishment of free universal and compulsory education. Before considering the contemporary situation and its developing professional consequences, it is necessary to set those changes in a historical context. So the first part of this chapter sketches out what we would call the struggle to create a profession.

The earliest attempt to address the question of making teaching a profession was as early as 1846 when the Society of Teachers was founded, which three years later gained a Royal Charter and was re-named the College of Preceptors. This move was addressed only to what we would now call secondary teachers and was originally concerned with certification. Even so, the history of the development of primary education is also the history of the struggle to create teaching as a profession. If we look back to 1870 and the establishment of universal education, which became compulsory in 1880, what we can see are the first attempts to ensure that teachers were trained, and more importantly were educated to a level sufficient to meet the needs of the pupils. Originally only a very tiny minority of teachers had any formal training of any length; the natural route into teaching was by becoming a pupil teacher, a sort of apprentice to your own school master or mistress. One of the things that teachers did throughout the nineteenth century was to identify the cleverest pupils and to persuade them to become pupil teachers. They then learned on the job in a system that was rigidly controlled by centrally set codes, what we would now call curriculum, and inspected on a yearly basis by Her Majesty's Inspectors. The development of the profession, in both training and education, can best be seen as coming about by the pressure of the teachers' union, but it was pressure that was acceptable to what might be described as the more enlightened authorities.

The nineteenth century was a period of educational development, not merely of elementary education but also what we might now describe as further and higher education. The establishment of University Colleges in London and Durham opened the way for the founding of the civic universities first, in the major industrial cities of Manchester and Liverpool, and then at the beginning of the twentieth century of almost all of what we call the 'red brick' universities. Oddly, the earliest teacher training colleges pre-date the establishment of the civic universities. In Bristol the college of St Matthias was established in 1853 to train women as teachers and St Lukes in Exeter established around the same date to train men; both of these were Church of England colleges. In London, Borough Road College was opened for non-conformists under the banner of the British and Foreign Bible Society. These colleges provided the earliest certification for elementary school teachers and in fact were the genesis of all teacher certification. This brief detour into the history of elementary education demonstrates how the profession sought to become a profession with specific training from its earliest years.

From around 1925 the battle to ensure that all entrants to teaching in elementary schools received specialised training had more or less been won. It was expected that all entering teaching would first undergo training in a college. The Church of England, non-conformist and Roman Catholics had all established thriving colleges by this time. The Burnham Committee advising on teacher training had established both the principle and practice of pre-entry training. It also established examination boards to ensure that certification was both at the right standard and that standards were consistent across the country. The success of this move to a profession can be judged by the opposition to the opening of emergency training routes after the Second World War. At its most extreme the opposition forecast classrooms being staffed by ill-equipped and untrained persons who would be burdens to their professional colleagues. More importantly, it was argued that the creation of the training was an attack on professionalism. Even so, the period after the Second World War right up to the 1960s was one in which schools expanded dramatically as result of the post-war baby boom. This led to the employment of untrained teachers, mainly in primary schools. On the whole they were women who had completed secondary education and who were deemed to be able to teach young children. This period was one in which the struggle for professionalisation was renewed. The teacher trade unions argued vociferously for a trained profession and then went beyond this to demand an all-graduate profession.

The struggle for a certificated profession in primary schools was completed by 1970 and in 1974 the old Certificate in Education came to an end and henceforth all entrants came into the profession either through a degree route or through taking a post-graduate qualification. The exception to this was those working with pupils deemed uneducable. Such pupils fell under the health service but in 1974 they were placed under the jurisdiction of the Department of Education and all those teaching in the sector were trained as teachers. The end of the 1970s saw all entrants to the profession being graduates. Large numbers of certificated teachers gained a degree through part time study of the In-service B.Ed. degree or took a degree via the Open University, so that effectively by the 1980s the goal of an all-graduate profession had been achieved.

In this brief review we argue that culmination of the struggle for professionalisation was the establishment of the General Teachers' Councils for England and for Wales. Scotland had had a council since the middle 1960s. The Council was the result of an ongoing debate which sought to provide teachers with the same professional recognition as lawyers and doctors. The General Council for England (GTCE) was established by the government with the intention of it dealing with professional discipline, in effect entrance and exit to the profession. In addition it has sought to engage with teacher Continuing Professional Development. By arguing for the right of every teacher to access, it has also set out a strategy for professional development that focuses on teacher involvement and empowerment and has sought government funding for teachers. The post Council period we might argue has finally established teaching as a profession equivalent to the older professions of medicine and law.

Reflection

From reading this account of the development of the profession and your own experience, what do you think are the key markers which denote professional status?

Pay reforms

The teaching profession entered the 1980s with some confidence but was almost immediately faced with severe professional challenges. The 1988 Education Reform Act (ERA) for the first time created a National Curriculum and was clearly a major challenge to professional autonomy. Although the debates at the time indicate very little support either from within or without the profession for a National Curriculum, the Conservative government went ahead and implemented one. Its impact was enormous. At first teachers resisted in the sense of protecting children from the curriculum and particularly its assessment procedures. A major study (Pollard et al. 1994) documented how infant teachers ameliorated the curriculum for their pupils. In doing this teachers themselves became not just recipients of policy but in Croll's (1996) words 'policymakers'. The effect of the National Curriculum and its attendant assessment procedures was to intensify teachers' work.

As the curriculum developed it became clear that teachers' workloads were increasing almost exponentially. The teachers' associations voiced grave concerns about overwork and the educational press reported experienced teachers leaving the profession early and usually giving the reasons as overwork and stress. A study published in 1994 (St John Neill and Campbell 1994) documented the working day of primary teachers and demonstrated both intensification and an extraordinary workload. This study was one of many, and all the surveys pointed to very high workloads and related those to national policy initiatives.

Government's first response to the workload issue was to 'slim down' the National Curriculum and this new or revised curriculum was implemented from 1995 (DfE 1995). Although the central policymakers were optimistic that the revision would reduce work pressure it did not prove to do so. The arrival of the Labour government in 1997 brought more policy initiatives:

first the National Literacy and Numeracy Strategies rapidly followed by calls for an extended school day and radical changes to the curriculum for children under five. Teachers' associations in particular continued to argue that teachers' workloads were unsustainable and in the end the government were persuaded of the case. Once central government had admitted the problem they were not in a position to ignore it; but what happened was not merely the reduction of work pressure but a policy aiming to radically reform the workforce, and it is to this reform we now turn.

The workforce reform began with massive changes in teachers' pay and conditions. Teachers, both primary and secondary, had traditionally been rewarded through promotion; the new system brought in performance-related pay, albeit in a rather muted form. Teachers had to apply to enter the performance-related system and in doing so received a threshold payment of £2000. Even though almost all experienced teachers applied and received the payment, 60 per cent of them according to a MORI poll were opposed to it on professional grounds. The process was time consuming and seen to be bureaucratic, the application forms taking between 20 and 22 hours to complete. The teachers' unions, although offering advice to their members, were sceptical of its professional development potential. Headteachers surveyed said that the system, rather than being motivational, had the opposite effect. One in seven of those who refused to apply for this pay boost also said it was the reason they were going to leave the profession. Even those teachers who received the £2000 threshold payment were uneasy about the scheme, with 60 per cent saying they were opposed to it on principle. What was most controversial was the use of pupil progress as a measure and nearly half of those surveyed by MORI who had failed to 'cross the threshold' failed to meet this measure. Headteachers and the General Secretary of the National Union of Teachers (NUT) were in agreement that the new pay would not improve the quality of teaching, rather it was leading to falling morale and de-motivation. Doug McAvoy, General Secretary of the NUT went further saying, 'We have told ministers that this was not going to work in terms of achieving the government's three targets of recruitment, retention and motivation' (NUT 2003).

At present, whilst teachers are still grappling with the complexities of the threshold payment and the potentiality of performance-related pay, they now face an overhaul in the way management roles are remunerated. Previously, the system was familiar and well known to teachers. The acceptance or pro-motion to a management role led to a stipulated increase in salary, a system that was easy to understand even by those who objected to its operation. The new system is a two-tier structure of Teaching and Learning Responsibility payments. The new system requires that teachers who receive the allowances have a responsibility for teaching and learning well beyond the responsibilities of the classroom teacher. Teachers receiving the allowances must be able to show that they influence the progress of many pupils, not just the ones in their class or classes. In effect the system will rank and grade teachers using criteria related to teaching, learning and pupil progress. As an essential part of the government's remodelling of the profession it has led to a major division opening up between the teachers' associations. The NUT has refused to sign this agreement and also the agreement with respect to classroom assistants, as we show later. It is the NUT's contention that because of its reasoned and professionally based opposition it has been excluded from membership of the Rewards and Incentive Group which designed and is implementing the new system.

We do not intend to engage with the politics of the situation here but simply to note that the profession is now divided over the matter of pay. Since the establishment of the Burnham Committee the profession has always been united around the issue of pay. The common pay scale and the management allowances that went along with it were symbolic of professional unity. The NUT's objections are based not just on the view that the government is seeking to save money on teachers' salaries, but also on the idea that the profession itself and only the profession can judge teachers against criteria related to teaching and learning. This reform provides a difficult challenge to hard won professionalism in the view of the NUT (NUT 2003).

We have to ask the question why is pay so important when we are concerned with professional development and the sustenance of the profession. It is very important. In a crude but important sense the level of pay that professionals receive indicates the status of that profession; arguably teachers are the proletariat of the professions. The new system of pay we argue places teachers in the positions of the 'hired hands' competing for 'bonuses' as rewards for extra work. We might compare that with recent changes in doctors' pay where government has clearly driven through workplace reforms by a massive change in doctors' salaries. 'Figures show that the average GP income was £106,000 in 2004–2005 – a rise of 30 per cent in one year. And reports have emerged that a small minority of family doctors are earning up to £250,000' (BBC News 2007). These sums represent the way in which GPs are now expected to deliver a wide range of new quality services, often of a preventative kind. Teachers may wonder why their pay deal is so much less.

Changing roles

Changes in the structure of pay are a challenge to professionalism and have produced a rift within the profession, but even more of a challenge are the radical changes in teachers' roles and teachers' assistants' roles. Consistently teachers and headteachers have pointed to overwork. Surveys conducted on the part of the teacher associations, detailed comments at annual conferences and powerful anecdotal evidence all indicate work overload leading to stress and de-motivation. Much of the evidence points to teachers having to complete an extraordinary amount of paper work on top of planning, preparing and assessing lessons. Teachers' leaders all point to the way in which central government is intruding into the classroom and in the name of accountability and standards loading ever more paper work on classroom teachers. Central government has accepted that there is a serious problem and in 2003 signed a new workplace agreement with employers and all school unions except the NUT. This agreement acknowledged the overwork problem and set three years as the period over which changes in work roles would solve the problem. In the words of the official document, the Workforce Agreement (TDA 2003):

> The Agreement acknowledged the pressure which schools were under to raise standards and tackle unacceptable levels of workload for teachers and introduced a series of significant changes to teachers' conditions of service to be introduced in three annual phases from September 2003. The Agreement has delivered joint action from all signatories to achieve its twin aims.

and further states:

> Significantly the Agreement does not focus solely on teachers. It acknowledges the vital role played by school support staff and has led directly to the establishment of Higher Level Teaching Assistant (HLTA) standards and the Certificate in School Business Management (CSBM). The Agreement has also helped create a wide range of other new roles in schools for adults who support teachers' work and pupils' learning.

In brief, the agreement negotiated the most radical change in how schools should be organised and who was qualified and able to teach classes alone. After many years of teaching being reserved for those trained and qualified to be teachers, the doors were opened to those with lower levels of qualifications. It was clear from the very start that this move would be difficult to implement and one of the difficulties would be role confusion.

Experience derived from Early Years settings shows that role confusion is a reality with the youngest children – often children and parents see no professional difference between qualified teachers and other workers. The proper desire to see all working with young children as a team further muddies these waters.

Not merely are we now facing the challenge of creating working relationships with learning support assistants (LSAs), but the demand for 'joined up care' adds even greater pressure. Recent changes in policy, originating in *Every Child Matters* (DfES 2004a), places classroom teachers and teacher leaders and managers in key positions in the delivery of a range of services. Teachers are now charged with extended provision and a wide ranging lifelong learning role. This will include for instance the teaching of parenting and a wide health education agenda. Regardless of how the associations viewed the reform, it is in the workplace that it must be implemented and it is to the teachers, headteachers and allied workers' views that we now turn.

Activity

Read Chapter 6 on 'Developing inclusive school communities'. Make a list of the roles of other professionals and support staff in schools. Share your thoughts with a colleague on the contribution which you make as a beginning teacher to children's learning and well being within school. Does your role overlap with other staff? Are there any potential tensions?

Teachers' associations

Two of the major teachers' associations, the National Association of School-masters and Women Teachers (NASUWT) and the Association of Teachers and Lecturers (ATL), along with three other teacher associations, were the first, and remain the only ones to sign the agreement. Although they welcomed the possibility of the reduction of workloads all of these associations were cautious and recognised the need to protect teacher professionality. They saw the use of teaching assistants to cover administrative and support work such as photocopying and organising resources as necessary and welcome. In the case of covering classes, each of these associations gave cautious welcomes and insisted that it should be clear that support staff would only teach whole classes under the supervision of qualified teachers. Concerns were expressed about the financing of the agreement; this most concerned the National Association of Head Teachers (NAHT) which initially signed the agreement, but then rejected it at its annual conference in 2005.

Headteachers' views

The role of the headteacher in any school reform is crucial; without their co-operation and indeed enthusiasm, reform is likely to run into the sand. We gathered data from two experienced headteachers who may be considered representative. The two informants have had considerable experience as teachers and headteachers and are professionally concerned to get the best possible outcomes for their pupils and staff. Each of them exhibit elements of what Hoyle (1969) calls 'extended professionalism', a concern for education in widest sense beyond school and classroom. One of the informants (Tony, head of a large school) puts it this way: *'It's* (Workforce Agreement) *not really about that. It is like having a bigger picture – a strategic plan for developing your school – then all these 'extra' things get absorbed into it, become a part of it.'*

He identified the positive benefits to pupils that the reduction in workload would bring. He also saw the agreement as strengthening staff development and already has time for planning as part of the school development plan. The new agreement for this headteacher offers probably for the first time the opportunity for teachers' professional development to be part of their role, not something they do in their own time. *'But having teachers who are even better prepared will benefit pupils – more relaxed, committed, motivated teachers – all that work/life balance stuff is important – this will all benefit pupils.'* In brief then, the reform is a positive opportunity for change – *'a way of starting with a clean sheet – not assimilating present structures into new ones.'*

Our second informant (Shona, headteacher of a small school) was equally enthused at the possibilities for maintaining and supporting staff morale by ensuring life/work balance. In spite of budget constraints she was clear that Planning, Preparation and Assessment Time (PPA) and other tasks, set out in the agreement, were not only reasonable but desirable. However, she was not so clear about implications of the Workforce Agreement and was expecting some further direction from the local authority on this. At the time she was interviewed she was working with bursar and staff to ensure PPA time.

It was in the implementation that Shona identified the real professional challenges. She had to struggle not just with the provision of PPA time but also the pay reform. The radical changes in pay were as professionally problematic as the PPA aspects of the agreement.

> *We found this process really difficult as a staff – moving from responsibility posts to the new Teaching and Learning Responsibility Allowances (TLR) – because the school is small, all members of staff had responsibility for one or more areas of the curriculum – but the expectations of staff to be 'moved over' to TLRs were high.*

The job descriptions had been returned to the school after scrutiny by the local authority and the unions because the teachers were expected to take on too much responsibility. This was problematic *'because union reps had no idea of the issues around curriculum management in a small school where the same curriculum load is shared between few staff'.*

In addition to these pay changes the teaching assistants in the school had moved to new pay scales tied to specific responsibilities, such as social play and health and safety.

Our other informant (Tony) had managed his clean sheet.

The new roles differ from any previous roles in a number of fundamental ways. Amongst these are: the accountability for the quality of teaching and learning for all pupils in the (designated) phase, including those not in the post-holder's class, and the associate responsibility for coaching of teachers within the phase. The role therefore also necessitates the demonstration of a record of personal teaching that is consistently good (2 – OfSTED) or better.

He was still very positive about the changes and took an optimistic view of future development. In contrast, the effects of the agreement on our other informant were negative. The reasons for professional optimism and pessimism can be seen to arise from the size of the school.

What can we make of these two small cases in terms of the professional challenges created by the reform? In the first instance the problem of finance for small schools was identified as it has been over the last thirty years or so. But we can see that Shona is able to identify the positive aspects of the reform in broad professional terms while at the same time having to face her local problems. Tony's optimism is founded in a similar broad professional vision but in his case finance does not create a local difficulty. There is a critical message for the profession and the government in both headteachers' responses to providing PPA. Both headteachers set their faces firmly against the use of Teaching Assistants as class teachers to provide the space for planning and preparation and struggled to create timetables such that qualified teachers covered classes of colleagues engaged in preparation and planning and other professional development activities.

Teaching assistants' views

We have discussed above the views of teachers as represented by their associations and also discussed the views of two headteachers. There is little comment in the education press about the views of teaching assistants on the reform. In the view of the policymakers they are key personnel in making the agreement work. The majority of workers in schools, including teaching assistants, belong to the trade union UNISON, and we were able to discuss the current roles and the proposed changed roles with a UNISON official. Teaching assistants are employed on three grades – the higher the grade, the more responsibility the assistant takes. The whole issue of PPA has become very problematic because of the refusal of the NUT to sign and the withdrawal of the NAHT from the agreement. This has left UNISON in a delicate position *viz-à-viz* its traditional relationship with the teachers' associations. In addition there is no national accredited training aligning teaching assistants to grades, although there are well-planned and useful courses locally, varying from those provided by the local authorities to university-validated courses offering certificates, diplomas and degrees. In the case of teaching assistants taking responsibility for classes as a result of the agreement, there is a requirement for training leading to the qualification of Higher Learning Teaching Assistant. It is the view of UNISON that what is now coming about is a tier of qualifications and this is to be welcomed.

The agreement is making changes to the work of teaching assistants. Their different roles and responsibilities are discussed more fully in Chapter 6. However, there is a real concern about assistants taking on the role of class teachers. At one level there is the fear that this is a way that major economies in the wage bills for education will come about, in short a fear that teaching assistants will simply be cheap labour. There is also a concern that the different levels of assistant may not be recognised in some schools. At the present the roles and responsibilities of the different grades are being established. It is clear that there is the potential for the blurring of roles. During our conversation the official made the point that assistants were taking on more specialised roles. There had already been a major move away from general assistant to assistants working in specialised roles with clear job descriptions. It is this increasing specialisation that may be the most problematic.

Since the drive towards full inclusion, teaching assistants have been employed more and more in specialised roles to support individual children. The process of full statementing of children's needs has already led to clearer definitions of assistants' roles. Under the system, funds follow the child who is deemed to be in need and very often this means that an individual child will be allocated a named number of hours of a teaching assistant's time. One result of this has been the building of expertise amongst some assistants. In our conversation with the union official he used the term SENCO to describe the role of more senior assistants working with pupils with Special Educational Needs. The descriptor Special Educational Needs Co-ordinator (SENCO) is a title for a teacher taking on that role. This role confusion is a challenge to the status of teachers and, as we argue later, needs to be faced. It is also worth noting that such role confusion is not confined to issues of specialisation, but is evident in the team working of many Nurseries. In this case it is often very difficult for outsiders, whether professionals or not, to determine the difference between the qualified teacher and the numerous assistants.

The advent of the Literacy and Numeracy Strategies in primary schools has also developed teaching assistants' roles in the classroom. In an infants' school in a suburb of Bristol, the first two listed roles and responsibilities of the teaching assistants are given as:

(a) To engage in learning activities with individual pupils or groups of pupils to re-inforce and extend appropriate aspects of teacher input.
(b) To assist the class teacher with the implementation of the National Strategies for literacy and numeracy by participating in prescribed activities.

Teaching assistants are highly trained to support class teachers. They work alongside class teachers and they also deliver scripted intervention lessons and 'booster classes' for literacy and numeracy. As OfSTED reports, they make a valuable contribution to teaching and learning in many schools. They are particularly effective where the teachers plan well-differentiated lessons and agree with the assistant the objectives for the pupils being supported. Main strengths noted by the report include the quality of relationships between staff and pupils, varied approaches to teaching and learning and a close match of work to pupils' needs. However, there can be issues over deployment where teaching assistants worked with individuals or groups of pupils rather than with particular teachers – limiting the opportunities for teachers and assistants to plan together (OfSTED 2004b: 15–16).

Summary

The reforms set in train by the Labour government should be welcomed. For the first time primary school teachers have been relieved of the time filling and tedious tasks that were thrust upon them in the past. No longer are they expected to collect dinner money, photocopy materials, and conduct the numerous little administrative tasks that used to fill the day. More importantly the system now recognises that preparation and planning are key roles and should be conducted during professional/paid time, not in the teachers' out of work time. Significantly it is now recognised as part of the agreement that continuing professional development is also part of the teachers' paid time. Having said that, the challenges to the profession we discuss above have not and will not go away. The determination of professionality, its protection and development we argue is and must remain in the hands of teachers, and it is to this we now turn.

Geoff Whitty in his welcome speech to the 2005 General Teaching Council's conference hosted at the Institute of Education, London, made the point that professional development should be for all school staff (Whitty 2005):

> We must ensure that the funding is there for all schools to put in place an effective development plan for their staff. This is in part about funding workforce remodelling: in practice, schools can struggle to find guaranteed professional time for their teachers.

It is a timely reminder to the profession that workforce remodelling is about more than giving teachers some school time for planning and relieving them of administrative duties. The profession needs to struggle for the time but it also needs to define what it means to be a professional in the circumstances where assistants are responsible, albeit under supervision, for the teaching of pupils. Professional development has to be a way in which the qualified teacher is distinguished from other workers in schools. It involves defining the roles and responsibilities of teachers and clarifying with much more provision the roles and responsibilities of teacher assistants.

We can identify a model which illustrates what this means by returning to Hoyle's (1969) perceptive description of the teacher as 'extended professional'. For Hoyle the notion that being professional focused only on the classroom and the school is inadequate. True professionals have a broader vision and are engaged in the development of the education system as whole. Such professionals are unafraid to engage with the politics of education and are prepared to examine reforms coolly and in a dispassionate manner. Alongside this we point to Schon's (1983) idea that proper professionalism lies in 'reflection in action'. Under this view the teachers do not simply engage in professional development but create and sustain it.

We identify the following actions that we believe will maintain and sustain teachers as professionals in times of radical change:

- in co-operation with their association and the GTCE, the teaching profession must define the tasks and responsibilities of teaching assistants;
- seize the professional development agenda from centralised control, which has been its main feature since the 1980s;
- establish professional unity rather than the current divisiveness that occurs as the result of inter-association conflicts;
- clarify how the management structure of schools operate such that proper regard is given to the teacher as a professional.

Reflection

In what ways has this chapter extended your understanding of the 'extended professional'? What does the notion of an 'extended professional' mean to you? List some of the ways which would enable you to demonstrate that you have a broader vision of your role beyond the classroom. This might include consideration of your own professional development, responses to government policies and initiatives, contributing to the work of your LA and more.

Further reading

1 The social distribution of school knowledge in primary classrooms

Mercer, N. (1995) *The Guided Construction of Knowledge: Talk Amongst Teachers and Learners*, Clevedon: Multilingual Matters.

Moyles, J., Hargreaves, L. Merry, R., Paterson, F. and Esarte-Sarries, V. (2003) *Interactive Teaching in the Primary School: Digging Deeper into Meanings*, Maidenhead: Open University Press.

Myhill, D., Jones, S. and Hopper, R. (2006) *Talking, Listening, Learning*, Maidenhead: Open University Press.

2 Support or straitjacket? A tale of three Strategies

ACME (2006) *Position Paper: Key Issues for the Future of Primary Mathematics Learning and Teaching*, available from: www.royalsoc.ac.uk/acme/ACME_position_paper_May-06.pdf (accessed 19 August 2007).

Alexander, R.J. (2006) *Towards Dialogic Teaching: Rethinking Classroom Talk*, 3rd edn, York: Dialogos (1st edn 2004).

Beard, R. (1999) *National Literacy Strategy: Review of Research and Other Related Evidence*, London: DfEE.

DfES (2006) *Primary Framework for Literacy and Mathematics*, London: DfES.

OfSTED (2005) *Primary National Strategy: An Evaluation of its Impact in Primary Schools 2004/5*, available from www.ofsted.gov.uk/assets/4117.doc (accessed 21 August 2007).

Reynolds, D. (1999) 'School Effectiveness, School Improvement and Contemporary Policies', in Demaine, J. (ed) (1999) *Educational Policy and Contemporary Politics*, Basingstoke: Macmillan Press.

3 Social care, childcare and education: Exploring issues in the Early Years

Athey, C. (2006) *Extending Thought in Children*, London: Paul Chapman.

Gopnik, A., Meltzoff, N. and Kuhl, P. (2001) *How Babies Think: The Science of Childhood*, London: Phoenix.

Moyles, J.R. (2005) *The Excellence of Play*, Maidenhead: Open University Press.

4 What makes a pedagogy fit for Key Stage 2?

Alexander, R., Rose, J. and Woodhead, C. (1992) *Curriculum Organisation and Classroom Practice in Primary Schools: A Discussion Paper*, London: DES.

Ashley, M. and Lee, J. (2003) *Women Teaching Boys: Caring and Working in the Primary School*, Stoke on Trent: Trentham.

Galton, M. (1995) *Crisis in the Primary Classroom*, London: Fulton.

5 Current assessment practice: Driving or supporting practice?

Black, P., Harrison, C., Lee, C., Marshal, B. and Wiliam, D. (2003) *Assessment for Learning: Putting it into Practice*, Maidenhead: Open University Press.

Clarke, S. (2001) *Unlocking Formative Assessment. Practical Strategies for Enhancing Pupils' Learning in the Primary Classroom*, London: Hodder & Stoughton.

Torrance, H. and Pryor, J. (1998) *Investigating Formative Assessment. Teaching Learning and Assessment in the Classroom*, Maidenhead: Open University Press.

6 Developing inclusive school communities

DfES (2001) *Special Educational Needs Code of Practice*, London: HMSO.

Gelsthorpe, T. and West-Burnham, J. (eds) (2003) *Educational Leadership and the Community: Strategies for School Improvement through Community Engagement*, Edinburgh: Pearson.

Thomas, G., Walker, D. and Webb, J. (1998) *The Making of the Inclusive School*, London: Routledge.

7 Space for learning?

Cox, M., Webb, M., Abbott, C., Blakeley, B., Beauchamp, T. and Rhodes, V. (2003) *ICT and Pedagogy: A Review of the Research Literature*, London: DfES, available from: www.becta.org.uk/page_documents/research/ict_pedagogy_summary.pdf (accessed 21 August 2007).

McFarlane, A. (ed) (1997) *Information Technology and Authentic Learning*, London: Routledge.

Mercer, N., Wegerif, R. and Dawes, L. (1999) 'Children's talk and the development of reasoning in the classroom', *British Educational Research Journal*, 25(1): 95–112.

8 What has happened to curriculum breadth and balance in primary schools?

Deakin Crick, R. (2006) *Learning Power in Practice. A Guide for Teachers*, London: Paul Chapman.

DfES (2003a) *Excellence and Enjoyment. A Strategy for Primary Schools*, London: DfES.

DES (1985) *The Curriculum from 5–16. Curriculum Matters 2* (an HMI series), London: HMSO.

Turner Bisset, R. (2003) *Expert Teaching: Knowledge and Pedagogy to Lead the Profession*, London: David Fulton.

9 Children's futures, our futures: Educating citizens for the twenty-first century

Bailey, A. and Kimber, D. (2001) 'Geography and SMSC', *Environmental Education*, 67: 27–31.
Bell, D. (2005) 'The value and importance of geography', *Primary Geographer*, 56: 4–5.
Eaude, T. (2006) *Children's Spiritual, Moral, Social and Cultural Development*, Exeter: Learning Matters.
Hicks, D. and Holden, C. (1995) *Visions of the Future: Why We Need to Teach for Tomorrow*, Stoke on Trent: Trentham.

10 Facing the future: The primary teacher in the twenty-first century

Hargreaves, A. (1994) *Changing Teachers, Changing Times*, London: Cassell.
MacBeath, J. (2004) *Democratic Learning: The Challenge to School Effectiveness*, London: Routledge Falmer.

General references

Abbot, L. and Pugh, G. (1999) *Training to Work in the Early Years: Building the Climbing Frame*, London: Paul Chapman.

ACME (2006) *Position Paper: Key Issues for The Future of Primary Mathematics Learning and Teaching*, available from: www.royalsoc.ac.uk/acme?ACME_position_paper_May-06.pdf (accessed 19 August 2007).

Ahmed, A. (1987) *Better Mathematics: A Curriculum Development Study Based on the Low Attainers in Mathematics Project*, London: HMSO.

Alexander, P., Schallert, D. and Hare, V. (1991) 'Coming to terms: How researchers in learning and literacy talk about knowledge', *Review of Educational Research*, 61(3): 315–343.

Alexander, R. (2000) *Culture and Pedagogy: International Comparisons in Primary Education*, Oxford: Blackwell Publishing.

Alexander, R., Rose, J. and Woodhead, C. (1992) *Curriculum Organisation and Classroom Practice in Primary Schools. A Discussion Paper*, London: DES.

Alexander, R. J. (2004) 'Still no pedagogy? Principle, pragmatism and compliance in primary education', *Cambridge Journal of Education*, 31(1): 7–33.

Alexander, R. J. (2005) *Culture, Dialogue and Learning. Notes on an Emerging Pedagogy*, available from: http://robinalexander.org.uk/docs/IACEP paper 050 612.pdf (accessed 19 August 2007).

Alexander, R. J. (2006) *Towards Dialogic Teaching: Rethinking Classroom Talk*, 3rd edn, York: Dialogos.

Ashley, M. (2005) 'Can KS2 teachers know enough? A comparative study', *Primary Practice*, 40: 36–40.

Ashley, M. and Lee, J. (2003) *Women Teaching Boys: Caring and Working in the Primary School*, Stoke on Trent: Trentham.

Ashton, P., Kneen, P. and Holley, B. (1975) *The Aims of Primary Education: a Study of Teachers' Opinions*, London: Macmillan Education.

Askew, M. (2001) 'Entitlement to attainment: Tensions in the National Numeracy Strategy', *Curriculum Journal*, 12: 5–28.

Assessment Reform Group (2002) *Assessment for Learning. 10 Principles. Research-based Principles to Guide Classroom Practice*, available from: www.aaia.org.uk/assessment.htm (accessed August 25 2007).

Athey, C. (2006) *Extending Thought in Young Children*, London: Paul Chapman.

Bach, P. and Christensen, C. (1992) 'From despair to optimism: The success story of Danish education', *Royal Society of Arts Journal*, June: 443–451.

Badock, E., Daniels, D., Islip, P. J., Razzell, A. and Ross, A. (1972) *Education in the Middle Years (Schools Council Working paper 42)*, London: Schools Council/ Evans Methuen.

Bailey, A. and Kimber, D. (2001) 'Geography and SMSC', *Environmental Education*, 67: 27–31.

Barber, M. (1997) *The Learning Game: Arguments for an Education Revolution*, London: Cassell.

Barber, M. (2001) 'High Expectations and Standards for All: No Matter What', in Fielding, M. (ed) (2001) *Taking Education Really Seriously*, London: Routledge Falmer.

Barratt, R., Scott, W. and Barratt Hacking, E. (2005) 'Listening to children (L2C): A collaborative school-based research project', *Teaching Geography*, 30: 3.

Batmanghelidjh, C. (2004) 'Working with vulnerable children and young people: the importance of relationships and loving care', *Spotlight, Issue 2*.

BBC News (2007) http://news.bbc.co.uk/1/hi/health/4918040.stm (accessed 25 August 2007).

Beard, R. (1999) *National Literacy Strategy: Review of Research and Other Related Evidence*, London: DfEE.

Beard, R. (2000) 'Long overdue? Another look at the National Literacy Strategy', *Journal of Research in Reading*, 23(3): 245–255.

Bearne, E. (2003) *Ways of* Showing – *Ways of Knowing: Children's Production of Multidimensional Texts*, available from: www.shef.ac.uk/content/1/c6/05/05/23/ bearne.pdf (accessed 19 August 2007).

Bearne, E. (2005) 'Multimodal Texts: What They Are and How Children Use Them', in Evans, J. (ed) *Literacy Moves On: Using Popular Culture, New Technologies and Critical Literacy in the Primary Classroom*, Portsmouth, NH: Heinemann.

BECTA (2005) *The BECTA Review 2005 – Evidence on the Progress of ICT in Education*, BECTA, available from: www.becta.org.uk/display/cfm?resID=25882 (accessed 19 August 2007).

Bell, D. (2003) 'Standards and Inspections in Independent schools', Keynote address, Brighton College Conference on Independent Schools, 29 April 2003, London: OfSTED.

Bell, D. (2005) 'The value and importance of geography', *Primary Geographer*, 56: 4–5.

Bennett, N. and Dunne, F. (1992) *Managing Classroom Groups*, Hemel Hempstead: Simon and Schuster Education.

Bernstein, B. (1990) *Class, Codes and Control*, vol IV: *The Structuring of Pedagogic Discourse*, London: Routledge.

Black, P. (1998) *Testing Friend or Foe? Theory and Practice of Assessment in Testing*, Brighton: Falmer Press.

Black, P. and Wiliam, D. (1998) *Inside the Black Box. Raising Standards through Classroom Assessment*, London: Kings College London.

Black, P., Harrison, C., Lee, C., Marshall, B. and Wiliam, D. (2003) *Assessment for Learning. Putting it into Practice*, Maidenhead: Open University Press.

Black, P., Wiliam, D., Harrison, C., Lee, C. and Marshall, B. (2002) *Working inside the Black Box. Assessment for Learning in the Classroom*, London: Kings College London.

Blair, A. (2005) 'Schools to encourage Emotional Intelligence', *The Times*, London, 28th November 2005.

Blair, T. (1998) *The Third Way*, London: Fabian Society.

Blair, T. (2005) Fabian Lecture on Education at the Institute of Education, London, 7 July 2005.

Board of Education (1931) *Report of the Consultative Committee on the Primary School (Hadow Report)*, London: HMSO.

Broadfoot, P., Osborn, M., Plannel, C. and Sharpe, K. (2000) *Promoting Quality in Learning. Does England Have the Answer? Findings from the Quest Project*, London: Cassel.

Broadhead, P. (2004) *Early Years Play and Learning: Developing Social Skills and Cooperation*, London: Routledge Falmer.

Bronfenbrenner, U. (1979) *The Ecology of Human Development*, Harvard: Harvard University Press.

Brooks, G., Pugh, A.K. and Schagen, I. (1996) *Reading Performance at 9*, Slough: National Foundation for Educational Research.

Brown, M., Askew, M., Baker, D., Denvir, H., Millet, A., et al. (1998) 'Is the Numeracy Strategy research-based?' *British Journal of Education Studies*, 46(4): 328–385.

Bruce, T. (2001) *Learning Through Play – Babies, Toddlers and the Foundation Years*, London: Hodder and Stoughton.

Bruce, T. (2004) *Developing Learning in Early Childhood*, London: Paul Chapman.

Bruner, J. and Haste, H. (1987) *Making Sense: The Child's Construction of the World*, London: Methuen.

Bruner, J., Jolly, A. and Sylva, K. (1976) (eds) *Play: Its Role in Development and Evolution*, Harmondsworth: Penguin.

Campbell, R. and Neill, S. (1991) *Workloads, Achievement and Stress. Second Report on Research in the Use of Teacher Time*, London: Assistant Masters and Mistresses Association.

Campbell, R. and Neill, S. (1992) *Teacher Time and Curriculum Manageability at Key Stage 1. Third Report on Research into the Use of Teacher Time*, London: Assistant Masters and Mistresses Association.

Carlgren, F. (1972) *Education Towards Freedom*, East Grinstead: Lanthorn Press.

Catling, S., Bowles, R., Haloca, J., Martin, F. and Rawlinson, S. (2003) *The State of Primary Geography in England*, Conference Paper, Geographical Association Annual Conference, Derby, 2003.

Cazdan, C.B. (2000) 'An Application of Basil Bernstein's Constructs of "Visible and Invisible Pedagogies"', in Power, S., Aggleton, P., Brannen, J., Brown, A., Chisholm, L. and Mace, J. (2000) *A Tribute to Basil Bernstein 1924–2000*, London: Institute of Education, University of London.

Central Advisory Council for Education (1967) *Children and their Primary Schools (The Plowden Report)*, London: HMSO.

Children's Fund (2004) The Children's Fund, available from: www.teachernet. gov.uk/management/atoz/c/childrensfund (accessed 26 August 2007).

Clark, A. and Moss, P. (2001) *Listening to Young Children: The Mosaic Approach*, London: Joseph Rowntree Foundation and the National Children's Bureau.

Clarke, S. (2001) *Unlocking Formative Assessment: Practical Strategies for Enhancing Pupils' Learning in the Classroom*, London: Hodder and Stoughton.

Cockcroft, W.H. (1982) *Mathematics Counts,* London: HMSO.

Cox, B. and Boyson, R. (1975) *Black Papers 1975: The Fight for Education,* London: Dent.

Cox, M., Webb, M., Abbott, C., Blakeley, B., Beauchamp, T. and Rhodes, V. (2003) *ICT and Pedagogy: A Review of the Research Literature,* London: DfES, available from: www.becta.org.uk/page_documents/research/ict_pedagogy_summary.pdf (accessed 21 August 2007).

Croll, P. (ed) (1996) *Teachers, Pupils and Primary Schooling. Continuity and Change,* London: Cassell.

Crook, C. (1994) *Computers and the Collaborative Experience of Learning,* London: Routledge.

Daniel, P. and Ivatts, J. (1998) *Children and Social Policy,* London: Macmillan.

David, T. (1999) *Young Children Learning,* London: Paul Chapman Publishing.

David, T. (ed) (2001) *Promoting Evidence Based Practice in Early Childhood Education 1. Research and its Implications,* Oxford: Elsevier.

Davies, M. and Edwards, G. (1999) 'Will the curriculum caterpillar ever learn to fly?' *Cambridge Journal of Education* 29(2): 265–275.

Dawes, L. (2002) 'Interthinking – The Power of Productive Thought', in Evans, J. (ed) *The Articulate Classroom,* London: David Fulton.

Deakin Crick, R. (2006) *Learning Power in Practice. A Guide for Teachers,* London: Paul Chapman.

Dearden, A. (2005) 'Knowledge of global warming and pollution', *Primary Science and Technology Today,* Autumn (29): 9–13.

Dearden, R. F. (1968) *Philosophy of Primary Education,* London: Routledge and Kegan Paul.

Denmark (1996a) *Act on the Folkeskole* (English language translation), Copenhagen: Ministry of Education.

Denmark (1996b) *Order on the Aims of the Teaching in the Subjects and Obligatory Topics of the Folkeskole with Indication of Central Knowledge and Proficiency Areas* (English language translation), Copenhagen: Ministry of Education.

DES (1978) *Primary Education in England,* London: HMSO.

DES (1985) *The Curriculum from 5–16. Curriculum Matters 2* (an HMI series), London: HMSO.

DES (1988) *Task Group on Assessment and Testing Report (TGAT). A Digest for Schools,* London: DES.

DES (1989) *Aspects of Primary Education: The Teaching and Learning of History and Geography,* London: HMSO.

Dewey (1916) *Democracy and Education,* New York: Free Press.

DfE (1995) *Key Stages 1 and 2 of the National Curriculum,* London: HMSO.

DfEE (1997) *Excellence in Schools,* London: HMSO.

DfEE (1998) *The National Literacy Strategy, Framework for Teaching,* London: DfEE.

DfEE (1999a) *The National Numeracy Strategy. Framework for Teaching,* London: DfEE.

DfEE (1999b) *NACCE Report: All our Futures – Creativity, Culture and Education,* London: DfEE.

DfEE (2000) *Sure Start: Making a Difference for Children and Families* London: DfEE.

DfEE and QCA (1999) *The National Curriculum Handbook for Primary Teachers in England*, London: HMSO.

DfEE and QCA (2000) *The Curriculum Guidance for the Foundation Stage*, London: HMSO.

DfES (2001) *Special Educational Needs Code of Practice*, London; HMSO.

DfES (2003a) *Excellence and Enjoyment: A Strategy for Primary Schools*, Nottingham: DfES.

DfES (2003b) *Fulfilling the Potential: Transforming Teaching and Learning through ICT in Schools*, Nottingham: DfES.

DfES (2003c) *The Foundation Stage Profile Handbook*, Nottingham: DfES.

DfES (2003d) *Speaking, Listening, Learning: Working with Children in Key Stages 1 and 2*, Nottingham: DfES.

DfES (2003e) *Birth to Three Matters*, Nottingham: DfES.

DfES (2004a) *Every Child Matters: Next Steps for Children*, Nottingham: DfES.

DfES (2004b) *Learning and Teaching in the Primary Years: Professional Development Resources*, Nottingham: DfES.

DfES (2004c) The Children Act, available from www.dfes.gov.uk/publications/childrenactreport/ (accessed 12 October 2007).

DfES (2005) *Key Elements of Effective Practice*, Nottingham: DfES.

DfES (2006a) http://www.standards.dfes.gov.uk/primary/publications/literacy/63293/nls_targetsettingsks2027502.pdf

DfES (2006b) *Primary Framework for Literacy and Maths*, Nottingham: DfES.

DfES (2007a) *Early Years Foundation Stage consultation*, May 2006, available from: www.standards.dfes.gov.uk/primary/features/foundation_stage/eyfs_consultation/ (accessed May 2007).

DfES (2007b) *The Early Years Foundation Stage*, Nottingham: DfES.

DfES and DWP (2006) *Choice for Parents, the Best Start for Children: Making it Happen – An Action Plan for the Ten Years Strategy: Sure Start Children's Centres. Extended Schools and Childcare*, London: DfES and DWP.

Dunn, J. (1988) *The Beginnings of Social Understanding*, Oxford: Blackwell.

Earl, L., Fullan, M., Leithwood, K., Watson, N. with Jantzi, D., Levin, B. and Torrance, N. (2000) *Watching and Learning. OISE/UT Evaluation of the National Literacy and Numeracy Strategies*, London: DfEE.

Earl, L., Levin, B., Leithwood, K., Fullan, M., Watson, N. with Torrance, N., Jantzi, D. and Mascall, B. (2001) *Watching and Learning 2: Evaluation of the National Literacy and National Numeracy Strategies*, London: DfES.

Earl, L., Watson, N., Levin, B., Leithwood, K., Fullan, M., and Torrance, N. with Jantzi, D., Mascall, B. and Volante, L. (2003) *Watching and Learning 3. Final Report of the External Evaluation of the Implementation of the National Literacy and Numeracy Strategies*, London: DfES.

Edwards, D. and Westgate, D. (1994) *Investigating Classroom Talk*, 2nd edn, London: Falmer Press.

Eisner, E. (1996) *Cognition and Curriculum Re-considered*, London: Paul Chapman.

Eke, R. and Lee. J, (2004) 'Pace and differentiation in the literacy hour: Some outcomes of an analysis of transcripts', *Curriculum Journal*, 15(3): 219–231.

Ellis, T. (1976) *William Tyndale: The Teachers' Story*, London: Readers' and Writers' Publishing Cooperative.

English, E., Hargreaves, L. and Hislam, H. (2002) 'Pedagogical dilemmas in the National Literacy Strategy; primary teachers' perceptions, reflections and classroom behaviour', *Cambridge Journal of Education*, 32(1): 9–26.

Every Child Matters (2003) *Every Child Matters*, Green Paper Cm5860, London: TSO.

Facer, K. and Williamson, B. (2004) *Designing Technologies to Support Creativity and Collaboration*, available from: www.futurelab.org.uk/research/handbooks/handbook_01/01_01.htm (accessed 19 August 2007).

Fisher, R. (2002) *Inside the Literacy Hour*, London: Routledge Falmer.

Fisher, R., Lewis, M. and Davis, B. (2000) 'Progress and performance in National Literacy Strategy classrooms', *Journal of Research in Reading*, 23(3): 250–266.

Fullan, M. (2000) 'The return of large scale reform', *Journal of Educational Change*, 1: 5–27.

Fullan, M. (2003) *Change Forces with a Vengeance*, London: Falmer Press.

Fullan, M. and Stiegelbauer, S. (1991) *The New Meaning of Educational Change*, London: Cassell.

Galton, M. (1995) *Crisis in the Primary Classroom*, London: Fulton.

Galton, M., Simon, B. and Croll, P. (1980) *Inside the Primary Classroom*, London: Routledge and Kegan Paul.

Galton, M., Hargreaves, L., Comber, C., Wall, D. and Pell, A. (1999) *Inside the Primary Classroom 20 Years On*, London/New York: Routledge.

Gardner, H. (1973) *The Arts and Human Development: A Psychological Study of the Artistic Process*, New York: Wiley.

Gelsthorpe, T. and West-Burnham, J. (2003) (eds) *Educational Leadership and the Community: Strategies for School Improvement through Community Engagement*, Edinburgh: Pearson Education Limited.

Geographical Association (2003) *Making Connections: Geography in the Foundation Stage, A Position Statement*, Sheffield: Geographical Association.

Gerhardt, S. (2004) *Why Love Matters: How Affection Shapes a Baby's Brain*, London, Brunner-Routledge.

Gibson, I.W. (2001) 'At the intersection of technology and pedagogy: Considering styles of learning and teaching', *Journal of Information Technology for Teacher Education*, 10(1&2): 37–61.

Goldstein, H. and Lewis, T. (1996) *Assessment: Problems, Developments and Statistical Issues*, Chichester: John Wiley & Sons.

Goodison, T.A. (2002) 'Learning with ICT at primary level: Pupils' perceptions', *Journal of Computer Assisted Learning*, 18: 282–295.

Grainger, J. (2003) 'Schools and the community', in Gelsthorpe, T. and West-Burnham, J. (eds) *Educational Leadership and the Community: Strategies for School Improvement through Community Engagement*, Edinburgh: Pearson Education Ltd.

Hancock, R. and Mansfield, M. (2002) 'The Literacy Hour: A case for listening to children', *The Curriculum Journal*, 13(2):183–200.

Harnett, P. and Newman, L. (2002) *Developing Children's Potential. Primary School Teachers' Views on their Professional Roles in the Twenty First Century*, paper presented at British Educational Research Association Conference, Exeter University.

Hart, D. (2005) 'Under 11s 'damaged' by all-rounder teaching tradition', *Times Educational Supplement*, Friday 14 October.

Hatcher, R. (1996) 'The Limitations of the New Social Democratic Agendas: Class, Equality and Agency', in Hatcher, R. and Jones, K. (eds) (1996) *Education After the Conservatives: The Response to the New Agenda of Reform*, Stoke on Trent: Trentham Books.

Hicks, D. (1998) 'Exploring Futures', in Carter, R. (ed) (1998) *Handbook of Primary Geography*, Sheffield: The Geographical Association.

Hicks, D. and Holden, C. (1995) *Visions of the Future: Why We Need to Teach for Tomorrow*, Stoke-on-Trent: Trentham Books.

Hohmann, M. and Weikart, D.P. (1995) *Educating Young Children: Active Learning Practices for Pre-School and Child Care Programmes*, Ypsilanti: High Scope Press.

Holden, C. (2003) 'Citizenship in the Primary School', in Gatt, S. and Vella, Y. (eds) (2003) *Constructivist Teaching in Primary School*, Malta: Agenda.

Hoyle, E. (1969) *The Role of the Teacher*, London: Routledge and Kegan Paul.

Isaacs, S. (1933) *Social Development in Young Children: A Study of Beginnings*, London: Routledge and Kegan Paul.

James, A. and Prout, A. (eds) (1990) *Constructing and Reconstructing Childhood*, Basingstoke: Falmer Press.

Jenkins, P. (1993) *Children's Rights – A Participative Exercise for Learning about Children's Rights in England and Wales*, London: Longman.

Jones, K. (1996) 'Cultural Politics and Education in the 1990s', in Hatcher, R. and Jones, K. (eds) (1996) *Education after the Conservatives: The Response to the New Agenda of Reform*, Stoke-on-Trent: Trentham Books.

Kimber, D., Clough, N., Forrest, M., Harnett, P., Menter, I. and Newman, E. (1995) *Humanities in the Primary School*, London: Fulton.

Krashen, S. (2005) *The 'Decline' of Reading in America, Poverty and Access to Books, and the use of Comics in Encouraging Reading*, available from: www.sdkrashen.com/articles/decline_of_reading/index.html (accessed 21 August 2007).

Laming (2003) *The Victoria Climbié Inquiry. Report of an Inquiry*, London: HMSO.

Lee, J. and Eke, R. (2004) 'The National Literacy Strategy and pupils with special educational needs', *Journal of Research in Special Educational Needs*, 4(1): 50–57.

Lee, J. and Withers, R. (1988) 'Power in Disguise', in Barton, L. (1988) *The Politics of Special Educational Needs*, London: Falmer.

McCallum, B. (2000) *Formative assessment: implications for classroom practice*, available from: www.qca.org.uk/qca_13440.aspx (accessed 19 August 2007).

McElroy, B.(1988) 'Learning Geography: A Route to Political Literacy', in Fien, J. and Gerber, R. (1988) *Teaching Geography for a Better World*, Edinburgh: Oliver & Boyd.

Machin, S. and McNally, S. (2004) *Large Benefits, Low Cost* (discussion paper), London: Centre for the Economics of Education.

McIntosh, A. (1981) *Developing Mathematical Thinking*, Buckingham: Open University Press.

MacIntyre, H. and Ireson, J. (2002) 'Within-class ability grouping: placement of pupils in groups and self-concept', *British Educational Research Journal,* 28(2): 249–263.

McNamara, D. (1994) *Classroom Pedagogy and Primary Practice,* London/New York: Routledge.

Maslow, A.H. (1999) *Towards a Psychology of Being,* 3rd edn, New York, Wiley.

Matthews, M.H. (1992) *Making Sense of Place: Children's Understanding of Large Scale Environments,* Hemel Hempstead: Harvester Wheatsheaf.

Medwell, J., Wray, D., Poulson, L. and Fox, R. (1998) *Effective Teachers of Literacy,* Exeter: Learning Matters.

Mercer, N. (1993) 'Computer based activities in classroom contexts' in Scrimshaw, P. (ed) (1993) *Language, Classrooms and Computers,* London: Routledge.

Mercer, N. (2000) *Words and Minds: How We Use Language to Think Together,* London: Routledge.

Montessori, M. (1995) *The Absorbent Mind,* New York: Henry Holt.

Moore, T.W. (1982) *Educational Theory – An Introduction,* Routledge and Kegan Paul: London.

Mortimore, P. (1992) 'Issues in School Effectiveness' in Reynolds, D. and Cuttance, P. (eds) (1992) *School Effectiveness: Research, Policy and Practice,* London: Cassell.

Mortimore, P., Sammons, P., Stoll, L., Lewis, D. and Ecob, R. (1988) *School Matters. The Junior Years,* Wells: Open Books.

Moseley, D., Higgins, S., Bramald, R., Hardman, F., Miller, J., Mroz, M., Tse, H., Newton, D., Thompson, I., Williamson, J., Halligan, J., Bramald, S., Newton, L. and Tymms, P. (1999) *Effective Pedagogy Using ICT For Literacy and Numeracy in Primary Schools,* Newcastle: University of Newcastle, available from: http://www.eric.ed.gov/ERICDocs/data/ericdocs2sq/content_storage_01/000001 9b/80/19/69/63.pdf (accessed 12 October 2007).

Moyles, J.R. (2005) *The Excellence of Play,* Maidenhead: Open University Press.

Mroz, M., Smith, F. and Hardman, F. (2000) 'The discourse of the Literacy Hour', *Cambridge Journal of Education,* 30(3): 379–390.

National Curriculum Council (1989) *Mathematics in the National Curriculum,* London: HMSO

Newman, F. and Holzman, L. (1993) *Lev Vygotsky. Revolutionary Scientist,* London: Routledge.

NfER (1998) *Evaluation of National Literacy Project: Summary report,* available from: www.standards.dfes.gov.uk/primary/publications/literacy/63545/918649 (accessed 21 August 2007).

Nicholson, M. (1990) *The Views of Five Local Industries on the Curriculum of One Secondary School,* Cardiff: University of Wales.

Nicholson, M. and Moss, D. (1990) 'Matching the curriculum to the needs of industry', *Education and Training,* 32(6): 3–8.

Nicholson, M.B. (2004) *A Comparative Study of the Attitudes of Beginning Teachers to Their Work in England and Denmark,* paper presented at the Comparative Education Society in Europe XXI Conference, Copenhagen, July.

Nolan, S. (2006) *Using ICT, in Particular the Internet, to Raise Global Awareness When Teaching About Distant Places,* Bristol, UWE Student Dissertation.

NUT (2003) *Protecting your Professionalism Guidance to NUT Members on the Government's Proposed Changes to the Teachers' Pay and Conditions Document,* London: NUT.

OECD (Organisation for Economic Co-operation and Development) (1997) *Education and Equity in OECD Countries,* Paris: OECD.

OECD (2001) *Starting Strong: Early Education and Care,* Paris: OECD.

OfSTED (1993) *History Key Stages 1, 2 and 3. Second Year 1992–1993,* London: HMSO.

OfSTED (1995) *History. A Review of Inspection Findings, 1993–1994,* London: HMSO.

OfSTED (2002a) *The National Literacy Strategy: The First Four Years 1998–2002,* London: HMSO.

OfSTED (2002b) *The Curriculum in Successful Primary Schools,* London: HMSO.

OfSTED (2003a) *The National Literacy and Numeracy Strategies and the Primary Curriculum,* London: HMSO.

OfSTED (2003b) *Annual Report of Her Majesty's Chief Inspector for Schools, 2001–2002,* London: HMSO.

OfSTED (2004a) *Subject Reports 2002/3: Geography in Primary Schools,* London, OfSTED.

OfSTED (2004b) *Transition from the Reception Year to Year 1: An Evaluation by HMI,* available from: www.ofsted.gov.uk/assets/3655.doc (accessed 21 August 2007).

OfSTED (2004c) *ICT in Schools: The Impact of Government Initiatives Five Years On,* London: OfSTED, available from: www.ofsted.gov.uk/assets/3652.pdf (accessed 21 August 2007).

OfSTED (2005a) *Annual Report of Her Majesty's Chief Inspector for Schools, 2003–2004,* London: HMSO.

OfSTED (2005b) *Primary National Strategy: An Evaluation of its Impact in Primary Schools 2004/5,* available from: www.ofsted.gov.uk/assets/4117.doc (accessed 21 August 2007).

OfSTED (2005c) *Geography in Primary Schools,* London: OFSTED.

OfSTED (2006a) *The Annual Report of Her Majesty's Chief Inspector for Schools 2004/5: Information and Communications Technology in Primary Schools,* OfSTED: London, available, from: www.ofsted.gov.uk/publications/annualreport 0405/4.1.6.html (accessed 21 August 2007).

OfSTED (2006b) *Early Years: Safe and Sound,* London: OfSTED.

Ogden, L. (2000) 'Collaborative tasks, collaborative children: An analysis of reciprocity during peer interaction at Key Stage 1', *British Educational Research Journal,* 26(2): 211–226.

Osborn, M., McNess, E., Broadfoot, P., with Pollard, A. and Triggs, P. (2000) *What Teachers Do. Changing Policy and Practice in Primary Education,* London: Continuum.

Osborn, M., Broadfoot, P., McNess, E., Ravn, B., Planel, C. and Triggs, P. (2003) *A World of Difference? Comparing Learners Across Europe,* Maidenhead: Open University Press.

Osborn, M., Croll, P., Broadfoot, P., Pollard, A., McNess, E. and Triggs, P. (1997) 'Policy into Practice and Practice into Policy: Creative Mediation in the Primary Classroom', in Helsby, G. and McCulloch, G. (eds) (1997) *Teachers and the National Curriculum,* London: Cassell.

Parlett, P. and Hamilton, D. (1977) *Beyond the Numbers Game*, Basingstoke: Macmillan Education.

Passey, D., Rogers, C., Machell, J. and McHugh, G. (2003) *The Motivational Effect of ICT in Pupils*, DfES: Nottingham, available from: www.dfes.gov.uk/data/ uploadfiles/RR523new.pdf (accessed 21 August 2007).

Peters, R.S. (1966) *Ethics and Education*, London: George Allen and Unwin Ltd.

Plender, J. (1997) 'A stake of one's own', *Prospect*, February 1997: 20–24.

Pollard, A. (2005) *Reflective Teaching: Evidence-Informed Professional Practice*, 2nd edn, London: Continuum.

Pollard, A., Broadfoot, P., Croll, P., Osborn, M., and Abbott, D. (1994) *Changing English Primary Schools. The Impact of the Education Reform Act at Key Stage One*, London: Cassell Education.

QCA (1996) *Model Syllabuses for Religious Education*, London: QCA.

QCA (1998) *Maintaining Breadth and Balance at Key Stages 1 and 2*, London: QCA.

QCA (2003) *New Perspectives on Spoken Language in the Classroom*, available from: www.qca.org.uk/libraryAssets/media//6111_new_perspec_in_spoken_eng_ class_room.pdf (accessed 21 August 2007).

QCA (2004a) *More Than Words: Multimodal Texts in the Classroom*, available from: www.qca.org.uk/libraryAssets/media/9053more_than_words.pdf (accessed 21 August 2007).

QCA (2004b) *Continuing the Learning Journey*, London: QCA.

QCA (2005) *More than Words 2, Creating Stories on Page and Screen*, available from: www.qca.org.uk/libraryAssets/media/More_than_Words_2_creating_ stories_on_page_and_screen.pdf (accessed 21 August 2007).

QCA (2006) *Assessment for Learning Guidance*, available from: www.qca.org. uk/qca_4334.aspx (accessed 25 August 2007).

QCA (2007) *A Big Picture of the Curriculum*, available from: www.qca.org. uk/libraryAssets/media/big_picture_of_the_curriculum.pdf (accessed 25 August 2007).

Rawson, M. and Richter, T. (2000) *The Educational Tasks and Content of the Steiner Waldorf Curriculum*, Forest Row: Steiner Waldorf Schools Fellowship.

Reynolds, D. (1999) School Effectiveness, School Improvement and Contemporary Policies, *in* Demaine, J. (ed) (1999) *Educational Policy and Contemporary Politics*, Basingstoke: Macmillan Press.

Richards, C. (2001) 'Cutting PANDAS down to size', *Education 3–13*, 29(3): 22–26.

Riley, J. (2001) 'The National Literacy Strategy: Success with literacy for all?' *The Curriculum Journal*, 12(1): 29–52.

Robinson, K. (1999) *All our Futures: Creativity, Culture and Education*, London: DfES.

Rose, J. (2006) *Independent Review of the Teaching of Early Reading*, available from: www.standards.dfes.gov.uk/phonics/report.pdf (accessed 21 August 2007).

SCAA (1994) *The Review of the National Curriculum. A Report on the 1994 Consultation*, London: SCAA.

SCAA (1996) *Nursery Education: Desirable Outcomes for Children's Learning on Entering Compulsory Education*, London: SCAA.

Schon, D. (1983) *The Reflective Practitioner: How Professionals Think in Action*, London: Basic Books.

Scottish Parliament (2006) *Education Committee Report SP Paper 596 ED/S2/ 06/R7 7th Report,* 2006 (Session 2), available from: www.scottish.parliament. uk/business/committees/education/reports_06/edr06-07.htm (accessed 27 August 2007).

Scrimshaw, P. (2004) *Enabling Teachers to Make Effective Use of ICT,* BECTA, available from: www.becta.org.uk/upload-dir/downloads/page_documents/research/ enablers.pdf (accessed 21 August 2007).

Shayer, M. (2006) 'Dumbing down', *Science,* 311(5763): 927.

Shulman, R. (1986) 'Those who understand: Knowledge growth in teaching', *Educational Researcher,* 15: 1–22.

Simon, B. (1994) *The State and Educational Change: Essays in the History of Education and Pedagogy,* London: Lawrence and Wishart.

Siraj-Blatchford, I., Sylva, K., Muttock, S., Gilden, R. and Bell, D. (2002) *Researching Effective Pedagogy in the Early Years,* DfES Research Report RR356.

Skrtic, T. M. (1995) *Disability and Democracy: Reconstructing (Special) Education for Postmodernity,* New York: Teachers College Press.

Slee, R. (1996) 'Disability, Class and Poverty: School Structures and Policing Identities', in Christensen, C. and Rizvi, F. (eds) (1996) *Disability and the Dilemmas of Education and Justice,* Buckingham: Open University Press.

Slee, R. and Weiner, G. (1998) *School Effectiveness for Whom? Challenges to the School Effectiveness and School Improvement Movement,* London: Falmer Press.

Smeaton, M. (2000) 'Questioning Geography', in Carter, R. (ed) *The Handbook of Primary Geography,* Sheffield: the Geographical Association.

St John Neill, S.R. and Campbell, R.J. (1994) *Primary Teachers at Work,* London: Routledge.

Stenhouse, L. (1975) *An Introduction to Curriculum Research and Development,* London: Heinemann.

Stenhouse, L. (1984) *Authority. Education and Emancipation,* London: Heinemann Educational.

Stobart, G. and Gipps, C. (1997) *Assessment. A Teachers' Guide to the Issues,* 3rd edn, London: Hodder and Stoughton

Sturman, L., Lewis, K., Morrison, J., Scott, E., Smith., P., Styles, B., Taggart, G. and Woodthorpe, A. (2005) *General Teaching Council Survey of Teachers 2005. Final Report,* available from: www.gtce.org.uk/research/tsurvey/2005survey (accessed 21 August 2007).

Sturman, L., Taggart, G. and Woodthorpe, A. (2004) *General Teaching Council Survey of Teachers 2004: Final Report,* available from: www.gtce.org.uk/ research/tsurvey/2004survey (accessed 21 August 2007).

Sylva, K. (1999) *Early Childhood Education to Ensure a 'Fair Start' for All,* London: Falmer Press.

Sylva, K., Melhuish, E., Sammons, P., Siraj-Blatchford, I., Taggart, B. and Elliot, K. (2003) *The Effective Provision of Pre-School Education (EPPE) Project: Findings from the Pre-school Period,* London: Institute of Education, University of London.

Tarr, J. (2000) 'Researching Children's Perspectives: A Sociological Dimension', in Lewis, A. and Lindsey, G. (2000) *Researching Children's Perspectives,* Buckingham: Open University Press.

TDA (2003) 'The National Agreement,' available from: www.tda.gov.uk/ remodelling/nationalagreement.aspx#access-content (accessed 25 August 2007).

Tharp, R. and Gallimore, R. (1988) *Rousing Minds to Life: Teaching, Learning and Schooling in Social Context,* New York: Cambridge University Press.

Tharp, R.G., Estrada, P., Dalton, S., S. and Yamauchi, L., A. (2000) *Teaching Transformed. Achieving Excellence, Fairness, Inclusion and Harmony,* Boulder, Colorado: Westview Press.

Thomas, G., Walker, D. and Webb, J. (1998) *The Making of the Inclusive School,* London: Routledge.

Tizard, B., (1988) *Young Children at School in the Inner City,* London: Lawrence Erlbaum.

Torrance, H. and Pryor, J. (2002) *Investigating Formative Assessment: Teaching, Learning and Assessment in the Classroom* (2nd Ed.), Maidenhead: Open University Press.

TTA (2002) *Training to Teach,* London: TTA.

Turner-Bisset, R. (1999) 'The knowledge bases of the expert teacher', *British Education Research Journal,* 25(1): 39–55.

United Nations Commission on Sustainable Development (1992) Agenda 21, Rio de Janeiro, available from: www.un.org./documents/ga/conference151/aconf15126-1annex1.htm (accessed 27 August 2007).

United Nations Convention on the Rights of the Child (UNCRC) (1989) *Convention on the Rights of the Child,* available from: www.unicef.org.uk/pages.asp?=page92 (accessed 27 August 2007).

Vincent, C. (1997) 'Community and collectivism: The role of parents' organisations in the education system', *British Journal of Sociology of Education,* 18(2): 271–283.

Vincett, K., Cremin, H. and Thomas, G. (2005) *Teachers and Assistants Working Together,* Maidenhead: Open University Press

Vygotsky, L. (1986) *Thought and Language,* London: MIT Press.

Vygotsky, L. V. (1978) *Mind in Society. Development of Higher Psychological Processes,* Harvard: Harvard University Press.

Wall, K. (2004) 'The National Literacy Strategy and setting: An investigation in one school', *Curriculum Journal,* 15(3): 233–246.

Water Aid (1998) *Buckets of Water,* video produced by Western Eye.

Wearmouth, J. and Soler, J. (2001) 'How inclusive is the Literacy Hour?' *British Journal of Special Education,* 28(3): 113–119.

Webb, R, (1993) *Eating the Elephant Bit by Bit: The National Curriculum at Key Stage 2. Final Report of Research Commissioned by the Association of Teachers and Lecturers (ATL),* London: ATL Publishers.

Webb, R. and Vulliamy, G. (1996) *Roles and Responsibilities in the Primary School: Changing Demands, Changing Practices,* Buckingham: Open University Press.

Wegerif, R. (2005) 'Reason and creativity in classroom dialogues', *Language and Education,* 19(3): 223–235, available from: www.rupertwegerif.name/ (accessed 19 August 2007).

Weldon, M. (2004) 'The Wider World', in Scoffham, S. (ed) (2004) *Primary Geography Handbook,* Sheffield: The Geographical Association.

Welsh Assembly (2003) *The Learning Country; Foundation Phase 3–7,* Cardiff: National Assembly for Wales.

Whitebread, D. (1997) 'Developing Children's Problem Solving: The Educational Uses of Adventure Games', in McFarlane, A. (ed) (1997) *Information Technology and Authentic Learning,* London: Routledge.

Whitty, G. (2005) Welcome speech, GTC/IOE Conference Workforce agreement, available from: www.gtce.org.uk/newsfeatures/features/whitty (accessed 27 August 2007).

Wiliam, D. (2001a) 'Reliability, validity and all that jazz', *Education 3–13*, 29(3): 17–21.

Wiliam, D. (2001b) 'What is wrong with our educational assessments and what can be done about it?' *Educational Review*, 15 (1): 57–62.

Winnicott, D. W. (1971) *Playing and Reality*, London: Tavistock.

Winther-Jensen, T. (2001) 'Changing Cultures and Schools in Denmark', in Cairns, J., Lawton, D. and Gardner, R. (eds) (2001) *Values, Culture and Education*, London: Kogan Page.

Wood, D. (1998) *How Children Think and Learn*, 2nd edn, Oxford: Blackwell.

Woods, P. (2005) *Democratic Leadership in Education*, London: Paul Chapman.

Woods, P. (2006) *Distributed Leadership Without Hierarchy*, London: British Academy.

Woods, P., Ashley, M. and Woods, G. (2005) *Steiner Schools in England*, London: DfES.

Wyse, D. (2001) 'Grammar for writing? A critical review of empirical evidence', *British Journal of Educational Studies*, 49(4): 411–427.

Wyse, D.(2003) 'The National Literacy Strategy: A critical review of empirical evidence', *British Educational Research Journal*, 29(6): 903–916.

Yates, L. (2004) *What does Good Education Research Look Like?* Maidenhead: Open University Press.

Young, R. (1992) *Critical Theory and Classroom Talk*, Clevedon: Multilingual Matters.

Young Writers (2004) *Once Upon a Rhyme*, Peterborough: Young Writers.

Index

eBooks - at www.eBookstore.tandf.co.uk

A library at your fingertips!

eBooks are electronic versions of print books. You can store them onto your PC/laptop or browse them online.

They have advantages for anyone needing rapid access to a wide variety of published, copyright information.

eBooks can help your research by enabling you to bookmark chapters, annotate and use instant searches to find specific words or phrases. Several eBook files would fit on even a small laptop or PDA.

NEW: Save money by eSubscribing: cheap, online acess to any eBook for as long as you need it.

Annual subscription packages

We now offer special low cost bulk subscriptions to packages of eBooks in certain subject areas. These are available to libraries or to individuals.

For more information please contact webmaster.ebooks@tandf.co.uk

We're continually developing the eBook concept, so keep up to date by visiting the website.

www.eBookstore.tandf.co.uk